access to history

Conflict and Reformation: The Establishment of the Anglican Church 1529–70

ROGER TURVEY

access to history

Conflict and Reformation: The Establishment of the Anglican Church 1529–70

ROGER TURVEY

HODDER EDUCATION
AN HACHETTE UK COMPANY

The Publishers would like to thank David Ferriby for his contribution to the Study Guide.

The Publishers would like to thank the following for permission to reproduce copyright material:

Photo credits: p7 British Library Board/TopFoto; **p36** Wellcome Library, London, Copyrighted work available under Creative Commons Attribution only licence CC BY 4.0 http://creativecommons.org/licenses/by/4.0/(detail of Cromwell); **p43** Titlepage, The Seventh Book, from 'Acts and Monuments' by John Foxe, ninth edition, pub. 1684 (litho), English School, (17th century)/Private Collection/The Stapleton Collection/Bridgeman Images; **p53** Wellcome Library, London, Copyrighted work available under Creative Commons Attribution only licence CC BY 4.0 http://creativecommons.org/licenses/by/4.0/(detail of More); **p54** Portrait of Sir Thomas More (1478-1535) (oil on panel), Holbein the Younger, Hans (1497/8-1543) (after)/National Portrait Gallery, London, UK/Bridgeman Images; **p82** Folger Shakespeare Library, Creative Commons Attribution-ShareAlike 4.0 International License http://creativecommons.org/licenses/by-sa/4.0/; **p93** Topical Press Agency/Hulton Archive/Getty Images; **p119** Portrait of Mary I or Mary Tudor (1516-58), daughter of Henry VIII, at the Age of 28, 1544 (panel), Master John (fl.1544)/National Portrait Gallery, London, UK/Bridgeman Images; **p122** Wellcome Library, London, Copyrighted work available under Creative Commons Attribution only licence CC BY 4.0 http://creativecommons.org/licenses/by/4.0/(detail of Gardiner); **p125** Wellcome Library, London, Copyrighted work available under Creative Commons Attribution only licence CC BY 4.0 http://creativecommons.org/licenses/by/4.0/(detail of Pole); **p127** The martyrdom of Dr. Thomas Cranmer at Oxford, illustration from 'Foxes Martyrs' c.1703 (litho), English School, (18th century)/Private Collection/The Stapleton Collection/Bridgeman Images; **p154** The Pope's Bull against the Queen in 1570 (engraving) (b&w photo), Hulsen, Friedrich van (c.1580-1660)/Private Collection/Bridgeman Images.

Acknowledgements: are listed on page 177.

Orders: please contact Bookpoint Ltd, 130 Milton Park, Abingdon, Oxon OX14 4SB. Telephone: +44 (0)1235 827720. Fax: +44 (0)1235 400454. Lines are open 9.00a.m.–5.00p.m., Monday to Saturday, with a 24-hour message answering service. Visit our website at www.hoddereducation.co.uk

First published in 2015 by
Hodder Education
An Hachette UK Company
338 Euston Road
London NW1 3BH

Impression number	10	9	8	7	6	5	4	3	2	1
Year	2019		2018		2017		2016		2015	

Cover photo: Bridgeman XCF99911 Copyright © The Bridgeman Art Library
Produced, illustrated and typeset in Palatino LT Std by Gray Publishing, Tunbridge Wells
Printed and bound by CPI Group (UK) Ltd, Croydon CR0 4YY

A catalogue record for this title is available from the British Library

ISBN 978 1471838736

Contents

Dedication

Keith Randell (1943–2002)

The *Access to History* series was conceived and developed by Keith, who created a series to 'cater for students as they are, not as we might wish them to be'. He leaves a living legacy of a series that for over 20 years has provided a trusted, stimulating and well-loved accompaniment to post-16 study. Our aim with these new editions is to continue to offer students the best possible support for their studies.

CHAPTER 1

The pre-Reformation Church before 1529

This chapter is intended to help you to understand what is meant by the terms and associated events connected with religion and religious change. The nature, state and authority of the pre-Reformation Church will be discussed, followed by an examination of the events that led to the Reformation in Church and religion. These issues are examined as three key themes:

★ The political and social role of the Church

★ Popular piety and the spiritual role of the Church

★ Humanists, reformers and criticisms of the Church

The key debate on *page 16* of this chapter asks the question: Why have historians adopted contrasting interpretations of the causes and nature of the Reformation?

Key dates

1503	William Warham appointed Archbishop of Canterbury
1514	Richard Hunne arrested and imprisoned, found dead in his cell
1516	Sir Thomas More published *Utopia*
1521	Bishop Fisher published *Sermon Against the Pernicious Doctrines of Martin Luther*
1520s	Wolsey closed 29 monasteries in England
1531	Sir Thomas Elyot published *The Book Named the Governor*

1 The political and social role of the Church

▶ *How significant was the political and social role of the Church?*

The pre-Reformation Church appeared to be powerful, stable and popular. It was the second largest landowner after the king in England. When Henry VIII ascended the throne in 1509 it is perhaps fair to say that the majority of the clergy in the English Roman Catholic Church split its allegiance equally between their king and the Pope in Rome. Although the Pope had no control over the day-to-day running of the Church in England, he had the spiritual authority to determine how the people worshipped and how Church **doctrine** was to be understood. The Pope also had the power to influence a kingdom's domestic and

KEY TERM

Doctrine The rules, principles and teachings of a belief system, in this case, the Church.

foreign politics by either offering or withholding his support for the ruler. The Church was a powerful organisation that can, for the sake of convenience, be divided into two component parts, secular and regular, staffed by some 45,000 clerics.

The secular Church

The **secular Church** consisted of several thousand parishes spread throughout the kingdom staffed by some 35,000 priests, led by some 40 bishops who administered their particular parts of the Church within a defined administrative area called a diocese. At the centre of the diocese was the cathedral to which was attached the bishop's administration, comprising both **clerks and clerics** entrusted with the task of administering the diocese and its courts. In administrative and legal terms, the pre-Reformation Church was so powerful and well organised that it is often said to have formed a state within a state, which rivalled the authority of the king. **Canon law** was practised alongside **common law** and each legal system had its own judges and courts.

The Church courts dealt with religious crimes such as adultery and **heresy** and crimes committed by churchmen. Although this was potentially an explosive situation, Crown and Church normally managed to exist side by side in relative harmony. Until his annulment, Henry VIII was a loyal member of the Church and he did little to jeopardise this harmonious relationship between Church and State. Two aspects of the Church's legal independence, **benefit of clergy** and **sanctuaries**, have normally been described as typifying the duality of the kingdom over which English kings ruled.

KEY TERMS

Secular Church That part of the Church which consisted of parish priests who lived and worked in the communities they served.

Clerks and clerics Clerks were involved in the administration of a diocese while clerics were responsible for spiritual matters.

Canon law Church laws that were administered in Church courts.

Common law Secular laws applying to the general population and administered in the king's courts.

Heresy Criticism or denial of the Church and its teachings.

Benefit of clergy An arrangement whereby any person charged in one of the king's courts could claim to be immune from prosecution if he was in holy orders.

Sanctuaries Areas of land, ranging in size from the county of Durham to the environs of particular churches or monasteries, which were outside the jurisdiction of the law of the land.

Benefit of clergy

As all those who played some official part, however minor, in Church life, and not just priests, were considered to be in holy orders. This benefit was extended to a large number of people. In the absence of documentation to prove a person's status, those who claimed benefit of clergy had only to be able to read a verse of Latin to escape the clutches of the law. This proved controversial because here was an obvious loophole for educated rogues to exploit and evade justice.

Sanctuaries

People whose normal place of residence was within a sanctuary could claim to be exempt from the normal processes of the common law wherever the crime of which they were charged had been committed. Some historians have suggested (or at least implied) that as long as such anomalies existed it would have been impossible for a fully fledged nation-state to have developed, and that the royal supremacy, by bringing the Church's legal system under the Crown's control, removed a bar to important constitutional developments. However, it is doubtful whether in reality the bar was of great significance. Not only had the numbers of people abusing the Church's legal privileges always been small, but legislation in the early Tudor period had also lessened the problem by removing some exemptions entirely – especially for major crimes such as murder and high treason – and by ensuring that those that remained were claimed only once by any individual (claimants were branded on the thumb to prevent them using the same 'escape' a second time).

The net result was that the existence of the clerical legal privileges has been assessed as being no more than a minor inconvenience, and certainly not one which would have seriously inhibited the emergence of England as a **unitary nation-state**.

Priests, people and problems

To ordinary people such matters meant very little. They were unaware or uncaring of the Church at a higher political level. England had few large towns or cities and the majority of its citizens lived a rural existence, populating a vast network of small villages spread throughout the country. Some of these villages were very small and the dwellings within them amounted to no more than a few dozen or less. One of the most enlightening studies of social and religious life in an English rural village is that published by Eamon Duffy. His study of the Devon hamlet of Morebath between 1520 and 1574 offers a 'unique window into a rural world in crisis as the reformation progressed'.

Duffy demonstrates that socially and religiously the church and its priest lay at the heart of people's lives. In most cases, the largest and most impressive building in any village was the stone-built church followed by, as in the case of Morebath, the 'church-house', which acted as the parish's place of public meetings and entertainment. Clearly, the life of the village revolved around the church and the priest's influence was often as great as that of the local landowner.

Nevertheless, despite its size, power and wealth (see below), the Church did have problems. The chief abuses were poverty, non-residence and ignorance. Many parish priests were poorly educated, some were illiterate, and their poverty contrasted with the wealth of the bishops. For example, 75 per cent of parish priests earned less than £15 a year while two-thirds of bishops earned more than £500. In order to survive, many priests were reluctant **pluralists** serving more than one parish (in extreme cases as many as five), which affected the quality of religious worship. It has been calculated that of the 10,000 parishes in England and Wales a quarter were likely to be without a resident clergyman. There were instances of neglect and criminal activity (such as bearing false witness and forging wills) by priests, which served to blacken the reputation of the Church. Nevertheless, in spite of its flaws the Church was generally popular with the people, whom it served reasonably well.

KEY TERMS

Unitary nation-state A country in which Church and State are united under a single authority or jurisdiction.

Pluralist A clergyman serving more than one parish or holding more than one office.

The regular Church

KEY TERM

Regular Church That part of the Church which consisted of monks, nuns and friars who lived and worked in monastic communities, usually in remote rural locations.

Upon Henry's ascension in 1509 there were more than 800 religious houses in England and Wales, with some 10,000 monks and nuns comprising the **regular Church**. The houses, consisting of monasteries, priories and nunneries, fell into one of two broad categories:

- There were those that were 'closed', in which the occupants – in theory at least – spent nearly all their time within the confines of the buildings and their adjacent fields and gardens, and devoted most of their energies to attending private religious services within their own chapel.
- The 'open' houses were the friaries, whose occupants were meant to work in the community at large, bringing spiritual comfort to the needy, be they the poor, the sick or merely those who were denied the services of an effective parish priest.

The two categories were also distinguished by other differences. The friaries were confined to the towns or their environs, were almost always small and were universally poor (it was against the rule of each of the four orders of friar to own property other than for their own immediate use). On the other hand, the 'closed' houses – now thought of as the typical monasteries – were more often situated in the countryside, were frequently large (in their buildings if not in their number of occupants) and were generally rich.

The wealth of the Church

The wealth of the 'typical' monasteries as a group was enormous. They possessed most of the Church's riches, normally estimated as including about one-third of the country's landed property. For example, the 30 or so richest monasteries each received an income approximating to that of one of the country's most powerful nobles. This money was derived mainly from 'temporal' sources, but one 'spiritual' source was significant:

- The 'temporal' element was overwhelmingly made up of rents from the agricultural land that the monastic orders owned.
- The 'spiritual' mainly took the form of profits from the parish priesthoods (benefices) that they held. These arose because very often the monastery would employ a vicar or curate to do the parish work, while retaining the lion's share of the value of the benefice for its own use.

A monastery had often acquired this wealth over several centuries, normally through dozens (in some cases even hundreds) of bequests made in the wills of property owners, large and small, in the hope that their generosity would help secure a place in heaven for their souls.

Most monasteries had been in existence for many generations and were accepted as an integral part of the community by almost the entire population which, mostly disliking change and having grown up with the religious houses, unquestioningly assumed that they were a normal part of life. Although a significant minority of the population lived and died without ever having seen a monastery, most people lived close enough to one, or to one of its outlying estates, to be aware of its activities. And although there were probably no more than a few hundred itinerant preaching friars active at any one time, it is unlikely that many adults would have escaped contact with them at some point during their lives. What evidence there is suggests that in the first half of Henry VIII's reign the popular expectation was that monasteries would always continue to exist.

The monastic dissolutions of the 1520s

During the 1520s, Cardinal **Wolsey** was responsible for dissolving 29 small religious houses because they were 'decayed', in that they had ceased to be viable in the terms envisaged by their founders because of a decline in the number of monks or nuns they contained. Their endowments were to be used for alternative charitable purposes and the dissolutions were carried out totally legally and with papal permission. Wolsey took over their property with the stated intention of using it to pay for the foundation of a grammar school in his hometown of Ipswich and a new college at his old university of Oxford. But there was nothing very remarkable or ominous in this. This was despite the fact that the scale of his activities was much greater than had been that of the bishops who had occasionally taken action to suppress individual religious houses during the past generation.

KEY FIGURE

Thomas Wolsey (c.1471–1530)

Wolsey served as the secretary of Bishop Fox before entering the service of Henry VIII. He held the office of Lord Chancellor of England between 1515 and 1529. He was as powerful a figure in the Church as he was in the State becoming Archbishop of York, Cardinal and later Papal Legate.

Politics and the Church

Wolsey's dissolution of the monasteries in the 1520s reveals the power that senior clerics still wielded in both Church and State. The Church and its most gifted clerics had long served the Crown in an administrative and political capacity. The government had been staffed by clerics for centuries and the royal council often contained men of the cloth. For example, the most influential advisers on Henry VII's council were churchmen, John Morton, Archbishop of Canterbury, and Richard Fox, Bishop of Winchester. This tradition of employing clerics as royal advisers continued under Henry VIII, who valued the advice given by men such as Stephen Gardiner, Bishop of Winchester (see page 122), and Cuthbert Tunstall, Bishop of London (he succeeded Wolsey as Bishop of Durham in 1530). Those clerics, who became the king's closest and most loyal advisers, were also employed as diplomats and ambassadors with the power to negotiate on behalf of their monarch.

Wolsey and the Church

Wolsey provides a fine example of what an ambitious and talented cleric could achieve. His humble background, the son of an Ipswich butcher, did not prevent him from rising through the clerical ranks to become the most

KEY FIGURE

William Warham (1450–1532)

Trained lawyer who became a priest and rose to become a minister in the government of Henry VII and, in 1503, Archbishop of Canterbury.

powerful churchman in England. As Archbishop of York he was second only to the Archbishop of Canterbury but by virtue of his other Church offices – **cardinal** and **papal legate** – he outranked him. Wolsey's appointment as Lord Chancellor made him the most powerful man in the kingdom after the king. Wolsey was especially trusted by Henry and, as a result, was able to exert a great deal of influence over government policy. He was an experienced administrator and possessed the leadership qualities Henry needed to run his government. Wolsey's control and management of the Church, even in the face of opposition from the Archbishop of Canterbury, **William Warham**, whom he detested, ensured that it and its senior clerics remained loyal to the king.

KEY TERMS

Cardinal Senior cleric in the Catholic Church.

Papal legate Personal representative of the Pope with the authority to act with full papal powers on ecclesiastical matters.

Ex officio Office holders who enjoy certain rights and privileges associated with or attached to their office.

Lords temporal The nobility who sat in the House of Lords.

Treason Betrayal of one's king and one's country.

Senior clergy

All bishops and abbots of large monasteries sat, by right of their offices or ***ex officio***, in the House of Lords. Sitting alongside the **lords temporal**, titled landowners such as barons, earls and dukes, whom they outnumbered, the lords spiritual took a full part in parliamentary business, be it political, legal or financial. Through their support for him, Henry was able to control and exploit the power and influence of the Church. The Church provided the king's coffers with substantial amounts of money raised through clerical taxation, loans and fines. The bishops also ensured that the parish clergy reminded the people of the importance of obedience to authority and the penalties for sinfulness and disorder. This was part of what was commonly held to be the divine order otherwise known as the Great Chain of Being.

The Great Chain of Being

According to the teachings of the Church, the chain started with God and progressed downward to angels, demons, stars, moon, kings, princes, nobles, men, wild animals, domesticated animals, trees, other plants, precious stones, precious metals and other minerals (see Source A). The Great Chain of Being conveyed the contemporary idea of God punishing those who rebelled against their ruler (**treason**) or who questioned the Church's teachings (heresy). It emphasised that those in authority held their power for the good of those below them, and subject to those above them. The concept is clearly expressed in Church doctrine and it was ordered to be taught as a normal part of the church service. In this way, the Church was able to exert a great deal of authority over the people, which was a vital element in upholding the rights of monarchical power. Thus, the Church was a key instrument of social control.

SOURCE A

The Great Chain of Being. Late fifteenth-century illustration showing animals and plants at the bottom topped by God and the angels. The people in the middle represent the various social classes.

Study Source A. What does this illustration reveal about the thinking of late medieval minds?

Monarchy and the Church

Regular pulpit sermons by the secular clergy reminded the people of the divine nature of monarchical authority since English monarchs claimed to rule *dei gratia* ('by the will of God'). This belief in divine right, that, as a person apart, the monarch was regarded as God's instrument on earth, was an integral part of Church teachings. Parish priests would regularly remind their parishioners of the terrible torments of hell that awaited those who dared rebel against the Crown. In practical terms, this meant that any rebellion against the monarch was regarded as being the same as a rebellion against God. Indeed, rebellion or any type of civil unrest was abhorrent to most people – from nobleman to peasant – because, as Sir **Thomas Elyot** wrote in his *The Book Named the Governor*, 'Where there is a lack of order there must needs be perpetual conflict.' This meant that the worst fear for most people was an outbreak of general anarchy.

KEY FIGURE

Thomas Elyot (1490–1546)

Bureaucrat and agent of Thomas Cromwell (see page 36) who served Henry VIII as a foreign diplomat. A friend of Thomas More (see page 53), Elyot was a scholar who published books on medicine, philosophy and government.

This is why the charge of treason, to betray one's king (or queen) and country, was regarded as a serious crime. This shows the importance of the law and the legal structure that had evolved in tandem with the development of the monarchy. The monarch was expected to act as the protector and enforcer of the laws of the kingdom. The old Latin maxim *Rex is Lex* and *Lex is Rex* ('the king is the law' and 'the law is the king') demonstrates the extent to which English monarchs had come to identify with the processes of law making. Although they came to hold a highly privileged position within the legal structure of the kingdom, they could not ignore or break the law but were expected to set a good example by acting within the accepted structure.

The monarch could not levy taxes or make laws at will or set aside the rights of the subject, or behave as a tyrant, especially as the Church had long taught that it was lawful to kill a tyrant. In short, the monarch had a duty to respect the notion that all who lived within the kingdom, from the lowliest peasant to the mightiest king, were bound by the common 'weal' or good. Even Henry VIII recognised the need to give legal basis to his break from Rome by seeking the consent of his people, via Parliament, and by framing the **schism** in English statute law. The fact that he may have bullied and harried his subjects, especially the regular clergy, into consenting to the break with Rome does not alter the fact that he had to be seen to be seeking their support. This balance of rights and duties between monarch and subject allowed for co-operation, compromise and even partnership.

KEY TERM

Schism Literally meaning 'break', but used by historians to describe England's break with the Pope in Rome.

Summary diagram: The political and social role of the Church

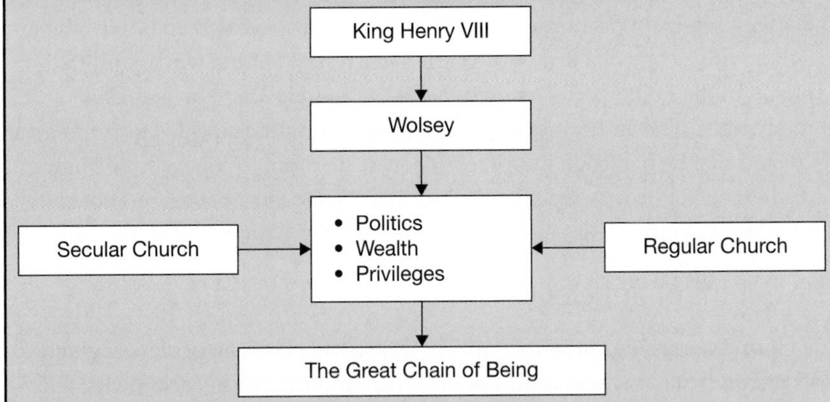

2 Popular piety and the spiritual role of the Church

▶ *How popular was the Church and how pious were the people?*

The Church ministered to the needs of its parishioners on a daily basis and provided essential services such as burials, marriages and christenings. Its parish priests offered advice, guidance and community leadership while its monks provided charity, education and employment. Unlike in Germany, where the Reformation began under **Martin Luther** and where the Church appeared weak, corrupt and neglectful of its parishioners, the English Church was generally well regarded. The English Church was not free from corruption and abuses such as pluralism, **nepotism**, **non-residence** and **simony** but it was not so widespread, and the Church was not as unpopular, as to produce a ruthless radical reformer like Luther in Germany. Luther's anti-papal preaching gave rise to widespread anti-papalism and anticlericalism in Germany, which in turn encouraged **iconoclasm**. The deliberate destruction of religious icons and other church symbols on the Continent was not repeated on such a large scale in England. There were no substantial riots or religious demonstrations in England, although the notorious Hunne case may be cited as an exception because it did induce an outburst of anticlericalism in London in 1511.

The Hunne case

After a bitter dispute with his local priest, Richard Hunne, a London merchant, had refused to pay the standard mortuary levied by the Church for conducting the funeral and burial of his baby son. Hunne was tried in the ecclesiastical

KEY FIGURE

Martin Luther (1483–1546)

A German friar and professor of theology, Luther campaigned against the corruption in the Catholic Church and advocated far-reaching religious reform. His support for the translation of the scriptures from Latin into German led to conflict with the papacy. His growing popularity in Germany was matched by the increasing hostility of the Pope, who eventually excommunicated him. The foundation of the Lutheran Church witnessed the beginnings of the Protestant Reformation in Germany which spread across Europe.

KEY TERMS

Nepotism The promotion or employment of family members and friends to important Church offices.

Non-residence Where priests did not live in their parish.

Simony The selling of Church offices and holy relics.

Iconoclasm Deliberate destruction of religious icons and other Church symbols in either community-inspired or State-organised attacks.

court, found guilty and **excommunicated**. He responded by suing the priest but the Church counter-sued and charged him with heresy. Hunne was arrested and after a search of his house the authorities found concealed an English Bible together with a copy of a text on Wycliffe's teachings. Hunne was committed to prison in the Lollards' Tower of St Paul's Cathedral, where he was later found hanged. The authorities claimed he had committed suicide but rumours circulated that he had been murdered. There is no proof to suggest that Hunne was a heretic but he may well have subscribed to reformist beliefs promoted by the **Lollards**, a radical dissenting sect dating from the late fourteenth century.

The extent of anticlericalism

The Hunne case aside, hard-core anticlericalism had little support in England. If Morebath be taken as an example, most parishioners readily acknowledged their obligations to their church and many seemed genuinely happy with the quality of their religious experience. Thus, the report, in 1529, by Eustace Chapuys, the Imperial ambassador, to his master, the Emperor Charles V, that 'nearly all the people here [England] hate the priests', is likely to have been exaggerated. (Charles V's interest in English affairs stemmed from the fact that he was the nephew of Henry VIII's wife, Catherine of Aragon.) Indeed, the popularity of religious **guilds** is testimony to this. The guilds were religious and community groups whose primary function was to assist in arranging funerals and intercessory masses for the souls of its departed members and their families. They also provided charity for widows and orphans, and assisted old and infirm people with gifts of money or food. Although they differed in size and wealth, the guilds were popular because they purported to protect their members from the dangers of **purgatory** by ensuring that the necessary masses were said as prescribed by Church doctrine.

KEY TERMS

Excommunicate To expel a person from the Church and deny them a Christian burial in consecrated ground, with the result that their souls would suffer everlasting torment in purgatory.

Lollards Followers of John Wycliffe (d. 1384), a university-trained philosopher and theologian whose unorthodox religious and social doctrines in some ways anticipated those of the sixteenth-century Protestant reformers.

Guild Religious or community group that provided its poorest members with assistance and charity.

Purgatory A place where the souls of the dead are sent in order to undergo purification so as to achieve the holiness necessary to enter heaven.

SOURCE B

Report by John Vaughan to Thomas Cromwell on the condition of Monmouth Priory, 1536. Vaughan was a younger member of the Vaughans of Golden Grove, the most powerful gentry family in Carmarthenshire. He became one of Cromwell's agents in south-east Wales and thereby established his fortune by purchasing the priory he dissolved: Monmouth.

I did see the said house and there is no pot nor pan nor bed nor bedstead nor no monk in the said house but one which does go to board in the town. The voice of the country is that while you have monks there you shall have neither good rule nor good order there; and I hear such saying by the common people of all the houses of monks that you have within Wales.

? How does Source B suggest that reports such as this one were a powerful weapon in the hands of anticlericalists?

The religious experience of the masses

It is important, however, to stress that the religious experience offered through the Church was not necessarily of a universally high quality and neither did the average parishioner think deeply about their religion (see Source C).

SOURCE C

From Glanmor Williams, *The Reformation in Wales*, Headstart History Publishing, 1991, p. 2.

The mass of the people were what might be described as 'community Christians' rather than individual believers. It was the customs which they absorbed from the community in which they were brought up much more than their own convictions which determined their religion. When they went to the parish church they worshipped as a communal group and were content to leave it to their priests to conduct services and administer the sacraments on their behalf in Latin, a language that most of them did not understand.

Study Source C. How far does this description of the religious experience of Welsh people in the early sixteenth century apply to England?

This suggests that much of their belief and practice was of necessity imitative and unthinking; in short, habit rather than conviction. Nevertheless, parish life was flourishing and the annual cycle of the great festivals, and the daily and weekly rituals of conventional worship – matins, mass and evensong – continued without any serious interruption.

Clearly, the parish church was the focal point of village life and its priest the most respected member of the community. While the priest's main preoccupation was the teaching and preaching on matters of death and judgement, heaven and hell, the parishioner was more concerned with baptism, marriage and burial. The religious fervour of the **laity** was frequently expressed in a materialistic way, and in the early sixteenth century many of England's 9000 parish churches were either built or improved by individuals hoping that their generosity would help reserve a place for them in heaven.

KEY TERM

Laity The main body of Church members who do not belong to the clergy but are part of the wider community.

It was this materialisation of religious belief that contributed to the demand for reform. In Germany it showed itself in the sale of indulgences by the Church to those willing to pay for salvation and thus avoid the pitfalls of purgatory. In England, indulgences were sold but the 'industry' was never as well established or as professionally organised as on the Continent, where vast sums of money changed hands.

Summary diagram: Popular piety and the spiritual role of the Church

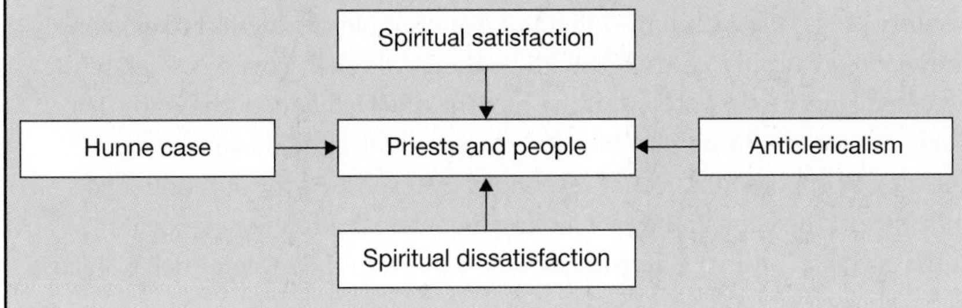

3 Humanists, reformers and criticisms of the Church

▶ *Why was there so much criticism of the Church?*

The relationship between the English Church and the Church in Rome was stable and generally harmonious. Indeed, the pre-Reformation Church enjoyed a degree of independence from Rome. Its senior leaders, archbishops and bishops, were chosen not by the Pope but by the monarch, often as a reward for loyal service. The Pope had the power to object, and block senior appointments in the Church, but this was rare. The good diplomatic relations established by Henry VII between the English Crown and the Pope served both parties well. Thus, the papacy could expect to receive regular payment of its clerical taxes and to receive the appeals of English litigants to its courts in Rome. The faithful took a great interest in events in Rome and when news of a papal election reached London it was celebrated by a procession to St Paul's Cathedral, where a service of thanksgiving took place.

The influence of Continental humanism

Only gradually did the influence of **Continental humanism** make its presence felt in England. The works of the Dutch humanist **Erasmus**, the greatest scholar of his day, and Luther, the radical German theologian, began to affect the thinking of the literate. The spread of literacy and the impact of the printing press provided greater access to religious literature and the fact that reading cannot be easily separated from thinking encouraged debate and growth in dissent. The paradox is that the Church encouraged education, which promoted free-thinking and debate, but it steadfastly refused to accept criticism.

The younger Henry, like the vast majority of his subjects, was pious and entirely **orthodox** in his religious belief and attitudes. Although he was aware of the weaknesses within the Church, he did not seriously question its authority nor did he try to reform it. He was keen to maintain good relations with the Church because it could be a powerful ally in his quest to maintain the stability and security of his rule within the kingdom. For example, in an effort to gain an international ally in his struggle with the heretic Luther, Pope Leo X gratefully accepted Henry's support, awarding him the title Defender of the Faith. The Pope, in turn, might support Henry by excommunicating those who dared threaten or oppose him. Henry responded by respecting the authority and influence of the Pope and by promoting the interests of senior clerics at the Papal Curia such as Cardinal **Campeggio**, who was given the revenue-rich bishopric of Salisbury.

KEY TERMS

Continental humanism Return to the study of the original classical texts and to the teaching of the humanities as the basis of civilised life. The movement began in fifteenth-century Italy and spread throughout Europe owing to the inspired leadership of intellectuals and scholars.

Orthodox Accepting doctrine without question, in this case of the Church.

KEY FIGURES

Desiderius Erasmus (1466–1536)

A Dutch Renaissance humanist, priest, scholar and theologian. He played a pivotal role in the establishment of humanism in universities. His influence on the English episcopal and aristocratic patrons under Henry VIII was immense, especially in education.

Lorenzo Campeggio (1474–1539)

A doctor of canon law and a senior cleric in the Catholic Church. He was a humanist scholar who wrote *De depravato statu ecclesiae*, which advocated reform of government in the papal states. In 1524 Henry VIII appointed him Bishop of Salisbury and thereby sought to employ him as an advocate of English matters in the Papal Curia.

Erastianism and Lollardy

The Church was certainly ripe for reform but not of the kind initiated by Henry VIII. English kingship was, in part, a religious office. Through his anointment at his coronation Henry VIII received God's blessing allied to divine power. As king, Henry was expected to set an example of piety and to protect the Christian faith and Church. Unlike his father Henry VII, Henry was an amateur theologian who could not resist meddling in the affairs of the Church which stemmed, in part, from his arrogance but mainly from his belief in the divine right of kings. Until the annulment (see Chapter 2, pages 22–4), the relationship between the king and the Church had been cordial and respectful but, thereafter, it deteriorated, becoming tense and fractious. The annulment changed Henry's attitude and thinking: he became critical of the Church, less orthodox in his beliefs and more amenable to the idea of reform. One key idea that appealed to Henry was that preached by Thomas Erastus, a Swiss theologian, who believed that the State had a duty to exercise control over the Church and religion. In his opinion the Church had no right to punish errant Christians in ecclesiastical courts; this was best left to the civil and criminal courts. Thus, **Erastianism** became a by-word to denote the doctrine of the supremacy of the State in ecclesiastical matters.

The only heretical idea to have acquired a significant following in England in the later Middle Ages was Lollardy. This laid stress on the reading of the Bible and urged the clergy to confine themselves to their **pastoral duties**. Systematic persecution in the fifteenth century had forced it underground but, encouraged by the spread of Continental reformist ideas, there was a resurgence of interest during the reign of Henry VIII. This, coupled with the influx of Lutheran texts into England, began to have an impact on the thinking of educated people who, in turn, began to question the power and authority wielded by the Church. It is perhaps no surprise to learn that areas where Lollardy still persisted were among the first to embrace the teaching and preaching associated with Lutheranism. It is difficult to estimate the impact Lutheranism had on religious belief and practice in England by the time of Henry's annulment but the king's very public quarrel with the Pope did stir some to seek an alternative belief system to the one into which they had been born and to which they had grown accustomed. According to the Venetian ambassador, the English people were 'raging against the clergy, or would be if the King's Majesty were not curbing their fury'. The evidence suggests that this assessment was exaggerated but not entirely without truth in some urban areas of the kingdom.

KEY TERMS

Erastianism Justification of a State-controlled Church, expounded by Thomas Erastus.

Pastoral duties The duty of care exercised by a priest to his parishioners, such as baptism, marriage and burial.

Renaissance An intellectual and cultural movement dedicated to the rediscovery and promotion of art, architecture and letters. It promoted education and critical thinking and ranged across subjects such as politics, government, religion and classical literature. Its spread was encouraged by humanist scholars such as Erasmus.

Humanism and the new learning

The dramatic cultural developments that were taking place on the Continent in a movement that we call the **Renaissance** came late to England. Mainly it took a literary form known as humanism, rather than the artistic form, which was more typical in Italy. Humanism was the return to the study of the original classical texts and to the teaching of the humanities as the basis of civilised life. It made its first appearance in England in the middle of the fifteenth century. Because literacy was confined to the upper levels of society, its followers were restricted to the educated class. The celebrated humanist scholar Erasmus visited England for the first time in 1499 and was impressed with the high standards of classical teaching being fostered by **John Colet**, Dean of St Paul's Cathedral and founder of St Paul's School. Soon an extended humanist circle emerged during the reign of Henry VIII. Among the more brilliant English scholars of their day were men such as Sir Thomas More (see page 54), Bishop John Fisher (see pages 51–2), Sir Thomas Elyot (see page 8) and **Roger Ascham**.

KEY FIGURES

John Colet (1467–1519)

A distinguished scholar, Renaissance humanist and theologian, who was an outspoken advocate of Church reform. Denounced by some as a heretic because of his support for religious reform, Colet was protected by his patron, Archbishop Warham.

Roger Ascham (1515–68)

A humanist scholar known for his educational theories and promotion of Latin and Greek classical literature. He was tutor to Princess Elizabeth.

Humanist publications

English humanism was responsible for major literary works such as More's *Utopia* (1516), which offers a model society based on reason and nature. Influenced by the humanist writings of Erasmus, More argued in his book that politics should be based on human nature and aimed exclusively at human happiness. Consequently, there are no lawyers in More's perfect world because of the law's simplicity and because social gatherings are in public view (encouraging participants to behave well). More also placed a great deal of emphasis on communal ownership rather than private property, and advocated the equal education of men and women. Given his fate during the Henrician Reformation (see page 54), it is perhaps ironic that in More's *Utopia* there is almost complete religious toleration where even atheists were tolerated but actively despised.

Elyot's contributions to English humanism included philosophical and moral essays, translations of ancient and contemporary writers, an important Latin–English dictionary, and a highly popular manual on human health and well-being. But perhaps his most famous work, based in large part on his experience as English ambassador to the Court of Charles V, was entitled *The Book Named the Governor* (1531), which acts almost as an advice manual to statesmen.

Ascham confined his talents to education, and his book *The Schoolmaster* (1563) sets out in detail what a good humanist education should aspire to be.

Bishop John Fisher

Fisher was a critic of the abuses in the Church but he was not prepared to acknowledge Henry VIII as supreme head of that Church. His writings up to the divorce crisis were mainly focused on improving the Church, with an emphasis on a better-educated clergy. Writing to Wolsey in 1518, Erasmus called Fisher 'a divine prelate' who was by far the most gifted scholar in the English Church. Two years later, Erasmus wrote to Reuchlin, the great Hebrew scholar of the day, expressing his opinion that 'there is not in that nation [England] a more learned man or a holier prelate'. Fisher had little sympathy with Luther, whom he denounced in a publication entitled *Sermon Against the Pernicious Doctrines of*

Martin Luther (1521). It is perhaps ironic that when Luther attacked Henry VIII for his publication *In Defence of the Seven Sacraments*, Fisher came to the king's aid by publishing *Defence of the Assertions of the King of England Against Luther.* During the divorce Fisher turned his hand to writing a series of brilliantly conceived papers on the rights of Catherine's case. However, he also laid bare the weaknesses of Henry's case and criticised the vindictiveness of the king and his advisers.

Propaganda and the printing press

The development and spread of humanist writings were greatly assisted by the printing press, brought to England from Germany in 1476 by William Caxton. Edward IV's patronage of printing was enthusiastically followed by his Tudor successors, who encouraged a steady stream of major English texts and translations from French and Latin. This led to the growth of a wider reading public, the beginnings of the standardisation of the English language and the circulation of the reformist ideas of Erasmus. Henry VIII also made use of the printing press to spread **propaganda** enhancing the prestige of the Tudor dynasty. Henry patronised learning and encouraged artists, musicians, poets and men of letters. Taking as his model the Renaissance court of the French king, Francis I, which was acknowledged to be the most magnificent in Europe, Henry wanted the English court to become the principal focus of cultural activity in the kingdom.

KEY TERM

Propaganda Method by which ideas are spread to support a particular point of view.

During the divorce crisis, Henry used the printing presses to publish books, pamphlets and tracts supporting his theological arguments and justifying his demand for an annulment of his marriage to Catherine of Aragon. However, as he was to find, the press could print equally influential tracts opposing his reasons for obtaining a divorce. The period witnessed a struggle by the Crown to win the hearts and minds of the reading public by publishing persuasive texts while censoring or even banning those that were critical. It became clear that Henry's quest for a divorce and subsequent quarrel with the Pope would have unintended consequences for the English Church and its religion.

Summary diagram: Humanists, reformers and criticisms of the Church

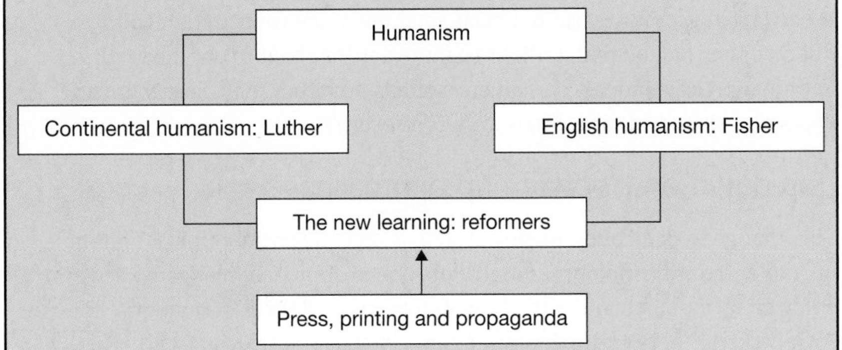

4 Key debate

▶ *Why have historians adopted contrasting interpretations of the causes and nature of the Reformation?*

Traditional view of the Reformation

The Reformation in England had traditionally been portrayed as a long, drawn-out event, lasting for more than 40 years (1529–70), but with the major actions all falling within the first half of the period. The problem was that it had been assumed that the individual happenings that comprised it were all linked together in a chain of cause and effect, giving unity and coherence to England's change from being a strongly Catholic country to being a Protestant nation, 'a land of whitewashed churches and anti-papal preaching' (Eamon Duffy, 2003). As a result, readers of histories of the Reformation could hardly avoid reaching the conclusion that the outcome of the story – the establishment of the Anglican Church – had been inevitable from the beginning. This was especially so as the majority of both authors and their readers regarded the Reformation as an account of 'change' and 'progress'.

Challenging the traditional view of the Reformation

Historians began to challenge these assumptions by becoming more objective (as opposed, in Reformation studies, to a commitment to either a Catholic or a Protestant point of view), and this was linked to a greater awareness of the dangers of hindsight. It became clear that the accepted ways of looking at the English Reformation were essentially flawed. Indeed, new research allied to revisionist thinking strongly suggested that the end-point – the Elizabethan Church Settlement leading to the establishment of a largely Protestant Anglican Church – had been reached as much by chance as by design and that the direction of events could have been altered by random factors at almost any time.

Many researchers, therefore, came to the conclusion that the coherence given to the events that made up the Reformation only existed in the minds of later observers and certainly had not been apparent at the time. In the light of this fact, they judged that it might be more accurate to think of the English Reformation as a 'process' (a sequence of related rather than closely linked happenings), and not as a single, coherent 'event'.

'Top-down' and 'bottom-up' approaches

This change in perception made particular sense when adopting a 'bottom-up' rather than the more traditional 'top-down' approach (instigated, led and enforced by monarch and government) to a study of the Reformation. Professor A.G. Dickens' 'bottom-up' interpretation (1964) certainly lent itself to this concept, and his research was effectively a charting of the 'process' by which Protestantism replaced Catholicism in England between 1529 and 1570.

For some time historians acted as if the concepts of 'event' and 'process' were incompatible, and that one must be 'right' and the other 'wrong'. However, it is now accepted that, as long as the dangers of assuming cause and effect and of using hindsight are kept in mind, both concepts are helpful in gaining an understanding of what the Reformation was, what were its causes and what were its effects.

Dickens argued that Henry VIII was able to carry out his political Reformation – breaking with Rome, establishing himself as the Supreme Head of the Church in England and **dissolving** the monasteries – largely because his actions coincided with both the advanced stages of a decline in popular support for the Catholic Church and a rapid spread of Protestant beliefs. His contention was that the Reformation from below happened early and speedily.

KEY TERM

Dissolving The dissolution or closure of the monasteries.

The impact of Revisionist historians

Revisionism has generally maintained the exact opposite in as much as it firmly believes that the Reformation brought Protestantism, not Protestantism the Reformation. Basing their conclusions mainly on a sequence of detailed local studies, revisionist historians have advanced the view that Protestantism was adopted by most of the people of England and Wales towards the end of the Reformation period (if at all) – 'late and slowly' as opposed to 'early and rapidly'. They have produced telling evidence to support the argument that Catholicism stubbornly remained the majority belief in some parts of the country throughout the Tudor period despite all the efforts of central government and the missionary activities of Protestant preachers.

It is a telling point that despite six years of Protestantism under Edward VI, Mary did not encounter significant resistance when she returned England to the authority of Rome and restored Catholic worship in the Church. Indeed, Christopher Haigh (1975), the best known of the revisionists, has contended that there was not just one English Reformation but several. He argues that there was a sequence of 'political' Reformations between 1529 and 1570. He claims that they should be treated as distinct happenings and that it is unhelpful to think of them as chapters in a single event. His view is that the English Reformations were separate but linked. It must not be thought that Haigh's is the final word on the Reformation for, as is the nature of historical research, the debate is set to continue.

The debate

The causes and nature of the English Reformation have provoked considerable debate and disagreement among historians. The generally accepted historical outline of events connected with the Reformation was established in the late nineteenth century by J.A. Froude. According to Froude, the Reformation was conceived, planned and executed by Henry VIII and his ministers in order to secure his divorce. In this 'top-down' approach to the study of what became known as the 'official' or 'political' Reformation, the doings and beliefs of the population at large were mentioned only in passing. This view was challenged by Dickens in his seminal work *The English Reformation*, published in 1964. Where earlier histories of the Reformation were often simple narratives and narrowly political, Dickens offered a persuasive account which took religious motivation seriously. In his 'bottom-up' approach, Dickens emphasised the preconditions of Reformation, such as popular anticlericalism and the native tradition of heresy, Lollardy.

By the 1980s, however, the tide had turned against Dickens' interpretation, and the local Reformation studies which he had done so much to establish were making his views hard to defend. Somewhat unfairly, 'Dickensianism' became a by-word for a blinkered account of the Reformation, which neglected both the vigour of the old and the unpopularity of the new religions in Tudor England. Dickens responded in 1989 with an extensively revised edition of *The English Reformation*. But he was unable to halt the establishment of a new orthodoxy in which his work featured as an interpretation to challenge rather than a point of departure. The following indicates some of the major contributions to the debate that has evolved in the past half century.

The Dickensian interpretation

Dickens concentrated on the activities and enthusiasms of ordinary people, which he believed would provide a more meaningful explanation of how England became Protestant than would an account of the monarch-inspired 'official' or 'political' Reformation. Dickens did not suggest that the actions of government were unimportant, he merely argued for a shift of emphasis in favour of the 'popular' Reformation. Dickens argued that Henry VIII was able to carry out his political Reformation – breaking with Rome, establishing himself as the Supreme Head of the Church in England and dissolving the monasteries – largely because his actions coincided with both the advanced stages of a decline in popular support for the Catholic Church and a rapid spread of Protestant beliefs. His contention was that the Reformation from below happened early and speedily because the seeds of popular religious change had been sown by the Lollards.

EXTRACT 1

From A.G. Dickens, *The English Reformation*, Collins, 1964, pp. 59–60.

Medieval men were faced by quite terrifying views of punishment in the life to come; it was small wonder that they felt more comfortable with the saints than with God, or that they came to regard the Blessed Virgin as a merciful mediatrix for ever seeking to placate the divine wrath of the Son as Judge. Popular theology suggested that those who looked on the host would prosper and avoid blindness or sudden death all that day.

From about 1490 we hear with ever-increasing frequency of Lollard heretics and of official attempts to obliterate the sect. That Lollardy thus survived and contributed in some significant degree towards the Protestant Reformation is a fact based upon incontrovertible evidence. By this time Protestant intellectuals had begun to see Lollard writings as serviceable additions to their arsenal of Reformation propaganda. It provided a springboard of critical dissent from which the Protestant Reformation could overleap the walls of orthodoxy. The Lollards were the allies and in some measure the begetters of the anticlerical forces which had made possible the Henrician revolution, yet they were something more, and the successes of Protestantism seem not wholly intelligible without reference to this earlier ground-swell of popular dissent.

Challenging the Dickensian interpretation

Duffy offers a revision of the standard Dickensian history of the popular Reformation. Whereas Dickens suggested that Lollardy was a significant influence on the religion practised by the common people, Duffy suggests that this has been grossly exaggerated. Duffy also played down the simplistic fear-driven nature of popular religious belief.

EXTRACT 2

From Eamon Duffy, *The Stripping of the Altars*, Yale University Press, 1992, pp. xiv–v.

Dickens's book begged many questions about the nature of late medieval piety. It never seems to have occurred to him that those who flocked and jostled to 'see their maker' at the elevation of the Mass could hardly be said to be remote from or uncomfortable with their God, or that the clergy who led prayers to the saints or who commended pilgrimage promoted also a religion focussed on their daily celebration of the ***Eucharist****. Dickens work therefore revealed the fundamentally negative assumptions which underlay much contemporary understanding of the pre-history of the English Reformation, as well as the course of that great revolution itself.*

The mainstream of fifteenth-century piety was indeed conventionally censorious of heresy, but not in my view greatly affected, much less shaped, by reaction to it, while the overwhelming majority of early Protestant activists were converts from devout Catholicism, not from Lollardy.

KEY TERM

Eucharist Also known as Holy Communion; a Catholic sacrament in which the bread and wine are taken in the belief that the body and blood of Christ are contained within.

The revisionist interpretation

Diarmaid MacCulloch has a more positive view of the Reformation than either Dickens or Duffy. His conclusions support Dickens in that he allows for greater influence of heretical movements like the Lollards but he also agrees with Duffy that the quality of religious worship was not as dire as was once thought.

EXTRACT 3

From Diarmaid MacCulloch, *The Later Reformation in England, 1547–1603*, Palgrave, 1990, pp. 105–6.

Outward show might nowadays seem a poor index to genuine piety, but traditional devotion cherished the tangible as a doorway to the intangible. How easily did the reformation sweep aside such devotional patterns to impose new priorities? In the past, disagreements about this largely depended on the confessional bias of the historical commentator; but the cooling of passions about the reformation has not ended the controversy. The English response to the Reformation was fragmented by region; one area might indeed furnish data for a quick reformation drawing on substantial support from below, another show a very late popular reaction to what successive Protestant regimes are attempting – slow and from above. One cannot deny that there is a striking coincidence between the areas where Lollardy had been strong and Dickens' 'great crescent' of early popular evangelicalism. Yet proof of definite links between Lollardy and the English academics who became spokesmen for the Reformation is the most difficult to substantiate.

? According to the historians quoted in Extracts 1–3, how significant was Lollardy in causing and sustaining the English Reformation?

Chapter summary

The nature, state and authority of the pre-Reformation Church have attracted a great deal of attention because historians cannot agree on the causes of the Reformation. There is no disputing the importance of the political and social role of the Church. The Church dominated the daily lives of the people; it preached, informed and educated them while also controlling them by the power and mystique of God-given authority. The Church also influenced the politics and government of the kingdom through Parliament in the House of Lords and by virtue of the appointment of clerics such as Cardinal Wolsey to run the government. The questionable depth and strength of 'popular' piety and the often misdirected spiritual role of the Church were significant factors in promoting religious reform. The influence of home-grown radical sects such as the Lollards and external reformists such as the humanist scholars Erasmus and Luther contributed to calls for religious change. The printing press and the spread of learning fuelled criticism of the Church which encouraged anticlericalism. However, the weaknesses of the Church and the strength of anticlericalism have been questioned by historians who dispute the effect each had in bringing about the Reformation.

Refresher questions

Use these questions to remind yourself of the key material covered in this chapter.

1. How satisfied were the people with the Church?
2. How influential were the Lollards?
3. What are the key features of the debate regarding the Reformation?
4. How powerful and influential was the pre-Reformation Church?
5. How have revisionist historians contributed to the debate on the Reformation?
6. What impact did the Hunne case have on contemporaries?
7. What was the Great Chain of Being and why was it so important?
8. What part did Erasmus and Luther play in influencing the English Reformation?
9. Why do historians dispute the impact of anticlericalism as a cause of the Reformation?
10. What is the difference between the secular and regular Church?

Question practice

ESSAY QUESTIONS

1. 'The pre-Reformation Church was ripe for reform because it was close to collapse.' Explain why you agree or disagree with this view.
2. 'Habit rather than conviction best sums up the religious motivation of the masses'. Explain why you agree or disagree with this view.
3. 'The Reformation happened because the people demanded the reform of an uncaring and corrupt Church.' Assess the validity of this view.
4. 'The contrast between the wealth of the Church and the poverty of the people encouraged the kind of criticism that led to the Reformation.' Assess the validity of this view.

Henry VIII and the break with Rome 1527–36

This chapter seeks to explain why the Reformation took place and the reasons why the English Church broke with Rome. The chapter will consider the influence and role of the king, Wolsey, Cromwell, the Pope and the campaign to secure an annulment in promoting change. The contribution of Catherine of Aragon, Anne Boleyn and factions at court will also be assessed. These issues are examined as three themes:

★ The annulment and the fall of Wolsey

★ The Reformation Parliament, royal supremacy and the rise of Cromwell

★ The influence of faction, opposition and the spectre of rebellion

Key dates

1527	Wolsey instructed to obtain an annulment of the king's union with Catherine of Aragon
1528–9	Failed attempt to obtain an annulment in England with Cardinal Campeggio
1529	Wolsey removed from power
1530	Wolsey died in Leicester while being taken to London to face trial for treason
1529–36	Reformation Parliament
1530	Church charged with *praemunire*
1531	Charge of *praemunire* withdrawn in return for a grant of £100,000
1532	Thomas Cromwell became the king's chief minister
	Submission of the Clergy
	Act in Restraint of Annates
1533	Act in Restraint of Appeals
1534	Act of Supremacy
	Execution of the Holy Maid of Kent
1534–7	Attack on the Observant Franciscans and the Carthusians
1535	Execution of John Fisher and Sir Thomas More

1 The annulment and the fall of Wolsey

▶ *How might the background and long-term causes of the Reformation be summarised?*

The annulment

The annulment or, as contemporaries came to call it, the king's 'great matter' has helped influence and shape attitudes to and concepts of the Reformation.

It is widely believed that the Reformation of the Church in England took place mainly because Henry VIII wished to obtain an annulment of his marriage to his Spanish wife, Catherine of Aragon, so that he could marry his English mistress, Anne Boleyn. The reason why this became such an issue is because only the Pope had the power to dissolve marriages and he appeared unwilling to do what Henry had requested. Given that the Catholic Church never granted divorce, only annulment, the Pope's reluctance is understandable. It was Wolsey's failure to get an annulment that left divorce (and a consequent break with Rome) the only option for Henry.

Despite years of debate, legal challenges and, ultimately, threats, it became clear to Henry that the only way in which he could obtain an annulment was to take over the Pope's powers within his own kingdom and arrange the separation for himself. This he did and the Reformation took place (in essence the establishment of an independent Church of England) as an unintended side-effect of political necessity and personal desire. Thus, historians are generally agreed that events in the years between 1527 and 1536 are a vital part of understanding the English Reformation.

Why did Henry feel compelled to seek an annulment?

Naturally, the events connected with the annulment and the break with Rome are rather more complex than this summary might suggest, but it serves a useful purpose in providing a starting point for asking searching questions. The key question, of course, is why Henry felt compelled to seek an annulment. This was due, in part, to the fact that by the mid-1520s, after more than fifteen years of marriage, a healthy daughter, and a number of miscarriages and stillbirths, contemporaries believed that the ageing Catherine of Aragon was unlikely ever again to bear children.

Catherine's failure to produce a son and heir weighed heavily on Henry's mind. He firmly believed that a woman could never rule England and that, if Mary succeeded him as queen, the kingdom would be plunged into dynastic civil war such as had happened during the Wars of the Roses. Believing that his marriage was cursed, Henry found Anne Boleyn to be the answer to his prayers. She was young, he was in love (or lust) and she promised him an heir. Henry was astute enough to recognise that a son born to Anne out of wedlock would at best have a contested claim to succeed him, so annulment became an urgent necessity. The man given the task of securing this was the king's chief minister, Cardinal Wolsey.

Wolsey and the king's 'great matter'

Wolsey may have become aware of his master's frustration with his marriage as early as 1521. It had been three years since Catherine's last pregnancy and, increasingly, it was becoming clear to Henry that he was unlikely to have another child, let alone the long hoped-for male heir, by his wife. Amid rumours at court and diplomatic gossip abroad that Henry intended to annul his marriage, the king sought solace in the company of Mary Boleyn (elder sister of Anne), whom he took as his mistress in 1522. Their two-year affair did little to ease Henry's concerns over the succession or the quest for a male heir. The end of his affair in 1524 coincided with Henry's decision to cease sleeping with his wife. On learning that Henry and Catherine were no longer bedfellows, Wolsey suggested that the king might consider the possibility of annulment and remarriage.

In sowing the seeds of doubt in Henry's mind about the long-term future of his relationship with Catherine, Wolsey hoped to persuade the king to take steps to provide for the succession. Apart from naming his daughter Mary as heir, in 1525 Wolsey advised Henry to designate his illegitimate son, Henry Fitzroy (born in 1519 and whom he had created the Duke of Richmond), as heir-apparent. However, Henry knew that following his death the claim of his illegitimate son to rule could be challenged and even set aside in favour of his legitimate offspring, Mary. The result would be the dynastic war he so feared. Wolsey too was aware of this but until the king could be persuaded to consider seriously the possibility of a remarriage, this interim measure would have to suffice.

Henry VIII's attitude to the annulment

In 1526 two events conspired to move Henry closer towards the annulment of his marriage:

- the advice provided by the royal physicians that the 41-year-old Catherine was unlikely ever to conceive again
- the public declaration of his love, at the Shrove Tuesday jousts, for a new mistress fifteen years his junior, Anne Boleyn.

Even then it took until May 1527, more than a year after meeting and falling for Anne Boleyn, that Henry finally made up his mind to seek an annulment.

?Study Source A. Why might Henry have had doubts about his relationship with Anne Boleyn?

SOURCE A

From Keith Randell, *Henry VIII and the Reformation in England*, Hodder, 1993, p. 10.

Anne let Henry know that she would not become his sexual partner until she was also his wife. It took Henry some time to become convinced that this stance was genuine and no mere example of courtly coyness. It is probable that once the reality of the situation became clear to him and that his infatuation was growing rather than diminishing, his mind turned increasingly to the doubts he had felt about the validity of his marriage.

The Levitical argument

Henry claimed that his doubts about the validity of his marriage stemmed from an Old Testament text of the Bible (Leviticus 20:21), the Latin translation of which read: 'If a man shall take his brother's wife, it is an unclean thing: he hath uncovered his brother's nakedness; they shall be without children.' To an amateur biblical scholar like Henry this was ample proof that his lack of surviving legitimate male children was God's punishment for marrying in defiance of divine law. This was because Catherine had previously been married to his elder brother, Arthur, whose early death in 1502 had made her a widow after five months of married life. However, it was pointed out to Henry that the Levitical tract did not apply because he had fathered a child, Mary, with Catherine. Having convinced himself that his marriage was cursed, Henry sought clarification in the Hebrew original, which he took to mean 'sons' rather than 'children'. In the opinion of historian Virginia Murphy (writing in 1995), 'By substituting the Hebrew for the Latin, Leviticus was thus cleverly made to fit Henry's situation exactly.' However, the majority of historians believe that the king's cynical manipulation of biblical texts did his cause more harm than good for it only served to antagonise his theological critics.

Apart from his infatuation with Anne Boleyn, the most plausible explanation of Henry's decision to free himself of Catherine appears to have been his unshakeable belief that he had been living in sin for some seventeen years. Henry believed that as punishment for this sinfulness his soul would suffer the torment of eternal damnation.

Henry VIII's religious convictions

The depth and sincerity of Henry's religious convictions have been the subject of intense debate but no firm conclusions can be drawn. It is fair to say that he was conventionally pious – attending church, abiding by prescribed doctrine and following the precepts of the clerical hierarchy – but the fact that he wrote a book (with the active collaboration of Sir Thomas More) attacking the early teachings of Martin Luther (see page 9) suggests that he had a deep interest in theology. When the book, entitled *In Defence of the Seven Sacraments*, was published in 1521, the Pope, Leo X (1513–21), awarded him the title 'Defender of the Faith'. Henry took great pride in this title and continued to use it even after the break with Rome.

In an effort to set the record straight and underline the reasons why he was pursuing the current course of action, Henry summoned the nobility and other worthies to a meeting at his palace of Bridewell in London in November 1528. According to **Edward Hall**'s *Chronicle*, the king made a public declaration in which he praised 'the great worthiness of his wife, both for her nobility and virtue and all princely qualities'. Henry went so far as to state that 'if he were to marry again he would marry her of all women, if the marriage were found to be good and lawful'.

KEY FIGURE

Edward Hall (1497–1547)

A lawyer and historian, who represented Much Wenlock and later Bridgnorth, Shropshire, in Parliament. He is best known for his book *The Union of the Two Noble and Illustre Families of Lancastre and Yorke*, commonly known as *Hall's Chronicle*, published in 1542.

Praise was accompanied by propaganda for, as Hall explained, the king declared that despite her worthiness and the fact that he had a 'fair daughter by her', he was 'wonderfully tormented in his conscience', for he 'understood from many great clerks whom he had consulted, that he had lived all this time in detestable and abominable adultery'. Therefore, according to Hall, to settle his 'conscience, and the sure and firm succession of the realm … he said that if by the law of God she should be judged to be his lawful wife, nothing would be more pleasant and acceptable to him in his whole life'.

Decision to annul the marriage

Once Henry had decided that the only solution to his dynastic and personal problems was the annulment of his marriage, events moved swiftly. Unknown to Catherine, in May 1527 Wolsey convened a secret court at his London residence, York House, to examine the validity of Henry's marriage. Exercising his authority as ***legatus a latere***, Wolsey focused his investigation on the legality of the papal dispensation issued by Pope Julius II (1503–13) permitting the marriage. After a month of deliberation Wolsey informed Henry that he had a strong case and that he could expect success in his quest for an annulment. Given his status as papal legate, Wolsey was confident that his **legatine powers** would help ensure that a favourable outcome would be speedily achieved. Reassured by Wolsey, in June, Henry informed Catherine of his intention to seek papal approval of his request to annul the marriage. A month later, in July 1527, Henry proposed to Anne, who accepted subject to the granting of the annulment.

KEY TERMS

Legatus a latere A position normally awarded for a specific purpose so that a representative with full papal powers could be present at a decision-making occasion far distant from Rome.

Legatine powers Authority delegated by the Pope.

The campaign to obtain an annulment

Henry's confidence in a swift and painless resolution to his 'great matter' suffered a serious setback when negotiations in Rome for the annulment became mired in legal arguments. What had been expected to be a formality, lasting no more than a few weeks, dragged on for months without any prospect of being resolved in the short or medium term. It became clear that the Pope, Clement VII (1523–34), was deliberately stalling, which caused a frustrated Henry to blame Wolsey for the delay. In the opinion of historian J.J. Scarisbrick (1997), Henry believed 'that it was not only his right to throw away his wife, but it was also his duty – to himself, to Catherine, to his people and to God'. Encouraged by Anne Boleyn and her allies at court, Henry demanded that Wolsey pursue a more aggressive policy in dealing with the Pope. In these pressured circumstances Wolsey adopted a dual strategy to persuade the Pope to grant the annulment.

The primary strategy

The primary strategy involved the forceful approach favoured by Henry. Wolsey asserted that the original dispensation, issued by Pope Julius II and accepted by both England and Spain, was insufficient in law. Henry's legal advisers claimed that no pope had the right to set aside divine law and nor could he simply ignore the prohibition contained in the biblical text of Leviticus. To support this theological and legal interpretation Henry enlisted the help of expert theologians who were commissioned to research and write treatises in favour of the Levitical argument.

This strategy was politically inept and unnecessarily confrontational. No pope was ever likely to admit publicly that one of his predecessors had erred by exceeding his legal powers. In an effort to counter the expert opinion Henry had paid for, the Pope, too, employed theologians who argued that the law laid down in Leviticus was subject to papal dispensation. This division of opinion served only to undermine Henry's case, especially when it became clear that the so-called experts could not even reach agreement on the exact meaning of the biblical instruction. Bishop Fisher of Rochester argued that the Levitical instruction had been misunderstood. In his opinion, the intention was that a man should not marry his brother's wife while his brother was still living. To support his argument Fisher cited an Old Testament text from the book of Deuteronomy (25:5) which stated: 'If brothers are living together and one of them dies without a son, his widow must not marry outside the family. Her husband's brother shall take her and marry her and fulfil the duty of a brother-in-law to her.'

Fisher's theological argument was considered to be the more persuasive and the fact that he had become Catherine's leading defender, publishing seven books in the process, angered Henry. The case had gained such a high international profile that it became almost impossible for either Henry or the papacy to give ground without a huge loss of face.

Adapting the strategy

Henry was persuaded by his advisers to adapt his original strategy by changing the focus of the attack, to concentrate more on the legal rather than the theological issues. In order to avoid any direct challenge to the powers of the papacy, Henry's legal team decided to object to the original dispensation on technical grounds, by arguing that it was invalid because it was incorrectly worded. It was hoped that this legal argument would appease Pope Clement and encourage him to accept it because it would require no more than a simple admission that a clerical error had been made.

Unfortunately for Henry, this too, after much delay, was rejected by the Pope. Although Clement's advisers urged him to consider this legal technicality as a means of resolving the deadlock they were undermined by the efforts of Catherine to prevent the annulment of her marriage. Agents working on her behalf were fortunate enough to locate an alternative version of the dispensation among the papers of her nephew, Charles V, in Spain. What is more, it was argued that this newly discovered version satisfied the legal criteria, unlike the copy held in England. To add to Henry's frustrations, Charles V denied the English ambassador access to the Spanish version of the dispensation and refused to allow it to leave the country. This forced the Pope to send his legal representatives to the Spanish court in Madrid to check the precise wording of the document. This episode made plain to Henry that Charles V had taken the side of his aunt in the affair and would likely prove to be a formidable adversary.

The secondary strategy

The secondary strategy was more straightforward and its success hinged on Wolsey's powers of persuasion. His intention was to:

- persuade the Pope to transfer the case to England
- delegate responsibility for the case to Wolsey.

As papal legate, Wolsey certainly had the status and power to preside over the case. Aware of the wider diplomatic situation, Wolsey sought to ease the pressure being brought to bear on the Pope by Charles V, by removing Clement from any personal involvement in the decision-making process.

After some delay in reaching his decision, Pope Clement appeared to favour this solution but he insisted on four key points:

- the case must be tried by two papal legates
- he reserved the right to appoint the second legate
- the judgement reached at the Legatine Court in England had to be arrived at jointly
- he reserved the right to either accept or reject the judgement reached by the legates.

The appointment of Cardinal Campeggio

In 1528 Henry and Wolsey accepted the Pope's terms and they welcomed the appointment of Cardinal Lorenzo Campeggio (see page 12) as the second legate. Henry and Wolsey knew Campeggio well, having worked with him some years before when negotiating the terms of Treaty of London in 1518. As a reward for his services Henry granted him the bishopric of Salisbury. In 1523 Campeggio was appointed Cardinal Protector of England by Pope Adrian VI (1522–3), which empowered him to represent English interests at the papal curia in Rome. Given their close personal and professional relationship, Wolsey was confident that Campeggio would be a compliant and co-operative partner.

Unfortunately for Wolsey, Campeggio proved to be anything but the pliant and acquiescent associate he had expected. Although Campeggio was known to be in poor health, his painfully slow journey to England was regarded by an increasingly impatient Henry as another stalling tactic by Clement. When he did arrive, in October 1528, the Cardinal Protector did not display the sense of urgency that Henry expected and demanded. Every delay was treated as a personal affront by the king, who unleashed his anger on Wolsey, the man who had promised him that there would be a swift resolution to the matter.

Campeggio and the Legatine Court at Blackfriars, London

It took seven months for the Legatine Court finally to meet at Blackfriars in May 1529. The delay was caused, in large part, by Campeggio's insistence that the case be tried according to the detailed procedures set out in canon law. As prescribed by law, Campeggio interviewed Henry and Catherine in turn before drawing up the necessary papers to conduct the case in open session. In his report to Pope Clement, Campeggio stated that Henry was so certain that his marriage was invalid that 'an angel descending from Heaven would be unable to convince him otherwise'.

Wolsey's attempts to speed up the process served only to antagonise Campeggio, who responded by delaying still further the legal procedure. An increasingly desperate Wolsey resorted to bribery and blackmail, both of which were resisted by the Cardinal Protector. By the time the case opened on 31 May Henry had not only come to distrust Campeggio but also lost faith in Wolsey. It took nearly three weeks, until 18 June, before Catherine was summoned to appear in court and when she did, she refused to recognise its right to hear the case. Registering her right to appeal directly to Rome, Catherine then withdrew. After one further brief appearance on 21 June, Catherine refused to attend or acknowledge the authority of the court. Four days later, on 25 June, she was charged with contempt of court.

Urged by Henry to continue the case in her absence, Campeggio reluctantly carried on for a further three weeks, until late July, when he suspended proceedings. On Wolsey's insistence, Campeggio agreed to resume the case in October but it was a futile gesture. Henry realised that Campeggio would never reach a verdict. A month before the court was due to reconvene at Blackfriars, Pope Clement recalled Campeggio and summoned the case to Rome.

Wolsey's political future

In short, Wolsey had no political future. Pope Clement's decision to preside over the case himself effectively ended Wolsey's career. Wolsey's promises of success had ended in complete failure, which made him vulnerable to the criticism of his enemies. Seeking a scapegoat, Henry was more prepared than before to listen to Anne Boleyn's accusation that Wolsey had always intended to sabotage the annulment. Henry may even have begun to believe the rumours circulating in the court that Wolsey, keen to secure the papal tiara for himself, had been secretly working with, rather than against, the Vatican.

Unfortunately, the evidence does not permit firm conclusions to be drawn but most historians believe that it is inconceivable that Wolsey would have deliberately undermined the case for the annulment. He was no friend of Anne Boleyn but neither was he in the business of opposing the will of the king. Privately Wolsey may well have disagreed with the king's choice of bride to replace Catherine but publicly he had no choice but to support it. Wolsey knew that his political future depended, as it always had, on pleasing the king and delivering what his royal master demanded.

Wolsey might have hoped that Henry would have tired of Anne Boleyn, as he had done with his other mistresses, but if so, he had seriously miscalculated. More importantly, he had underestimated Anne Boleyn, who had proven to be a formidable opponent. From a diplomatic standpoint, it is known that Wolsey favoured a foreign match and it is likely that following the papal blessing of the annulment he hoped to persuade Henry to marry a French princess. Therefore, it is possible to conclude that Wolsey's failure to secure the annulment was not through want of trying, it was simply beyond him to achieve.

Wolsey's fall from power

Undoubtedly, the major reason why Wolsey fell from power was due to his failure to secure for Henry the annulment of his marriage to Catherine of Aragon. It seems that this was the issue at the forefront of the king's mind for the whole of the two years prior to Wolsey's fall. The minister had promised that this would be a matter easily resolved because of his influence with the papacy, from which all annulments of marriages must come, but every attempt had resulted in disappointment.

In the circumstances, Henry had been very patient. Anne Boleyn was refusing to have sex with him until he could guarantee to make 'an honest woman' of her by marrying her. It was obvious to everybody at court that this caused Henry great frustration. And Henry was increasingly aware that the passage of time was endangering his aspiration of passing his crown to an adult male when he died. It is an indication of the depth of Henry's faith in Wolsey, and the skill with which the minister explained away the delays, that the breakdown in their relationship was so long delayed. When the final failure of Wolsey's efforts to secure the annulment became apparent, the king turned on his once faithful and most trusted servant.

Removing Wolsey from power

In October 1529 Henry decided that the most efficient way of removing Wolsey from power was to charge him with ***praemunire***. A series of Acts of Parliament in the fourteenth century had created the crime of *praemunire*, which in essence was any action taken to exercise papal powers in England to the disadvantage of the king or any of his subjects. From the time he had acquired his appointment as *legatus a latere*, Wolsey had clearly been open to a *praemunire* charge, and to the punishments associated with it – the confiscation of all property and imprisonment during the king's pleasure.

Wolsey was arrested and all his possessions were confiscated. However, he was soon released and allowed to live in modest comfort away from court. It was only some months later that he was rearrested and taken towards London from

KEY TERM

Praemunire A legal provision, arising from three fourteenth-century laws, which forbade clerics to take any action that cut across the powers of the Crown – especially recognising any external authority without the monarch's explicit permission.

his archdiocese of York, to which he had been 'exiled' by Henry. But his health was broken and he died at Leicester on 29 November 1530. During the period of his disgrace he had done all he could to engineer his reinstatement. He had sent a stream of pleading letters to the king and had attempted to gather support among his 'friends' throughout Europe. But all had been to no avail. Henry had slowly become convinced that his long-time leading servant must suffer the only fitting end to his period of dominance: death as well as disgrace. Wolsey's premature end at Leicester had in fact spared him from the show trial and execution that almost certainly awaited him in London.

That Wolsey managed to survive all attacks on his position for fifteen years is remarkable. This was due in large part to both the minister's outstanding abilities and the king's trust in him. Thus, the relationship between Henry VIII and Wolsey was a real (if very unequal) partnership that depended on the achievements of both parties for its success. Wolsey's failure to deliver the one thing most desired by the king – the annulment – resulted in the dissolution of that partnership.

Summary diagram: The annulment and the fall of Wolsey

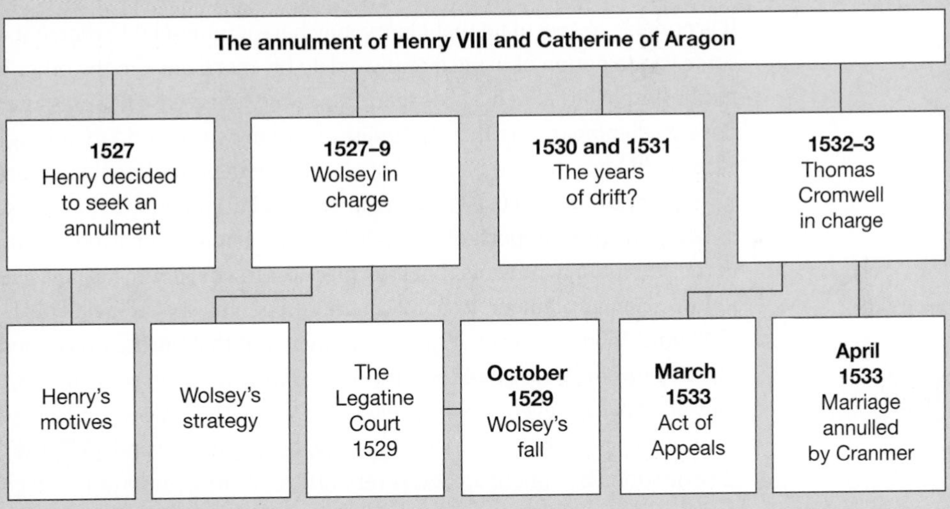

2 The royal supremacy and the rise of Cromwell

▶ *What was the Reformation Parliament and how effective was it?*

The Reformation Parliament

In November 1529 the king summoned Parliament for the first time in six years. Traditionally, parliaments were called to grant taxes and to pass new laws but in times of crisis the Crown sought reassurance by securing the support of the governing classes for its policies. This was just such a time. Failure to secure the annulment followed by Wolsey's disgrace had shaken Henry's confidence but quite what he expected from this Parliament is unclear. Contemporaries, too, were not sure of the purpose of this Parliament. The French ambassador believed it was summoned to draw up charges against Wolsey, whereas the Spanish ambassador thought it was to be used against Queen Catherine. Even Sir Thomas More, Wolsey's successor as Lord Chancellor, was vague in his opening speech to Parliament, stating only that new laws were required to deal with 'divers new enormities'.

It is possible to speculate that Henry may have summoned Parliament on some vague notion of using it to invalidate his marriage. On the other hand, it might simply have been a propaganda exercise to increase the pressure on the Pope by demonstrating that the 'political nation' was behind their king. It is clear that Henry had no plan on how to resolve the annulment crisis and was unsure of how best to use Parliament. Yet this Parliament has been described as being the most important in English history because it played a central role in the revolutionary events that took place during its lifetime. Known as the Reformation Parliament, it sat for an unprecedented six and a half years, from 1529 until 1536. However, it must be pointed out that during this period its meetings were **prorogued** for much longer than it was in session, meeting for only 484 days in seven separate sessions. During the time when Henry VIII assumed responsibility for policy making, between 1529 and 1532, the Reformation Parliament achieved very little of lasting importance. In contrast, during Cromwell's period in power, between 1533 and 1536, the legislation enacted proved to be of considerable significance.

KEY TERM

Prorogue Temporary suspension of Parliament.

From Wolsey to Cromwell: a period of drift?

The years between the fall of Wolsey in 1530 and the rise of Cromwell by 1532 have been described as a period during which the campaign to obtain the annulment was conducted aimlessly and with no clear plan. This lack of direction is evident from the observations of Eustace Chapuys, Charles V's ambassador. Reporting on the second session of the Reformation Parliament

(1531), Chapuys observed that its members 'do not know their own minds about the measures to be proposed therein'. Chapuys was especially critical of three of Henry's leading advisers – the Dukes of Norfolk (**Thomas Howard**) and Suffolk (Charles Brandon) and the Earl of Wiltshire (Thomas Boleyn, father of Anne) – whom he blamed for the failures of government.

The period between 1530 and 1532 demonstrates that Henry had no strategy and neither did his closest advisers. It also revealed that Henry was as dependent on able ministers as they were on him. Certainly, Norfolk, Suffolk and Wiltshire lacked the political skills and strategic judgement of either Wolsey or his most talented adviser, Thomas Cromwell. The one man with talent enough to suggest an alternative course of action, the Lord Chancellor, Sir Thomas More, was unwilling to do so because he sympathised with Catherine and wished to defend the Church.

KEY FIGURE

Thomas Howard (1473–1554)

As Duke of Norfolk he was the most powerful nobleman in England, with significant influence at court. He was leader of the conservative faction and uncle to two of Henry VIII's wives: Anne Boleyn and Catherine Howard.

Collectanea satis copiosa

During this period only one major initiative was taken in an attempt to win a victory in the debates on the meaning of the Leviticus text (see page 25) and on the Pope's power to issue a dispensation for a man to marry his brother's widow. This initiative was led by a relatively unknown priest and academic, Thomas Cranmer (see page 106), who had impressed Henry with his theories on the jurisdictional rights of kings over the Church in secular and spiritual matters.

Cranmer, assisted by Edward Foxe, Dean of Salisbury (see page 37), was instructed to undertake research and to compile a treatise based on collected historical evidence to help resolve the annulment crisis. The result was the *collectanea satis copiosa* or 'the sufficiently large collection'.

By means of the *collectanea satis copiosa*, Henry had procured a degree of learned support for his case. This was followed by a concerted effort by Cranmer to secure formal 'judgements' on the issue from the most prestigious European universities. Large sums of money were spent bribing theologians to vote in Henry's favour and ten verdicts were obtained. But the overall impact of the campaign was minimal, especially as it was widely known that coin rather than conscience had decided many of the outcomes. Some of the participants were even prepared to be bribed by Catherine's supporters (the so-called Aragonese faction) to declare publicly that they really believed the dispensation to be valid and that they had only said otherwise because they had been paid to do so. In this poisoned atmosphere of claim and counter-claim, the credibility of the exercise – which had never been high – was almost totally destroyed.

Thomas Cranmer, Christopher St German and 'caesaro-papism'

Inspired by his extensive research and by the debates he had with distinguished theologians, Cranmer wrote another treatise, entitled *The Determinations*, published in 1531. In this treatise Cranmer argued strongly that the king should 'be master in his own house', in effect, the head of all institutions within his kingdom, including the Church. According to Cranmer, the divinely ordained king of England ruled by the will of God, with the consent of his people and according to his conscience. Therefore, the Pope had no right to question, much less interfere, in the internal affairs of Henry's kingdom.

KEY FIGURE

Christopher St German (1460–1540)

Lawyer, humanist scholar and doctor of divinity, St German was one of England's leading intellectuals whose writings proved influential in shaping English common law.

Cranmer was ably supported by the scholar and legal expert **Christopher St German**, one of the most influential writers of his generation. In his *Treatise Concerning the Division between the Spirituality and the Temporality*, published in 1532, St German argued that the king's conflict with the Pope over the annulment was more legal than theological and could, in theory, be resolved by English common law rather than Roman canon law. In effect, he was providing a legal justification for the elimination of the Pope's authority in England.

Having no strategy of his own and lacking a clear direction, Henry was immediately drawn to the works of Cranmer and St German. Their idea of combining secular government with that of the Church under the authority of the monarch impressed Henry. The term used by historians to describe this idea – that the same person can be both the temporal leader (the Roman Emperor Caesar) and the religious leader (the Pope) – is 'caesaro-papism'. Inspired by their work Henry, encouraged them to undertake further research to refine their ideas.

Henry's promotion of Cranmer

Henry had unearthed a talent, Cranmer, who would later become instrumental in securing the king's annulment by virtue of his promotion, in 1532, to the archbishopric of Canterbury. However, until Cromwell arrived on the scene Cranmer simply followed the approach adopted by the king, which was no more than an elaboration of the failed strategy that Wolsey had attempted to implement. The aim was still to persuade the Pope to declare in Henry's favour by convincing him of the rightness of the king's case, despite the clear-cut evidence that the papal curia was likely neither to be swayed by public opinion, however eminent its spokesmen, nor to be unduly influenced by the facts of the case, one way or the other. Henry's objectives and Rome's aims were too far apart.

But at least these years witnessed one success of sorts. The great fear in London, after the case had been revoked to Rome in the summer of 1529, had been that a verdict in favour of Catherine would be issued. So the king's agents in Italy were instructed to reverse the direction of their efforts, and instead of trying to speed up the process they were told to slow it down. They managed to initiate some additional delays in what was already a very slow and complicated process, but it is unlikely that, even without their work, any final decision would have been forthcoming for a very long time; both sides had arrived at a stalemate.

Breaking the stalemate: Cromwell's 'new idea'

In late 1531 or early 1532, Thomas Cromwell came up with a new idea about how best to resolve the king's 'great matter'. Since the papacy would never be persuaded to rule in Henry's favour, Cromwell believed that the only way forward was to remove the Pope's power in such matters and give it to someone or some group willing to be persuaded by the king. In effect, Cromwell was proposing to divorce England from the papacy. For this to be accomplished the clerical hierarchy in the English Church would either have to support actively the proposal or quietly acquiesce. Cromwell made it clear that clerical opposition would not be tolerated and those seeking to frustrate the proposal would be punished. This proved too much for Sir Thomas More (see page 54) who, expressing his distaste for any threat against the Church, resigned his Lord Chancellorship. The way was now clear for Cromwell to succeed More as the king's chief minister.

From annulment to divorce

The new chief minister gradually became the major influence on Henry and it is to him that historians turn to explain why the decision to break completely with Rome was eventually taken. Cromwell probably used the arguments that this was the only way of being sure that the annulment would be granted and that the king owed it to himself and his successors to regain the powers that had been stolen from his ancestors by fraudulent means. Cromwell's first success was in persuading Cranmer to support him so that the two of them might better influence the king.

Cromwell was a talented lawyer, parliamentarian and dedicated bureaucrat who had served Wolsey well. Anticipating the fall of his master, Cromwell left Wolsey's service and entered the king's household. It was here, while working his way up the career ladder, that Cromwell presented the king with his idea. Cromwell's strength was that besides being able to describe clearly what needed to be done he was also able both to indicate how it could be done and to guarantee to do it himself.

It seems that, although Henry was quick to recognise the talent of this relatively low-born former lieutenant of his fallen minister and to see that he was a man whose services could be used, he was unwilling to accept the total package – a complete break with Rome – that was on offer. It became apparent to Cromwell that his royal master still harboured hopes of reaching some agreement with Rome. Consequently, it was necessary to persuade the king of the merits of his 'new idea' in piecemeal fashion. Therefore, there was no sudden change of direction leading to speedy success; rather, there was an edging towards a new way forward. This was done with much wavering and hesitation, until events – a mixture of papal intransigence and English diplomatic clumsiness – took on a momentum of their own, leading to a resolution of the king's 'great matter'.

Thomas Cromwell

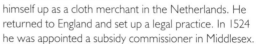

1485	Born the son of Walter Cromwell of Putney in London, a blacksmith and cloth merchant
1520	Established in London mercantile and legal circles
1523	Entered the House of Commons for the first time
1524	Entered Wolsey's service
1531	Took charge of the king's legal and parliamentary affairs
1532	Became master of the king's jewels
1534	Confirmed as Henry VIII's principal secretary and chief minister
1535	Appointed royal vicegerent, or vicar-general
1540	Granted the earldom of Essex (April). Imprisoned in the Tower of London (June) prior to his trial and execution for treason in July

Early in his life, Cromwell left England and joined the French army. In 1503 he marched with his French comrades to campaign in Italy. His period of service as a mercenary soldier was short, for in 1504 he entered the household of the Italian merchant-banker Francesco Frescobaldi. In 1513 he left Frescobaldi's service to set himself up as a cloth merchant in the Netherlands. He returned to England and set up a legal practice. In 1524 he was appointed a subsidy commissioner in Middlesex.

In 1524 he entered Wolsey's household as his solicitor but he quickly rose to become the cardinal's chief adviser. Cromwell was a dedicated bureaucrat who served Wolsey well. In the cardinal's service he attracted the attention of Henry VIII, who would later employ him in the royal household. In 1530, after Wolsey's fall from power, Cromwell became a member of the king's council.

Cromwell's greatest achievements were in securing the divorce and the break with Rome. He was responsible for drawing up and piloting through Parliament the Act of Supremacy in 1534, thereby making Henry VIII the Supreme Head of the Church in England. He was executed on trumped-up charges of treason in 1540.

Cromwell and the Reformation Parliament

Cromwell's key decision was to use Parliament to pass laws restricting papal powers by recognising that these powers in fact resided in the Crown of England, and stipulating the punishments that would be meted out to those who opposed or acted contrary to the new arrangements. The uniqueness of the approach suggested by Cromwell appealed to Henry. At the time it was generally accepted that Parliament was a rarely and briefly used component of political life (it had played no significant part in the first twenty years of Henry's reign) whose main functions were to grant extraordinary taxes and to pass new laws. The idea of using it to bring about a revolution in the relationship between Church and State was highly innovative. It was also very shrewd. It ensured that the representatives of the landed and merchant classes, on whom the king depended to exercise his authority throughout the country, would be fully implicated in and beneficiaries of whatever was done.

The steps taken to reduce the Pope's influence in England

The passing of two pieces of vital parliamentary legislation marked the first official steps in the process of reducing the Pope's influence in England: the Act in Restraint of Annates (1532) and the Act in Restraint of Appeals (1533). The Act in Restraint of Annates forbade the payment to the Vatican of up to 95 per cent of **annates**. Henry hoped that this financial penalty would encourage the Pope to reconsider his position in regard to the annulment or risk losing the payment of annates entirely.

KEY TERM

Annates Money equivalent to about one-third of the annual income paid to the Pope by all new holders of senior posts within the Church in England and Wales.

Pope Clement did not respond, so greater pressure was applied the following year with the passing of the Act in Restraint of Appeals, which declared that final authority in all legal matters, lay and clerical, resided in the monarch and that it was therefore illegal to appeal to any authority outside the kingdom on any such matters. This was a significant measure for the following reasons:

- It ensured that the final verdict on the validity of Henry and Catherine's marriage would be taken out of Rome's hands.
- In order to justify the change, the right of the Pope to make decisions affecting Henry and his subjects was publicly denied.

The fact that Anne Boleyn had become pregnant injected a sense of urgency into the work of securing the passage of this necessary legislation, which explains why it passed swiftly through both houses of Parliament and received the royal assent.

SOURCE B

The preamble to the Act in Restraint of Appeals (1533). This Act of Parliament justified what was being done.

... that this realm of England is an empire, and so hath been accepted in the world, governed by one supreme head and king having the dignity and royal estate of the imperial crown of the same, unto whom ... all sorts and degrees of people divided in terms of spirituality and temporality, be bounden and owe to bear next to God a natural and humble obedience to the king ...

Study Source B. Why might the Pope object to this Act?

Key personnel

The way was now clear for the annulment to be decided finally without the involvement of the Pope or his bureaucracy. Crucially, the people were in place who could be relied on to carry out the work speedily and with the desired outcome:

- Thomas Cromwell, the king's chief minister
- Edward Foxe, Dean of Salisbury and later Bishop of Hereford
- Sir Thomas Audley, the Lord Chancellor
- Thomas Cranmer, Archbishop of Canterbury.

Taking his lead from Cromwell's carefully drafted text of the Act in Restraint of Appeals, Cranmer, in his capacity as Archbishop of Canterbury, made three important decisions:

- he assumed the legal powers over Church matters that had previously resided in the Pope
- he announced that the papal dispensation allowing Henry and Catherine to marry was invalid
- he declared that Henry and Catherine had never been legally husband and wife.

Cranmer was supported by Lord Chancellor Audley, who ensured that the archbishop had the legal backing of the State. Pope Clement was rattled but did not immediately react to the challenges to his authority. He hoped to arrive at a compromise with Henry but after months of tense negotiation it became clear that this would not be possible.

In 1534 Clement finally delivered his verdict and declared that the papal dispensation issued by Pope Julius II was valid and that Catherine was lawfully Henry's wife. An infuriated Henry instructed Cromwell to set in motion plans to eliminate every trace of papal power in England. In the opinion of historian G.R. Elton (1953), the Cromwell-drafted Act in Restraint of Appeals was a 'masterpiece in statute-making' because it marked the beginning of the process whereby England was able to separate itself from the papacy.

The Reformation Parliament and the Church

In order to secure the annulment and eliminate every trace of papal power in England, Cromwell had first to ensure that the Church was pliant and complicit in this undertaking. He was assisted by the work that already been done prior to his emergence as the king's chief minister.

From the very first meeting of the Reformation Parliament it was clear that the Church would be put under pressure to comply with whatever policy the king deemed fit to force the Pope to grant him the annulment. During the first parliamentary session a small group of MPs, mainly London merchants and lawyers, launched an attack on abuses they claimed were widespread within the Church. A contemporary who witnessed the events, Edward Hall (see page 25), gives the impression that his fellow MPs were motivated by genuine anger at the scale of clerical corruption, resulting in demands for legislation to deal with the matter. Although it is likely that Hall exaggerated both the anger and the actions taken by MPs, there is no doubting the anticlericalist tone of the Commons. Consequently, the session witnessed the passage of three bills attempting to limit pluralism, simony and non-residence.

It has been claimed that Henry allowed this very public attack on the Church to take place because he wished to harness the anticlericalist sentiment in the Commons. This would enable him to suggest to the Pope that the country was in a state of fervent anticlericalism which could only be controlled by a monarch publicly backed by papal authority. Thus, Henry posed as the defender of the Church, echoing the title conferred on him by Pope Leo X some eight years before (see page 12). In this way, the king hoped to persuade the Pope to grant him the annulment of his marriage.

Increasing the pressure on the Church

It cannot be known for sure how far this episode was orchestrated by the king, but it seems Henry did little to dissuade those who managed the Commons on his behalf to curb whatever strength of feeling existed. Tellingly, he consented to the three anticlerical bills becoming law. Whether this inspired the king to undertake a more general attack on the Church's position is not known. What little evidence there is suggests that Henry was encouraged to increase pressure on the Church and thus weaken its will to resist. He did so by applying pressure in two ways:

- legally: the king threatened to take legal action against any clerics, either individually or collectively, who might oppose the Crown
- financially: the Church was expected to comply with the king's demands for generous financial support for the 'good governance' of the nation.

Not content with these measures, Henry decided to pursue a more radical course of action. A few months later, towards the end of 1530, he indicted the clergy, both secular and regular, on a charge of *praemunire* (see page 30). The indictment was phrased in such a way – acknowledging Wolsey's legatine powers without seeking the king's permission – that it was virtually impossible for any cleric to escape punishment under the law. A precedent had been set in the toppling of Wolsey when he, too, had been charged and found guilty of *praemunire*. Henry reasoned that what had succeeded against one cleric, especially one so mighty, might also be applied to them all. A critical Chapuys reported to his master, Charles V, that the indictment 'rests on the imagination of the king, who comments and amplifies it at pleasure connecting with it any cause he chooses'.

'Sole protector and supreme head of the English Church and clergy'

The relentless pressure applied by Henry finally took its toll and the Church caved in. When **Convocation** met in January 1531, the majority of its members were eager to compromise. The price of their pliancy was high. They were informed that the king would withdraw the indictment of *praemunire* in return for:

- a grant of £118,000
- the awarding to him of the title of 'sole protector and supreme head of the English Church and clergy'.

After some hard bargaining both sides managed to reach a compromise. Negotiating on behalf of Convocation, Bishop Fisher (see pages 51–2) failed to achieve a reduction in the huge sum demanded but he did persuade the king to

KEY TERM

Convocation Church equivalent of Parliament where clerics meet in two houses to discuss and transact Church affairs.

accept payment over five years. Arguably Fisher's most significant achievement was in amending the title Henry had claimed for himself. Convocation agreed to accept the king as their 'supreme head' but only on condition that a qualifying clause was added to the title, namely, 'as far as the law of Christ allows'. This concession made it possible for each cleric to interpret for himself what (if anything) the king's new title meant in practice.

The agreement between the Crown and the Church was enshrined in an Act of Parliament passed in January 1531. The Pardon of the Clergy absolved the Church of any wrongdoing and the indictment was withdrawn. Despite Fisher's concessions there was only one winner in this contest and that was the king.

The Supplication against the Ordinaries

If the clergy thought that the king's pardon had ended the conflict between Church and Crown they were mistaken. A year later, early in 1532, it seems that Parliament took the lead in attacking the Church when the House of Commons presented the king with a petition known as the Supplication against the Ordinaries (bishops). The petition's attack on the Church was two-fold:

- it claimed that the Church was riddled with corruption
- it challenged the Church's right to have its own courts and laws independent of the Crown and State.

The petitioners urged the king to root out this corruption and end the legal and legislative independence of the Church by bringing it firmly under the control of the State. There is some dispute among historians regarding the origin of the Supplication but the majority believe that it was engineered by Thomas Cromwell and pushed through Parliament in order to give the impression that the king had the support of his people.

Henry agreed to consider the petition and passed a copy to Convocation requesting them to respond to the complaints. Henry was cynically manipulating events by pretending, in the opinion of historian Keith Randell (1993), 'to be the impartial judge in a dispute between two groups of his subjects'. Convocation responded by rejecting completely the complaints and countered by asserting the Church's ancient right to enact and enforce canon law. The defiant tone of the reply angered the king who abandoned the pretence of impartiality and aligned himself with the Commons. Henry demanded that Convocation agree to respect his kingly authority and to acknowledge his right to govern the Church as he did the State. With the legislative independence of the Church under threat, the more militant bishops in Convocation urged their fellow clerics to resist the king's demands. Unfortunately for them the Archbishop of Canterbury, William Warham, was weak and indecisive, and he failed to provide the kind of leadership required to resist the Crown.

The submission of the clergy

Henry pressed home the attack by demanding the submission of the clergy. Unable to resist the pressure any longer, in May 1532 Convocation reluctantly agreed to the terms of the submission. The Church did the following:

- surrendered its right to make ecclesiastical laws independently of the king
- promised not to issue new laws currently being drafted without royal licence
- agreed to submit existing laws to a royally appointed committee for revision.

The terms of the submission were confirmed in an Act of Parliament, at which point Sir Thomas More, a defender of the Church's right to autonomy, resigned as Lord Chancellor. The clergy's will to resist had been crushed.

The royal supremacy

The royal supremacy asserted that the king of England had a God-given right of **cure of souls** of his subjects, was head of the national Church and owed no obedience to the 'Bishop of Rome'. This was based on the premise, expounded in the Act in Restraint of Appeals, that 'this realm of England is an empire ... governed by one Supreme head and King'. It claimed this had always been so and that the papacy had usurped jurisdiction over the English Church. Thus, the Act of Supremacy sought to re-establish the king's territories as a 'sovereign empire' within which no other ruler could exercise control of any sort. Much of the force of the argument underpinning this policy lay in the word 're-establish'. Those who urged the king in this direction believed that the rulers of England had enjoyed sole power in their kingdoms until sometime in the early Middle Ages, when the Pope (unjustifiably in their opinion) had established a variety of legal and financial claims because of his headship of the Western Church. These, it was argued, were spurious and should be rejected out of hand.

KEY TERM

Cure of souls God-given authority to safeguard the salvation of men as part of Christ's mission on earth.

When Cromwell and his team of advisers finally prevailed on Henry, who had often vacillated, to assent to the passing of the Act in November 1534, a complete break with Rome was achieved. Cromwell's success, of course, was only possible because the Pope was unprepared to bow to any threat, thus enabling Henry to be persuaded that it was only by throwing off allegiance to Rome that his annulment could be achieved. Once it had been accepted by the king that there could be no going back, the task of those who wished to see an end to papal power in England for reasons unconnected to Anne Boleyn became much more straightforward.

Supremacy and vicegerent (vicar-general)

The terms of the Act of Supremacy empowered the king 'to reform and redress all errors, heresies and abuses in the same'. This was significant because the routine management of the Church in spiritual as well as temporal matters passed from clerical into lay hands. Henceforth, it would be the king and his representative rather than the Archbishop of Canterbury and the clerical hierarchy who would direct the nation's religious affairs. The king's authority was emphasised in the Act's opening sentences (see Source C).

? Study Source C. How does this Act suggest that Parliament had grown in power?

SOURCE C

Extract from the preamble of the Act of Supremacy (1534).

Albeit the king's Majesty justly and rightfully is and oweth to be the supreme head of the Church of England, and so is recognized by the clergy of this realm in their Convocations; be it enacted by authority of this present parliament that the king our sovereign lord, his heirs and successors kings of this realm, shall be taken, accepted and reputed the only supreme head in earth of the Church of England called Anglicana Ecclesia …

KEY TERM

Vicegerent The king's deputy in Church affairs.

Henry wasted little time in exercising his new powers and one of his first acts as Supreme Head was to appoint his representative to oversee the Church. In January 1535, Cromwell was appointed as the king's **vicegerent** in spiritual matters. This gave him enormous power since it meant that he was in a position to exercise the authority that legally belonged to the king. Much to their dismay, the senior clergy found Cromwell to be an energetic and intrusive vicegerent. Any hopes that they had that the royal supremacy would be a distant, light-touch affair were soon dispelled when Cromwell involved himself in day-to-day matters. Even Cranmer, as Archbishop of Canterbury, found himself subject to the forceful opinion of the vicegerent on such matters as clerical appointments.

Extinguishing the authority of the Bishop of Rome

Inspired by St German's *Treatise Concerning the Power of the Clergy and the Laws of the Realm*, published in 1535, Cromwell sought to eradicate every vestige of papal authority in England. Through his careful management of the Reformation Parliament a number of acts were passed that, collectively, led to the enhancement of royal authority and the extinction of papal power. The most important of these acts was the aptly named 'Act Extinguishing the Authority of the Bishop of Rome' (1536), under the terms of which the following were denied to the Pope:

- access to and collection of clerical taxes
- the power of appointment to Church offices
- the authority to determine matters of religious doctrine
- the right to grant dispensations and personal exemptions
- the use of his title in England, being known, henceforth, as the Bishop of Rome.

Needless to say, any clerics who persisted in recognising or defending papal authority were deemed to be traitors and were dealt with by means of the Treason Act (see page 51). Drawn up by Cromwell immediately after the Act of Supremacy, the Act made it treason to deny or question the validity of the

SOURCE D

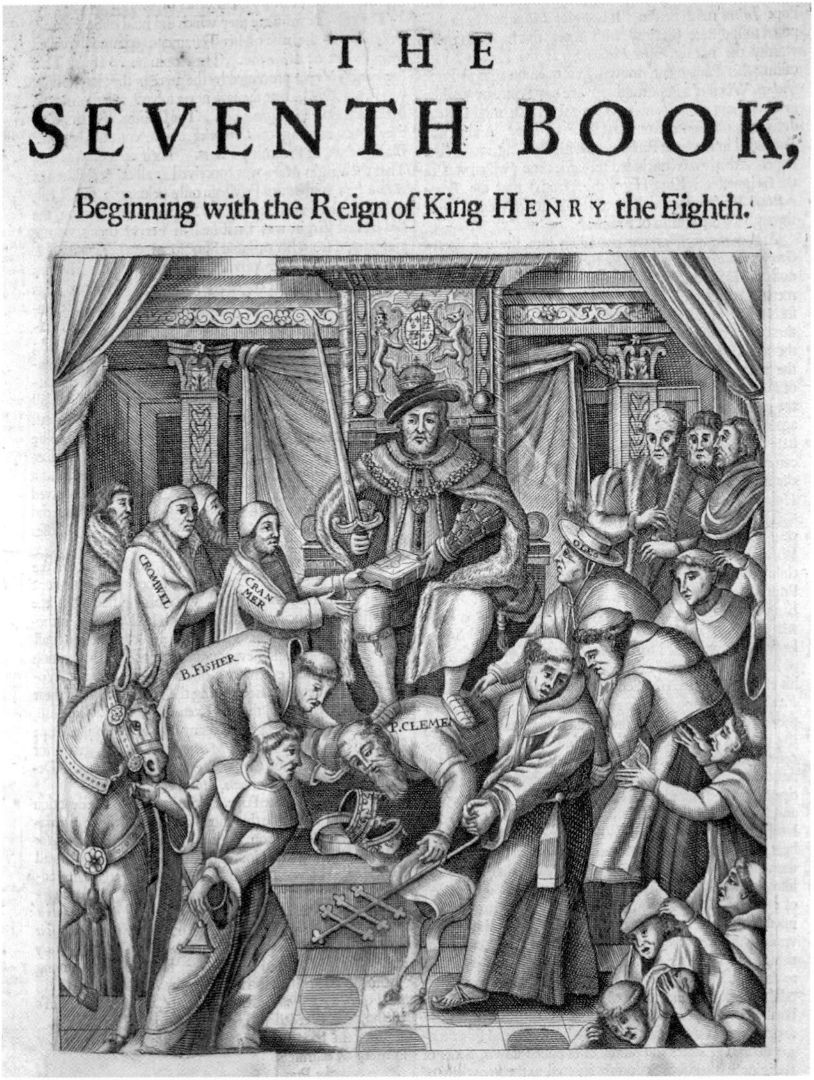

The 'Seventh Book'. An allegory of the Reformation from John Foxe's *Book of Martyrs*, first published in 1563, a massively influential piece of Protestant literature published during the reign of Elizabeth I.

Study Source D. Why might the Pope have regarded this image distasteful?

king's supremacy. For those who broke the law by daring 'to slanderously and maliciously publish and pronounce, by express writing or words, that the king should be heretic, schismatic, tyrant, infidel or usurper', there was only one punishment: death.

In the opinion of historian W.J. Sheils (1989), the significance of the royal supremacy is that it 'came to be exercised by the King in Parliament, rather than by the King in his own right'. It was, he continued, 'essentially a personal supremacy' that involved 'Parliament not only in matters of jurisdiction but also in matters of doctrine'. To some historians such as Elton, this amounted to a constitutional revolution because it redefined the Crown's relationship not just with the Church but also with Parliament. The Church became subject to the power of the State and the king's authority over the Church was expressed through legislation enacted in Parliament.

Summary diagram: The Reformation Parliament, royal supremacy and the rise of Cromwell

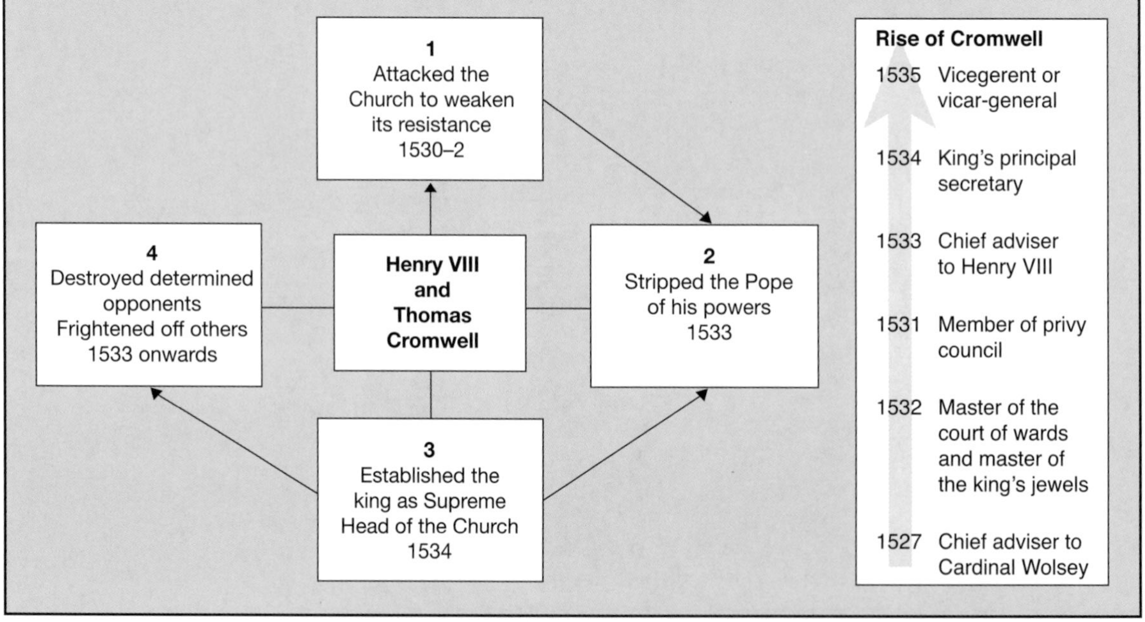

3 Faction, opposition and rebellion

▶ *What motives lay behind the actions of those involved in the conflict between England and the papacy?*

Faction

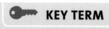

KEY TERM

Faction Political groups working against each other at the royal court and in government.

As the king's 'great matter' progressed and turned into an attack on the Church there developed a division of opinion within the ranks of the nobility and clerical hierarchy. This division was, in some respects, to be expected when one considers the factional nature of English politics and government. Although the nature and significance of **faction** are fiercely debated by historians there is little doubt that there existed competition for office and personal power. Faction was closely linked to patronage, which enabled the powerful at court to reward their followers. Of course, the most powerful were those who held senior office in the government or in the royal household, or who were held in special affection by the king since the Crown was the ultimate fount of all patronage.

Wolsey had long been opposed by rivals who sought either to disgrace or to displace him and he responded in kind, but the period after 1527 witnessed a reshaping of the traditional lines of conflict. Removing Wolsey from power was no longer in itself a means to an end since his replacement would have to contend with the problems and pitfalls connected with the king's 'great matter'. Thus, there developed three broad groupings at court:

- the Boleyn group led by Anne and her father, Sir Thomas
- the Aragonese group which formed around Queen Catherine
- the Norfolk group which was led by Thomas Howard, Duke of Norfolk.

Although the Boleyn and Aragonese groups were bitter enemies they shared a common antipathy towards Wolsey, whom they blamed for either hindering or promoting the king's 'great matter'. Norfolk had long been opposed to Wolsey so either group might expect to gain his support. However, Norfolk's sympathy with Catherine of Aragon was outweighed by ties of blood since Anne Boleyn was his niece. Therefore, the Boleyn/Norfolk axis sought to secure the annulment while the Aragonese faction worked against it.

The fall of Wolsey and changing faction groups

Following the fall of Wolsey, the annulment remained centre stage but the increasing attacks on the Church led to a gradual redrawing of the battle lines so that, generally speaking, it is possible to identify two broad groups competing at court: conservatives and reformers. Norfolk, in conjunction with Stephen Gardiner, Bishop of Winchester, assumed the headship of the conservatives while the reformers or progressives were led by the Boleyns. Other groups emerged to champion one side or the other, such as the group that gathered around Cromwell, who led the reformers until his fall, after which the Seymours took up the cause of reform. The conservatives too embraced change, particularly after the passing of the Act of Supremacy and following the death of Catherine of Aragon.

Although faction did play a part in courtly politics, a group was only ever as influential as the individual who led it. Thus, the roles of Thomas Cranmer, Catherine of Aragon, Anne Boleyn, Norfolk and Gardiner need to be assessed if the role of faction is to be properly understood.

Religious differences deepened the rift between political factions at court, particularly when the king appointed a 'progressive', Thomas Cranmer, to lead the Church on the death of William Warham in 1532. While he had lived, there had always been the possibility that he would summon up enough courage to refuse to do as he was directed by Henry. Certainly, he was not in favour of the annulment and he had proved himself willing to be obstructive to the king, even if his resolve often crumbled in the face of royal pressure. But with the old man dead, the way was clear for Henry to choose a totally pliable replacement (as long as the Pope could be prevailed on to endorse the man chosen). The conservatives considered Gardiner a fitting choice for the archbishopric of Canterbury but the king saw things differently.

Thomas Cranmer

In Henry's opinion, Thomas Cranmer appeared to have all the right attributes to lead the Church. He had shown a marked lack of personal ambition, was intellectually very able and had shown himself to be strongly in favour of the annulment. He had already been useful to the king, carrying out his instructions to the letter, whether it was in writing a book supporting Henry's case (in 1529), acting as an agent buying support in European universities (in 1530) or (as now) serving as England's ambassador at the court of Charles V.

Given his reformist views, Cranmer became a junior member of the Boleyn faction and was thus totally acceptable to the queen-in-waiting. Once the Act in Restraint of Appeals had become law there was a need for rapid action. Anne Boleyn, convinced that the divorce would soon be achieved, had finally consented to share her monarch's bed at some time in 1532. By January 1533 she knew that she was pregnant, and Cranmer was instructed to perform a secret marriage ceremony. It was now important that the annulment be finalised and the new marriage declared legal before the baby was born in the early autumn. Cranmer acted with speed, tact and efficiency. A hearing of the case was arranged for late May and, when Catherine refused to attend, a swift judgement was delivered against her. It was announced that the papal dispensation had been invalid, that Henry and Catherine had therefore never been legally married, and that the secret marriage of Henry and Anne was legal. The king was well satisfied and was not in the least displeased that six years of endeavour on his 'great matter' had ended in such a tame victory. The anticlimax was to come when the baby turned out to be a girl!

Catherine of Aragon

If Henry expected Catherine to simply accept that the marriage was over and quietly step aside he was to be bitterly disappointed. In fact, Catherine's defiance surprised and angered him. Henry blamed those around the queen, her close advisers such as Bishop John Fisher, for encouraging her to resist the annulment. Henry was powerless to stop Catherine writing to Pope Clement and her nephew Charles V. Some letters were intercepted but others got through, mainly with the covert assistance of ambassador Chapuys. Unable to block all her channels of communication, Henry instructed his agents in Rome and at the Imperial Court to counter the negative reports by putting the king's side of the affair. Refusing to accept the legality of the proceedings being taken against her, Catherine only appeared before Campeggio and Wolsey at the Legatine Court at Blackfriars to address Henry directly and plead with him to dismiss the case for annulment. Her dignity and self-assurance in such a pressured and public environment impressed those who witnessed her conduct. Thereafter, she refused to attend or to be represented in what she considered to be an illegal tribunal. Her request that the matter be transferred to Rome eventually brought the proceedings to an end and resulted in Wolsey's disgrace.

Besides her calm and dignified personality, Catherine's greatest asset was her popularity. Much to Henry's fury Catherine was as loved by the people as Anne Boleyn was hated. To ensure that she retained the sympathy and support of the people Catherine set herself strict limits to the scale and nature of her opposition. She refused the advice of those who willed her to become more aggressive in her conflict with the king. She was careful to disassociate herself from those who might encourage violent protest or who claimed to act in her name. She denounced Chapuys when she learnt that he was urging Charles V to provide military and financial aid in support of a rebellion he was trying to organise.

Anne Boleyn

Henry's passion for Anne Boleyn was her greatest asset. That she managed to keep the king interested for so long while other mistresses fell quite quickly by the wayside, her sister Mary among them, amazed Anne's contemporaries. Had she provided Henry with the son she promised her life and career might have been very different. Anne was well educated and, unlike many of her female contemporaries, she possessed the strength of mind that enabled her to compete in a man's world. According to historian David Starkey (writing in 1993), 'Anne was not the unthinking vehicle of the Reformation – the pretty face that dissolved a thousand monasteries … she functioned … as an honorary man.' Anne had the instincts of a politician and the skill to make a meaningful contribution to the tactics used by her faction to disgrace Wolsey and isolate Catherine. Anne's alliance with Cromwell proved useful in the short term and her manipulation of the king was especially effective during the darkest days of the annulment crisis.

There is no doubt that Anne played an importance role in Henry's life, but she and her faction may not always have been the principal driving force behind Henry's actions throughout the struggle for the annulment. The king's love for her was deep and enduring but it only intermittently provided the major motivation for his actions. The primary motivation was securing the dynasty.

Norfolk and Gardiner

Gardiner was a talented government minister, and respected thinker and theologian. Although he supported Henry VIII's divorce and break from

Rome, he opposed any major changes in religion. Gardiner did not agree with the religious direction and doctrinal changes proposed by the Henrician government, which alienated the king. Nevertheless, he proved to be an able leader of the conservative faction at court and he succeeded in bringing about the downfall of Cromwell. His opposition to the Seymours in the final years of Henry VIII's reign reduced his influence and resulted in his fall from power after the king's death.

Gardiner was closely allied to Thomas Howard, Duke of Norfolk, one of the most powerful and influential figures at court. Norfolk came to prominence by leading the faction opposed to Henry's chief minister, Cardinal Wolsey. His effort to discredit the cleric paid off when, on Wolsey's fall in 1529, Norfolk became president of the royal council. He supported the marriage of his niece Anne Boleyn to Henry in 1533, but Anne's fall in 1536, coupled with Cromwell's growing power, weakened his position. He regained royal favour by suppressing the rebellion known as the Pilgrimage of Grace. A conservative in religion, Norfolk became a leading and outspoken opponent of the reformers Thomas Cromwell and Thomas Cranmer. On Cromwell's execution in 1540, Norfolk emerged for a time to become the king's chief adviser but his position was again weakened when Henry's fifth wife, Catherine Howard – another of Norfolk's nieces – was put to death in 1542 for infidelity. In December 1546 Norfolk was accused of being an accessory to the alleged treasonable activities of his son and heir, Henry Howard, Earl of Surrey. Surrey was executed and Norfolk condemned, but before the sentence could be carried out Henry VIII died in January 1547.

Conservatives versus reformers

The division between the conservative and reformist factions at court took a bitter turn with the passing of the Act of Supremacy in 1534. Having already lost ground, it became evident to the conservative faction that the Boleyns were no longer the primary focus of the reformist group. Cromwell and his supporters had gained ground by forming an alliance with the Boleyns. By securing the divorce, promoting the marriage and the passage of the royal supremacy, Cromwell was very much in the ascendancy. As he grew stronger, the Boleyns grew weaker. Anne's failure to give Henry the son he craved, allied to his growing dissatisfaction with his wife, led to a decline in their influence. The Aragonese faction, too, lost its influence after the divorce although it tried to make ground by championing the claims of Catherine's daughter, Mary. In 1536 both the Aragonese and Boleyn factions suffered fatal blows to their power when both Catherine of Aragon and Anne Boleyn died: Catherine from natural causes and Anne by execution. The end of the Boleyn faction was hastened by Cromwell who, anticipating Henry's desire to rid himself of Anne in favour of his new love interest, Jane Seymour, turned on his erstwhile allies. Anne's arrest, trial and execution were orchestrated by Cromwell, who saw to it that no impediment lay between the king and his third wife.

Cromwell's tactical masterstroke seemingly cemented his position as the undisputed power at Henry's court. However, as the conservatives bided their time a new reformist group emerged, the Seymours. Cromwell allied himself with this group and when he fell from power they took the leading role in organising the reformers. Cromwell's fall from power was due in part to international intrigue (see pages 56–7), which indicates that foreign politics played a significant role in faction at the English court.

Faction, reformation and the influence of foreign politics

Apart from the Pope, the most important person in influencing the outcome of Henry's 'great matter' was Emperor Charles V. Certainly his influence was strongest in the years during which the king of England accepted that the decision on his marital fate lay with the Pope in Rome.

Charles V

Working through his ambassador, Eustace Chapuys, Charles sought to influence English affairs in two ways:

- first, by supporting the Aragonese faction in their fight to prevent the annulment
- secondly, by supporting the conservatives in opposing the religious changes.

It has long been maintained that Charles prevented the Pope from reaching a decision that would prejudice the interests of Catherine of Aragon by threats and intimidation. According to this interpretation, Charles V did this to protect the honour of his family and because he could not allow Henry to publicly disgrace such a close relative. (Catherine was his mother's sister.) Charles was in a position to do this after imperial troops had ransacked Rome in 1527 and taken the Pope prisoner. Having satisfied himself that Pope Clement was now a compliant client of imperial power, Charles freed him and allowed him to retire to his country retreat at Orvieto. For the next five years, 1527–32, Clement was diplomatically isolated and, militarily, at the mercy of Charles. Thus, the Pope could be prevented from doing anything of which Charles did not approve, which included granting Henry his annulment.

Revisionists have challenged this traditional view, however. According to them, there is little evidence to suggest that Charles cared for Catherine, a relative he hardly knew, nor did he do much to defend her honour in the three years following the annulment of her marriage in 1533 and before her death in 1536.

It is probably fair to say that Charles was motivated by a combination of political self-interest and aristocratic pride. It may be argued that once the annulment had become a matter of widespread international debate, Charles was perhaps unwillingly drawn into the affair. Diplomatic pressure, personal pride and public expectation may have gathered momentum and conspired to force Charles into declaring himself opposed to the annulment.

The Pope

History has been unkind to Pope Clement VII. His reputation has suffered because he found himself amidst political crises over which he could exercise little control. His indecisive approach to the problem of Henry VIII's annulment was compounded by his failure to escape defeat and imprisonment at the hands of Charles V. Clement was no more successful in his relations with the French king, Francis I, who dismissed the pontiff as being weak and of no consequence in international affairs. Clement had no answer to the growing threat of Lutheranism, which served only to encourage the spread of the Protestant Reformation.

Unsurprisingly, some historians have described Clement as being a weak and pathetic figure. The description of Clement given by Archdeacon William Knight, one of Henry VIII's envoys to Rome in 1527, of a dithering and distressed old man unable to reach a decision, seems to support this unflattering image. However, this is perhaps unfair for while there is some truth in this portrait of Clement, a learned and cultured man, he was not consistently indecisive. Following the **Sack of Rome** in 1527 his determination not to act as a tool of Charles V was impressive. He was equally determined not to be bullied by Henry VIII or Francis I.

KEY TERM

Sack of Rome Attack on and looting of Rome by Habsburg troops under Charles V. The attack was a result of the war between Francis and Charles for the control of Italy.

Pope Clement's attitude to the divorce

Clement was unprepared for Henry's request for an annulment. He realised how significant it was and he was aware of the consequences should he make an error in delivering his verdict. Given that the parties concerned all represented the cream of European royalty, Clement had to tread carefully. Clement sympathised with Henry's need for an heir to secure the succession but he felt the annulment was a step too far. In the face of mounting pressure, Clement adopted a 'wait and see' policy, hence the slow pace of papal proceedings.

From letters written by Clement at the time is it clear that, in private, his own sense of justice disposed him to favour Queen Catherine but in public he had to maintain an air of impartiality. Clement proposed two possible solutions to resolving the conflict over the annulment:

- Persuade Catherine to enter a nunnery freely, thus enabling Henry to marry again. By taking the monastic vow of chastity Catherine's marriage would be annulled by default.
- Convince Henry that any children he had with Anne Boleyn could be legitimised by papal dispensation (presumably after Catherine's death, leaving him free to marry Anne).

The Pope's proposal was delivered to Catherine by Campeggio (see page 12) during his interview with her prior to the opening of the court at Blackfriars. It was rejected. Henry, too, rejected the Pope's proposal. Given his policy of questioning the validity of an earlier papal dispensation he had little faith in the legal authority of such documents.

Thus, Clement pursued his policy of delay at all costs in the hope that at some future time, the dispute might be settled by other means. When he did eventually deliver his verdict in Catherine's favour, shortly before his death in 1534, he only did so because Henry had taken the law into his own hands by enforcing the Act in Restraint of Appeals.

Opposition and the Treason Act

Henry and Cromwell were acutely aware that the political and religious policies they were pursuing were likely to be unpopular. What they could not anticipate was the potential scale and seriousness of that opposition. Cromwell had calculated that the opposition would come from a minority of hardliners who would refuse to accept the changes and who preferred martyrdom to submission. This group was likely to consist of devout clerics, like Bishop John Fisher, and politicians of conscience, such as Sir Thomas More. The king's chief minister believed that with a little 'persuasion' the majority of the population would accept the changes without protest. To ensure that the reaction of the Crown would be seen to be proportionate and legally justified, he drew up the Treason Act, which he steered through Parliament in 1534.

The key clause in the Act specified that any person who 'do maliciously wish, will or desire by words or writing, or by craft imagine, invent, practise, or attempt any bodily harm to be done or committed to the king's most royal person, the queen's [Anne Boleyn] or their heir's apparent [Elizabeth]' was guilty of high treason for which they would be put to death.

Not only were people forbidden to speak or write anything that might be critical of the king and his policies, they must, if required by a magistrate or judge, swear oaths accepting the changes and pledging their allegiance to the Crown.

Cromwell was confident that the terms of the Act would be sufficient to deter all but the most determined of the king's opponents.

John Fisher, Bishop of Rochester

Two of the most influential and determined opponents of the king were Bishop John Fisher and Sir Thomas More (see page 54). Their harsh treatment at the hands of the king shocked contemporaries, who blamed both Anne Boleyn and Thomas Cromwell for their trial and execution. They were both canonised (made saints) by the Church in 1935.

Fisher was one of the most senior and well-respected clerics in the English Church. He was a humanist scholar and theologian of international repute. He was a particular favourite of Henry VIII's grandmother, Margaret Beaufort, and he gave the oration at Henry VII's funeral. As a young man Henry VIII admired the charismatic and learned bishop but this turned into a deep loathing once the depth of Fisher's opposition to the annulment became clear. He was the only bishop in Convocation who, from the beginning, consistently opposed the king and his policies. Described as unskilled in politics, he nonetheless vigorously opposed the anticlerical legislation passing through the Reformation Parliament.

Initially, Henry tolerated Fisher's theological and intellectual arguments against accepting the annulment and for rejecting the invalidity of the papal dispensation. Henry even granted Fisher's request to serve as one of Queen Catherine's legal counsel at the annulment tribunal at Blackfriars. However, Fisher's increasing outspokenness, both in public and in print, on the matter of the annulment caused Henry to abandon the restraint he had shown thus far.

KEY FIGURE

Elizabeth Barton (1506–34)

Known as the Holy Maid of Kent, Barton was a nun at St Sepulchre's Convent in Canterbury. She was known for her prophecies and claims to be in contact with the Virgin Mary. Barton had a remarkably wide following among the English clergy and nobility.

Enemy of the king

Henry was furious when Fisher declared his support for the Holy Maid of Kent, **Elizabeth Barton**. Barton had attracted the attention of the government when she denounced Henry's attempts to annul his marriage. Fisher believed that Barton's visions and prophesies were divinely inspired. However, when Barton began prophesying that if Henry remarried he would die shortly thereafter and go straight to hell, Fisher distanced himself from her. Fisher was not prepared to go as far as to discuss in public the king's mortality or any sin he may have committed, but in private he began corresponding with Charles V, whom he encouraged to invade England and remove Henry. When Barton publicly stated that Henry 'should no longer be king of this realm ... and should die a villain's death' she was arrested, tried and convicted of heresy. In April 1534 she was executed at Tyburn in London.

In the same month that Henry disposed of Barton he moved against Fisher. Henry realised that he could not simply punish Fisher without just cause as this might encourage protest both at home and abroad, so he charged him with treason on two counts:

- meeting with the heretic Elizabeth Barton and failing to disclose the treasonous nature of her prophesies
- refusing to swear the oath of supremacy accepting the annulment of the king's marriage and the succession of his offspring by Anne Boleyn.

Fisher was imprisoned in the Tower of London and Henry was prepared, at first, to leave him there. However, this changed when Pope Paul III (1534–49), Clement's successor, appointed Fisher a cardinal. It is thought that Pope Paul did this in an effort to save Fisher's life by deterring Henry from punishing a newly appointed 'prince of the Church'. It had the opposite effect for Henry resented the pontiff's attempts to interfere in the internal affairs of England. On being informed of Fisher's promotion, Henry is reported to have said that he would 'give Fisher a red hat of his own, or else see that he had nowhere to put it'. Fisher was tried for treason and executed in 1535.

Sir Thomas More

Sir Thomas More was a lawyer by trade and a scholar by inclination. His literary activities had earned for him a reputation as one of Europe's leading scholars. He attracted the attention and patronage of Henry VIII, who came to regard him as a friend. His political interests drew him to court, where Henry employed him as an adviser and diplomat. However, in the cut and thrust of Tudor politics More's strict moral code prevented him from doing the things needed to become a front-line political figure. This explains why many of his contemporaries were surprised when Henry offered him the post of Lord Chancellor. To succeed Wolsey at such a critical juncture in the annulment process was very risky. More could offer no solution to a problem for which he had little sympathy. Like Fisher, he was not convinced by the king's reasons for seeking the annulment but unlike his clerical friend, More was willing to remain silent.

During his two-year tenure as Lord Chancellor (1530–2) More worked behind the scenes to frustrate Henry's cause but to little practical effect. However, it was not the annulment itself that caused him to resign but the king's mounting attack on the independence of the Church. Henry's bullying of Convocation

Sir Thomas More

1478	Born the son of a lawyer, Sir John More, in London
1504	Entered Parliament
1510	Appointed under-sheriff of London
1515	Joined the royal delegation to Flanders to negotiate new agreements on the wool trade
1518	Admitted to the king's council as an adviser to the king
1521	Knighted by Henry VIII. Co-author with the king of *Defence of the Seven Sacraments*, a rejection of Luther and Protestantism
1523	Appointed speaker of the House of Commons
1525	Appointed to government office as Chancellor of the Duchy of Lancaster
1530	Appointed Lord Chancellor (king's chief minister)
1532	Resigned from the government after refusing to support the king's annulment and for opposing the king's attack on the Church
1535	Tried and found guilty of treason. Executed by beheading

More was educated at St Anthony's School, London, and served as a teenage page in the household of Archbishop John Morton. Between c.1494 and 1496 he attended Oxford University, after which he was admitted to Lincoln's Inn to study law. In 1501 more became a barrister-at-law. In 1505 he became friends with Desiderius Erasmus (see page 12), the international scholar and humanist. In 1511 his first wife died in childbirth and he married for a second time.

As Lord Chancellor, More could not support the king's divorce and opposed the attack on the Church. He resigned. In 1534 he refused to swear to the Act of Succession and Oath of Supremacy, for which he was committed to the Tower of London.

More was a reluctant martyr and Henry VIII was a reluctant executioner. More's last words on the scaffold were: 'I die the king's good servant, but God's first.' He is important because he is seen as a man of conscience and he refused to compromise or betray his principles.

Study Source E. Why might More have commissioned this portrait?

SOURCE E

A painting by Hans Holbein (the Younger) painted in 1530 of Sir Thomas More wearing his chain of office as Lord Chancellor.

followed by the Pardon of the Clergy and Parliament's Supplication of the Ordinaries caused More to feel uncomfortable about remaining in office. He did not believe that the Church's best interests would be served if it passed into the hands of laymen.

More's resignation and execution

More's resignation coincided with the Submission of the Clergy because he felt no longer able to serve a king who had so offended against the laws of God and the Church. He intended to retire from public life and protect himself by remaining silent. Unfortunately for him, Henry was not satisfied and he requested that More swear to the oath of succession. Like Fisher, More refused and he joined the bishop in the Tower. He was later tried and was found guilty on a legal technicality aided by the perjury of Cromwell's agent Richard Rich. More was executed in July 1535, a month after Fisher.

Monastic opposition: Franciscans and Carthusians

Among the most outspoken critics of the king's treatment of Catherine and of the Pope were two religious orders of the regular clergy: the Observant Franciscan friars and the Carthusian monks. They were dangerous because they were respected and well connected. Geographically, the London Carthusians were in a strong position to influence public opinion because unlike many of the other monastic orders, they were not situated in isolated rural locations. They were to be found at the heart of the capital city, close to the government and the court, a visibility they used to their advantage to remind the powers that be that not all of the king's subjects approved of the royal supremacy. The leading Carthusian, Prior John Houghton, became a target of Cromwell's agents because of his refusal to deny papal authority. Over a three-year period Houghton and seventeen fellow Carthusians were arrested and executed for their opposition to the supremacy.

The Observant Franciscan friars were feared by the government because they had so much support and to move against them might have invited public protest or even rebellion. Attempts were made to discredit them as in 1528, when a discontented friar confessed that many of his brethren were guilty of Lutheranism and spoke ill of the king and of Wolsey. Cromwell stepped up the pressure on the Franciscans by offering them immunity from prosecution if they would publicly declare their support for the royal supremacy; few did. One of their leaders, Friar John Forest, had been confessor to Catherine of Aragon, so he was unwavering in his support of the queen. He was arrested after a letter he wrote to the queen was intercepted by Cromwell's agents. From the contents of the letter and under the terms of the Treason Act, Cromwell was able to charge Forest and his fellow Franciscans with being 'disciples of the Bishop of Rome and sowers of sedition'. Following their forced removal from public view it is thought that up to 30 of the 200 Franciscans died unnoticed in captivity; Forest was among them.

Fear of rebellion

Besides the possibility of invasion, Henry's greatest fear was the outbreak of rebellion. The changes introduced were such that some people might be pushed into armed opposition to the Crown and its ministers. In the event, the long feared rebellion broke out in northern England in late 1536. The Pilgrimage of Grace was the largest and, potentially, the most serious rebellion of the sixteenth century. The rebellion grew in strength to nearly 40,000 people and it broadened geographically to include half a dozen counties in northern England. Henry ordered the dukes of Norfolk and Suffolk to deal with the insurgents but their forces, no more than 8000, were vastly outnumbered by the rebels. Henry turned to diplomacy and managed to persuade the rebel leader, Robert Aske, of his good intentions. Negotiating through Norfolk, who posed as a sympathiser, Henry conceded their demands: monastic lands to be restored, Cromwell to be removed and a Parliament called to address their wider concerns. Henry also promised a free pardon for all rebels who agreed to disperse and return to their homes. Duped by a deliberately deceitful king, the rebels dispersed but in the weeks following the end of the rebellion many, including Aske, were hunted down, arrested, tried and executed.

? Why might some historians consider Hall's opinion of the Pilgrimage of Grace, as expressed in Source F, to be biased?

SOURCE F

From Edward Hall, *The Union of the Two Noble and Illustrious Families of Lancaster and York*, commonly known as *Hall's Chronicle* and published in 1542.

But the northern men refused to end their wicked rebellion. But, as if by a great miracle of God, the water suddenly rose to such a height and breadth, so that on the day, even when the hour of battle should have come, it was impossible for one army to get at the other.

Then a consultation was held and a pardon obtained from the King's majesty for all the leaders of this insurrection. They were promised that their petition would be presented to the King and their grievances would be gently heard and their reasonable requests granted, so that by the King's authority all things should be brought to good order and conclusion. And with this promise every man quietly departed.

The Reformation and fall of Cromwell

There is wide agreement that Henry VIII's motives in breaking away from Rome were much more political than religious. The English Reformation put the Church firmly under the control of the State. It also removed England from the authority of the Pope; a source of outside interference which was highly resented among the English ruling elites. The resulting royal supremacy made Henry VIII more independent and more powerful than any monarch in English history. It enabled him to rule an undivided kingdom where Church and State were merged into a single sovereign state. Henry VIII was able to reduce the political power of the Church and exploit its vast wealth. Ecclesiastical wealth replenished the Exchequer, which had been almost bankrupted by Henry's unsuccessful attempts to secure the French throne.

On the surface, the Crown was the main beneficiary of the English Reformation. Yet, once religion had come to the forefront of the political arena, it created problems for the monarchy. Religious differences deepened the rift between political factions at court. The most notable casualty of this rivalry was the 'architect of the Reformation', Thomas Cromwell. Cromwell's greatest achievement was in planning and piloting the legislation responsible for the break with Rome. His survey, closure and eventual destruction of the monasteries represent a model of administrative speed and efficiency. Unfortunately, his skill and effectiveness in government, his promotion of the key aspects of Protestantism and his leadership of the religious reform movement at court caused jealousy and made him powerful enemies. When he made mistakes, such as arranging the marriage between Henry VIII and Anne of Cleves, his enemies pounced and ruined his reputation with the king. Barely three months after being ennobled as Earl of Essex he was executed on trumped-up charges of treason in July 1540.

Thereafter, Henry VIII had to tread a cautious path between the conservative Catholic and reforming Protestant parties. By 1546 he had decided that the safest way to protect the succession and the royal supremacy was to give control of the privy council to Somerset and the reformers.

Summary diagram: The influence of faction, opposition and the spectre of rebellion

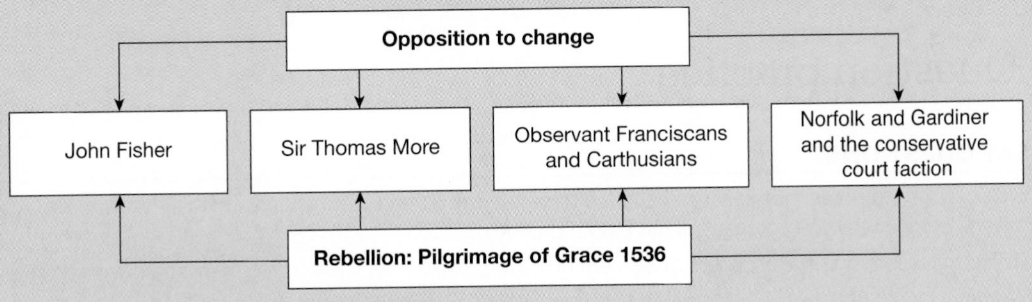

Chapter summary

Historians continue to debate the reasons why the Reformation took place and why the English Church broke with Rome. The role and influence of Henry VIII, Cardinal Wolsey, Cromwell and the Pope are pivotal in reaching an understanding why the Reformation occurred. There is wide agreement on the impact the divorce had in promoting change. Henry VIII's instruction to Wolsey to explore with the Pope the possibility of obtaining an annulment from Catherine of Aragon set in motion a chain of events culminating in the unintended break with Rome. Wolsey's failure to obtain an annulment, combined with opposition from factions or groups supporting Catherine of Aragon and Anne Boleyn, led to his fall from power. His replacement as chief minister, Sir Thomas More, fared equally badly, which led to his resignation and eventual execution for opposing the king's treatment of the Church. Owing to Cromwell's skilful handling of the Reformation Parliament, the Church was cowed into submission and the Act of Supremacy was passed. Following the break with Rome, Henry became head of the Church, secured his divorce and, with the assistance of Archbishop Thomas Cranmer, set about doctrinal reform. This led to conflict between conservatives and reformers at court.

Refresher questions

Use these questions to remind yourself of the key material covered in this chapter.

1 What was the king's 'great matter'?
2 Why did Henry VIII want an annulment?
3 What steps did Henry take to obtain an annulment?
4 Why did Wolsey fail to secure the annulment?
5 How and why did Wolsey fall from power?
6 What was Cromwell's 'new idea' to break the deadlock between king and Pope?
7 How significant was Cranmer's role in the annulment issue?
8 Why did the Crown attack the Church?
9 How was the king's 'great matter' resolved?
10 How significant was Cromwell's role in the Reformation?
11 What was meant by the royal supremacy and how was it achieved?
12 Did the royal supremacy influence constitutional change?
13 What impact did court faction have on the progress of the Reformation?

Question practice

ESSAY QUESTIONS

1 'Wolsey fell from power not because he failed to secure the divorce but because he failed to win over Anne Boleyn.' Explain why you agree or disagree with this view.
2 'Sir Thomas More was the architect of his own downfall.' Explain why you agree or disagree with this view.
3 To what extent was the desire for religious reform mainly responsible for the break with Rome?
4 'From archbishop to parish priest the English clergy fully supported the Act of Supremacy in 1534.' Assess the validity of this view.

SOURCE ANALYSIS QUESTIONS

1 With reference to Sources 1 and 2 below, and your understanding of the historical context, which of these two sources is more valuable in explaining why Henry VIII felt the need to control the Church?
2 With reference to Sources 1, 2 and 3 below, and your understanding of the historical context, assess the value of these sources to a historian studying the relationship between Henry VIII and the Church.

SOURCE 1

From the Act for the Pardon of the Clergy passed in the Reformation Parliament in 1531.

The King, our Sovereign Lord, calling to his blessed and most gracious remembrance that his good and loving subjects the most reverend father in God Archbishop of Canterbury and other bishops, prelates and other spiritual persons of the province of the archbishopric of Canterbury which have exercised, practised or executed in spiritual [Church] courts and other spiritual jurisdictions within the said province [of Canterbury] have incurred His Highness's anger by ignoring and committing acts contrary to the order of the King's laws and specially contrary to the Statute of Praemunire. His Highness by authority of his Parliament, hath given and granted his liberal and free pardon to his said good and loving spiritual subjects on condition that henceforth they abide by the authority of his laws as enacted by this his present Parliament.

SOURCE 2

From reports of suspected dissident priests sent to Cromwell published in the *Calendar of State Papers: Henry VIII (1534–6)*. Royal agents were instructed to gather evidence of sermons preached in church services that appeared to be critical of the Crown's religious policy.

Unnamed Priest from St. Albans (1535). If it fortune the king to die, you shall see this world turned up-so down or clear changed.

Unnamed Priest from London (1536). Be you of good comfort, and be steadfast in your faith and be not wavering, and God shall reward us the more. For these things will not last long, I warrant you; you shall see the world changed shortly.

Dr. John London (1534). Remember how often in times past these ways hath been attempted, and what end the authors thereof hath come unto. Remember this world will not continue long. For although the king hath now conceived a little malice against the bishop of Rome because he would not agree to this marriage, yet I trust that the blessed king will wear harness on his own back to fight against heretics.

SOURCE 3

From the Act for the Submission of the Clergy to the King's Majesty passed in the Reformation Parliament in 1534.

Where the King's humble and obedient subjects, the clergy of this realm of England, have not only acknowledged, according to the truth; that the Convocations of the same clergy is always, hath been, and ought to be assembled only by the King's writ, but also, submitting themselves to the King's Majesty, have promised that they will never from henceforth presume to enact, pass or promulgate any new canons [Church laws] unless the King has given them his Royal assent to do so. Be it therefore now enacted by this Present Parliament, according to the said submission and petition of the said clergy that no manner of appeals shall be had or sent out of this realm to the Bishop of Rome, nor to the see of Rome. Henceforth all appeals and petitions shall be heard within this realm and for lack of justice in the Church courts it shall be legal for all complainants to appeal to the King's Majesty in the King's Court of Chancery.

A Church half-reformed: religious change and continuity 1535–47

This chapter considers change and continuity in religion, the nature of worship and the evolution of doctrine. The reaction to change will also be examined, especially the faction struggle between conservatives and reformers and the causes and consequences of the dissolution of the monasteries. It has been argued that by 1547 the Church was only 'half-reformed' because the impact of religious change had not been deep enough. These issues are examined as three themes:

- ★ The dissolution of the monasteries
- ★ Cromwell, Cranmer and the progress of the Reformation after 1534
- ★ Change and continuity in doctrine: the state of the English Church by 1547

The key debate on *page 69* of this chapter asks the question: To what extent was the dissolution of the monasteries planned?

Key dates

1535		Visitations to the monasteries; *Valor Ecclesiasticus*
1536		First Act for the Dissolution of the Monasteries
		Act of Ten Articles
1537		Publication of *The Bishops' Book*
1539		Second Act for the Dissolution of the Monasteries
		Act of Six Articles
1542	**Nov.**	Battle of Solway Moss
	Dec.	James V died; succeeded by Mary
1543		Treaty of Greenwich
1544		Invasion of France; Boulogne captured
1545		Cranmer's Litany and *King's Prymer*
1546		Treaty of Camp
1547		Henry VIII died

1 The dissolution of the monasteries

▶ *Why were the monasteries dissolved?*

Causes of the dissolution

The majority of historians agree that the principal cause of the dissolution of the monasteries was financial. The Crown was in dire need of an additional permanent source of income. Henry and Wolsey had struggled to finance the French war of 1522–3, when taxpayers resisted what they considered to be excessive financial demands. The monasteries were thought to be an easy target because they were already in crisis and it was rumoured that the monastic orders preferred papal primacy to royal supremacy. Humanists had condemned them as a drain on the Commonwealth and the monastic vocation had declined to such an extent that many houses were staffed by dwindling numbers of inmates. Fewer than 10,000 monks, friars and nuns, inhabiting over 800 monastic institutions, were sustained by perhaps one-fifth of the cultivated land in England and Wales. As events were to prove, the closure, confiscation of goods and subsequent sale and lease of monastic land did much to enrich the English Crown.

As early as 1533, there had been talk of the Crown assuming control of Church property and estates, both monastic and secular, and of employing bishops as salaried officials. There was a generally held perception that the monasteries no longer commanded enough respect to justify the great wealth with which they were endowed. The fact that Wolsey met with no opposition when he dissolved some 29 houses in the 1520s might be cited as proof of this. However, it was not until 1535, after Henry had become head of the Church, that a plan was put forward to survey the wealth and possessions of the monasteries before any subsequent action was taken. That action would be taken against the monasteries was inevitable given the cutting remark by Charles V's ambassador Chapuys (see page 49), that Cromwell's rise to power was due to a promise he made Henry that he would make him 'the richest king in Christendom'.

Visitation and the compilation of the *Comperta Monastica*

In 1535 Cromwell began to flex his ecclesiastical muscle by exercising his powers as the king's vicegerent. His first objective was to assess the state of the monasteries, so he assembled a team of agents who were entrusted with the task of visiting the vast majority of the nation's religious houses. Monastic visitations were nothing new; they had a long history and were an accepted part of Church administration. Traditionally, such visitations had been conducted either under the authority of the bishop in whose diocese the particular monastic community was located or by the head of the religious order to which the clerics belonged.

KEY TERM

Comperta Monastica
A book compiled by Cromwell's agents which contained lists of transgressions and abuses admitted by monks and nuns.

The difference between the more traditional visitations and those ordered by Cromwell was the searching nature of the enquiry and the attitude of the agents delegated to compile the reports.

Much of the work done in compiling the ***Comperta Monastica*** (also known as the *Compendium Compertorum*) was carried out by some of Cromwell's most trusted 'servants', Thomas Legh, Richard Layton, John ap Rhys, John Tregonwell and John Vaughan. They were handpicked by Cromwell because they were able, ambitious and supported his reformist agenda. They were mainly secular clergy who had expressed doubts about the value and quality of the monastic vocation. Rhys and Vaughan, Cromwell's Welsh agents, were especially dismissive of relics, pilgrimages and miraculous tokens. In addition, the commissioners were instructed to record whether or not the monasteries were complying with the Oath of Supremacy and to detail any alleged offences against the Crown. Clearly, these were men in whom Cromwell had complete trust.

Visitation

To ensure a measure of consistency in the reports that each agent or royal commissioner was expected to provide they were issued with a list of questions by Cromwell. Motivated by a twin desire to please their master and prove the irrelevance of monasticism, Cromwell's commissioners performed their task with brisk efficiency. Lacking tact and sympathy for those whom they 'interrogated', the commissioners often spent only a few hours in each institution they visited. Reports of bullying and intimidation soon reached Cromwell, who feigned interest and promised to investigate but never did so. His main concern was how the king might react should he receive copies of these complaints, so Cromwell tried to control the flow of information to the king. By carefully selecting the most damning reports highlighting evidence of moral laxity (especially sexual) and the prevalence of superstitious religious observances such as the veneration of relics, Cromwell was able to maintain the king's support.

Nevertheless, the complaints kept coming and some of Cromwell's commissioners were even included in a list of the king's 'evil counsellors', drawn up by the rebel leader Robert Aske during the Pilgrimage of Grace in 1536 (see Chapter 2, page 67, and Source A on page 67).

Although Cromwell's programme of visitations was never completed, his agents had collected a mass of information that proved useful in conveying an impression of monastic laxity and decline. At the end of 1535 a truncated edition of the *Comperta Monastica* was completed and submitted to the king. The fuller version envisaged by Cromwell never appeared because it was superseded by another even more ambitious undertaking, the *Valor Ecclesiasticus* or 'church valuation'.

The *Valor Ecclesiasticus*

The *Valor Ecclesiasticus* represented Cromwell's most ambitious project to date. It was the greatest survey of ecclesiastical wealth and property ever undertaken and has been described a kind of Tudor Domesday Book. The *Valor* valued taxes paid to the Crown from ecclesiastical property and income that had previously been paid to the Pope. Unlike the handpicked commissioners who worked on the *Comperta*, the work of the *Valor* was undertaken by local gentry.

In what was a colossal undertaking, every parish and every monastic institution in England and Wales was visited. As a result of its work, the government gained a solid understanding of the scale of the wealth of the Church as a whole and of the monasteries in particular.

According to the *Valor*, the net annual income of the Church was put at £320,000, a figure that can be revised upwards by at least £60,000 when omissions are taken into account (in today's values this would range from £103 million to £122 million). The division of income between the regular and secular Church was roughly 60/40, making the numerically inferior monks and nuns far wealthier that their more numerous counterparts working as parish priests and chaplains.

The impact of the *Valor Ecclesiasticus* and *Comperta Monastica*

The *Valor* and the *Comperta* provided the ammunition for those determined to close the monasteries. The *Valor* provided a list of itemised expenditure as well as income that Cromwell manipulated and then used to show evidence of widespread corruption. Cromwell was able to demonstrate the bankruptcy of monasticism by revealing that in spite of the considerable income enjoyed by the religious orders, only three per cent was regularly allocated to charitable works. The misapplication of funds, fraud and clerical corruption were highlighted by Cromwell, who managed to convince an initially sceptical king of the necessity and value of the exercise.

Even more damning, and without question more sensational, were the tales of widespread immorality and sexual perversion contained in the *Comperta*. To help ensure that the reports compiled by his agents would be believed, Cromwell was able to provide the signed confessions of monks and nuns who had admitted breaking their vows of chastity. The more lurid tales dwelt on the stories of monks taking part in homosexual practices and nuns who had borne children.

While historians have been impressed by the information provided by the *Valor* they have been more cautious in accepting at face value the reports contained in the *Comperta*. Historical research has shown that the monasteries were not nearly as bad as was once thought. Although less than ten per cent of houses were centres of spiritual excellence, the majority were adequately following the way of life prescribed by the religious order to which they belonged.

Consequently, the *Comperta* must be treated with care because although the commissioners did conduct their investigations with efficiency, they did so with little regard for fairness.

Declining popularity

There is evidence to suggest that monasteries were not as popular at the time of their dissolution as they had been in former times. There was certainly a decline in the number of men and women wishing to become monks or nuns in the late fifteenth and early sixteenth centuries. Humanist scholars such as Erasmus had undermined public confidence in the monasteries by questioning their right to exist, particularly where it could be shown that they were leading lives incompatible with the vows they had taken.

On the other hand, recent research has suggested that the public attitude towards the religious houses was marginally more supportive of them continuing than not. There was little popular opposition to the continued existence of the religious houses and those who complained about specific abuses which adversely affected them were content merely to grumble. In short, there was no indication of widespread anger and indignation. In fact, it should be remembered that the people who took part in the largest rebellion in the sixteenth century, the Pilgrimage of Grace (see page 67), were motivated by a desire to protect a way of life in which the monasteries played a significant part.

The dissolution of the smaller monasteries 1536

The test of Henry's supremacy over the Church was whether it could be imposed on the people and in the localities. The work of Cromwell's commissioners fuelled rumours that the government intended to close the monasteries and to seize their wealth. These fears were realised in part by the passing of the Act for the Dissolution of the Smaller Monasteries in March 1536. According to the preamble of the Act, the smaller monasteries were being closed because of the 'manifest sin, vicious, carnal and abominable living [that] is daily used and committed among the little and small abbeys, priories and other religious houses'.

As the Act made clear in a later, more significant, section, the real reason for their dissolution was financial. The test of their fitness to continue was whether they had an annual income of more than £200. Those houses that failed to meet this financial target were to be dissolved and their property was to pass to the Crown. As a consequence, 399 houses were suppressed, with the inmates given two options: to continue their vocation by transferring to a larger monastery or to abandon their vocation and rejoin society. To avoid protest or opposition the heads of the dissolved houses were more generously provided for by being pensioned off. Some religious houses, 67 in total, were exempted from dissolution but the price of their continued existence was high in that they had to pay a heavy financial penalty.

Implementing the closures

The dissolved monasteries were stripped of their assets such as gold or silver, followed by the lead from roofs and the bronze from church bells. All other saleable items such as glass, slates, doors and even the books from the monastic library were often auctioned locally. The most valuable asset, of course, was the land: the landed estate and attached farms, together with the livestock, were either put up for lease or sold. Only the most favoured individuals were granted the privilege of purchasing the landed estates outright. John Vaughan, Cromwell's agent, was among those favoured by the Crown. He successfully petitioned the king for the dissolved priory of Monmouth in Wales, which was said to be worth £60 a year. Another was Sir Thomas Jones, a member of the king's household and a loyal servant of Cromwell, who purchased Talley Abbey in west Wales for the enormous sum of £737 (the equivalent of nearly £227,000 today).

In some areas, most notably in northern England, there was a violent reaction against the closures. There were far fewer petitions to buy or lease monastic property in the north mainly because the religious houses were held in greater esteem. In some instances, Cromwell's commissioners were prevented from conducting their business by angry mobs determined to defend the monasteries.

Those commissioners who continued to operate in the face of local protests were partly responsible for stirring up the Pilgrimage of Grace in October 1536 (see page 67). The size and geographical scale of this rebellion shocked Henry and for a while the dissolution process was halted. Once the dust had settled and the ringleaders had been dealt with the dissolution began again. The first to be closed were those houses that had supported the rebels but this gave way to a more widespread dissolution that took no account of size, wealth or whether they had been obedient or not.

Second Act for the Dissolution of the Monasteries

In 1539 an Act of Parliament was passed making legal what had already occurred, namely the closure of the remaining monasteries. Following the suppression of the Pilgrimage of Grace the process of dissolution was revived but conducted piecemeal. Cromwell's commissioners were instructed that all monasteries regardless of their size, wealth or powerful connections were to be closed and their property seized. The majority of the remaining religious communities went quietly but for those who resisted there could only be one outcome: death. Among those who suffered under the terms of the unforgiving Treason Act was Richard Whiting, Abbot of Glastonbury, head of one of the richest monasteries in the country. His execution at his abbey was followed by that of his colleagues at the abbeys of Colchester and Reading. Even as the last of the monasteries were being closed the Crown was denying the destruction that was taking place. In a confidential report sent in May 1539 to Francis I by the French ambassador, Marillac, it was said that Parliament was 'discussing the reduction of certain abbeys of which they wish to make bishoprics, the foundation of schools for children and hospitals for the poor'. By 1540 every one of the 800 monastic houses had been closed but only a small percentage of them had been transformed into the bishoprics, schools and hospitals mentioned by Marillac.

Reaction of the monasteries to the dissolution

Apart from those few institutions which lent support to the Pilgrimage of Grace, the majority of the religious houses acquiesced in their dissolution. Indeed, after the initial dissolution of the smaller monasteries, the evidence suggests that many of the larger monasteries were expecting to be dissolved in the near future and were dispersing their assets among friends and well-wishers so that they would not fall into the king's hands. This seems to have caused Cromwell to amend his judgement that the richer religious houses would be too powerful to destroy without risking widespread political unrest. The piecemeal closures of late 1538 and early 1539 were probably intended to test the resolve of the remaining monastic communities. Much to Cromwell's relief, he found that most were willing to surrender to the Crown without a struggle.

Violent action was necessary only against the few who resisted, such as the abbots of Glastonbury, Reading and Colchester. In any event, Cromwell, the highly skilled, pragmatic politician, made it difficult for the monasteries to resist because he opted to avoid a full-frontal attack in favour of a gradual process of closure. This denied his potential enemies time to plan or organise any serious resistance.

Lack of opposition to the dissolution

In the final analysis, the monasteries offered little opposition to their dissolution because Henry had the law on his side. As Supreme Head of the Church the king had the power to deal with them as he wished, a position that the monks and nuns had accepted by swearing the Oath of Supremacy in 1535. Moreover, the majority of the senior clerics – the abbots, priors and other heads of houses – had been bought off, which deprived the rank and file of the leadership they needed to resist. The truth is that the will to resist had been broken when Convocation caved in to royal pressure in the Submission of the Clergy. The abbots outnumbered their secular counterparts, the bishops, in Convocation so that monastic submission to the will of the king was already well established by the time the dissolutions took place. Although the Pilgrimage of Grace received some support from a number of northern monasteries it was really a rebellion of the laity rather than of the clergy.

The consequences of the dissolution

It is very difficult to make an objective assessment of the religious effect of the dissolution. What criteria does one apply, and what relevant evidence exists?

These are issues that have not greatly interested recent historians of the English Reformation, who have generally satisfied themselves with the judgement that the dissolution of the monasteries was probably the part of the Reformation that had the least effect on the quality of the religious experience in England and Wales.

Social and economic consequences

It has been claimed by some historians that the dissolution of the monasteries amounted to a revolution in land ownership. There were also social and economic consequences since the monasteries had been employers of large numbers of farm workers and had provided a stimulus to the local economy. Religious houses also offered hospitality for pilgrims and charity for the old and infirm. Monasteries had also supplied alms for the poor and destitute, and it has been argued that the removal of this and other charitable resources, amounting to about five per cent of net monastic income, contributed to the legions of 'sturdy beggars' that plagued late Tudor England, leading to crime and social instability.

Pilgrimage of Grace

The outbreak of the Pilgrimage of Grace might suggest that the dissolution had serious consequences for the king and his kingdom (see pages 55–6). The rebellion never seriously threatened the king but it did threaten the maintenance of law and order in the north of England.

SOURCE A

From the Pontefract Articles drawn up in December 1536 by Robert Aske, the leader of the Pilgrimage of Grace.

We humbly beseech our most dread sovereign lord that the Lady Mary may be made legitimate and the former statute [Act of Succession] be annulled in Parliament.

Touching our faith, to have the heresies of Luther, Wyclife and the works of Tyndale and other such heresies within this realm to be annulled and destroyed.

To have the supreme head reserved unto the see of Rome, as before it was accustomed.

To have the abbeys suppressed restored – houses, lands and goods.

To have the heretics and their sect to have punishment by fire.

That the privileges and rights of the Church be confirmed by act of Parliament.

Study Source A. Why did Robert Aske believe that Henry VIII would accept these articles?

On a more positive note, the dissolution did witness the survival of some of the more impressive abbey churches, which were transformed into cathedrals in newly created dioceses such as Bristol, Gloucester, Chester and Westminster. Many others were purchased by their local communities to serve as parish churches, such as in Abergavenny, Bath and Tewkesbury. By the same token, the loss of such great abbeys as Glastonbury, Fountains, Rievaulx and Tintern cannot be so easily explained or excused and may amount to what some historians have described as 'cultural vandalism'.

When considering other possible long-term consequences of the dissolution, historians have traditionally focused attention on the effect of the disappearance of the monasteries on the relative wealth of the Crown. This is because the seizures made between 1536 and 1540 had the potential of virtually doubling the king's regular income and of freeing him from any dependence on parliamentary grants, except in very exceptional circumstances. That this did not happen is due to the fact that a vast amount of monastic property was sold quickly and at far less than its market value. Henry wanted a quick fix to solve his immediate financial problems and had no long-term plan to put the Crown's finances on a more secure footing. In the opinion of historian Denys Cook (1980), the sale of monastic property might have been an example of 'poor economics' but politically at least it was 'a master stroke ensuring the permanence of the Henrician Reformation by the simple expedient of selling shares in it'.

Summary diagram: The dissolution of the monasteries

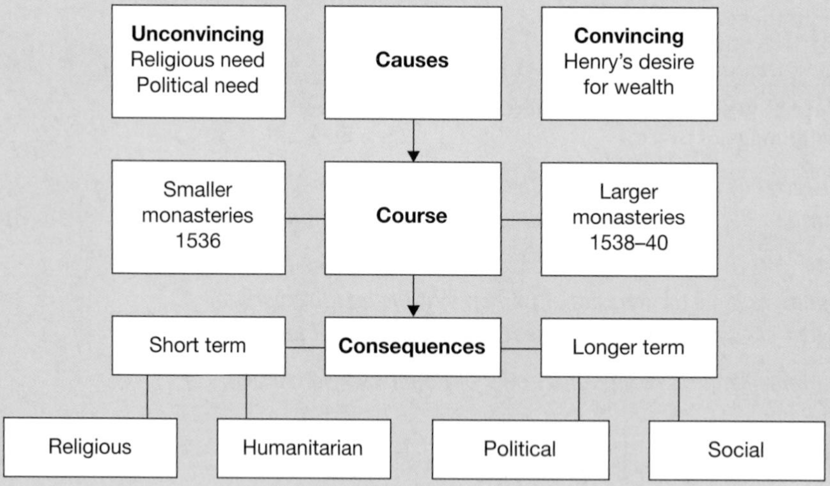

2 Key debate

▶ *To what extent was the dissolution of the monasteries planned?*

Most historians agree that the monasteries were dissolved because of Henry VIII's desire to acquire the monasteries' enormous riches. Contemporary claims that the monasteries were dissolved because they were unpopular or were no longer fulfilling their religious mission were merely a smokescreen to cover the real reason for their closure. The idea that they were part of a wider religious reform programme has also been questioned by historians who see no evidence of reform but only of complete closure. The man considered most responsible for the dissolution was the king's chief minister, Thomas Cromwell. Apart from a desire to serve and please the king, it is thought that Cromwell was motivated by his Protestantism, believing that any form of monastic life was a perversion of the true religion. That the king was solidly behind Cromwell and supported each of the stages in the dissolution process suggests that he, too, might have shared some of his minister's antipathy for the monastic vocation.

The traditional view

Historians once believed that the dissolution of the monasteries had been planned from the beginning by the Lutheran-leaning Thomas Cromwell. It was believed that the king's chief minister planned and managed the dissolution with the full knowledge and consent of the king. Having promised Henry that he would help him acquire the wealth of the monasteries, Cromwell then spent the next seven or eight years putting his plan into operation. This planning and organisation fitted in well with G.R. Elton's portrayal of Cromwell as the skilled bureaucrat with the vision and talent to undertake such an enormous task.

EXTRACT 1

From G.W.O. Woodward, *The Dissolution of the Monasteries*, Blandford Press, 1966, pp. 54–5.

That Cromwell had the dissolution of the monasteries in mind from quite early on in his career in the king's service is made clear by a document which dates from 1534 and details the most sweeping scheme for the conversion of ecclesiastical property to secular uses. Not only were the smaller religious houses to be expropriated, but the larger ones were to have their incomes seized, and the bishops and other clergy were to be deprived of their endowments. The dissolution began as a modest campaign against the smaller and more defenceless abbeys. For the time being the larger abbeys were left untouched. They had their champions in the parliamentary abbots who might readily accept a partial dissolution which did not affect their own houses, especially if it could be presented in the guise of reform.

The revisionist view

This traditional view is no longer thought to be the case. Revisionist historians claim that the evidence that Cromwell planned the dissolution is highly unreliable because it is based on hostile reports compiled after the event. In addition, there seems to have been no intention to implement a programme of complete closure on the part of either Henry or Cromwell when the order was issued to compile the information that would become the *Valor Ecclesiasticus*.

The fact that Cromwell had not had time to draw together all the evidence against the smaller monasteries by the time Parliament came to debate the legislation dissolving them suggests that the chief minister was not working according to a carefully laid plan. It is much more likely that he was reacting to a sequence of the king's hastily made decisions – even though they were decisions of which he heartily approved and which he had probably done much to encourage.

EXTRACT 2

From Denys Cook, *Sixteenth-century England 1450–1600*, Macmillan, 1988, pp. 42–3.

An earlier generation of historians saw the dissolution as the essential concomitant of the Henrician Reformation. Their view was that once Henry VIII had assumed the Supreme Headship of the Church then monastic communities represented a political threat to the crown as cells of papal cancer in need of excision. Research over a quarter of a century has altered this picture at practically every point. The dissolution is now seen as neither an integral, nor an essential, part of the Henrician Reformation.

If the 1536 Act was merely the first stage in a planned total dissolution then it would hardly have been worthwhile to provide alternative accommodation: it would have been simpler (but not cheaper) to provide a pension without option (as was done between 1538–40). The presence of an option clause, it has been argued, seems to indicate therefore that no more than a partial dissolution was intended in 1536. In late 1537 and early in 1538 there began to appear signs which strongly suggest that total dissolution was by then the ultimate aim.

The post-revisionist view

It can never be proved that Henry and Cromwell had not planned the destruction of all the monasteries from the outset, which is why some historians have questioned the conclusions of revisionist historians. To the post-revisionists it is possible that Cromwell had early on envisioned a complete dissolution, although he might not have drawn up a blueprint for turning such an aspiration into reality until the process had already begun.

EXTRACT 3

From Ian Dawson, *The Tudor Century*, Nelson, 1993, pp. 165–6.

To convinced Protestants the monasteries were a clear reminder of the survival of Catholic ideals. One of their main functions was to pray for the souls of the dead – an intercession thought unnecessary by Protestants. The monasteries were also members of international organisations, owing obedience to their mother houses as well as the Pope. They might well find it more difficult than others to accept the king's supremacy. Therefore, the abolition of the monasteries would be a real measure of the triumph of Protestantism. However the dissolution was not simply a matter of religion – money, foreign policy and the need to ensure the loyalty of the landed classes to the new church all helped to close the monasteries.

And so, in 1536, those monasteries worth less than £200 a year were closed following visitations by the king's men, whose reports provided the justification for closure. In fact, Cromwell always intended to close the rest of the monasteries, despite the statement in 1536 that in them 'thanks be to God, religion is right well kept and observed'.

According to the historians quoted in Extracts 1–3, how significant was Henry VIII's contribution to the dissolution of the monasteries?

3 Cromwell, Cranmer and the Reformation after 1534

▶ *How far can Cromwell and Cranmer be described as the architects of the Henrician Reformation?*

From the time Henry had made himself head of the English Church in 1534 he had been under pressure to formulate an acceptable doctrine. Senior clerics in the Church now sought to exert their influence over the thorny issue of religious reform. The royal supremacy was regarded as the means by which fundamental reforms could be carried out with the full weight of the law behind the changes. Needless to say, the Church hierarchy was divided over the issue of reform, and the struggle to gain control over the direction in which religious reformation should take was fought largely between two groups led by two intellectually gifted and inspirational leaders: Thomas Cranmer, Archbishop of Canterbury, and Stephen Gardiner, Bishop of Winchester. The competing aims of the two groups would inevitably lead to bitter conflict:

- The Protestant-leaning reform party led by Cranmer advocated the introduction of moderate Lutheran ideas.
- The pro-Catholic, conservative faction led by Gardiner favoured a policy of minimum change to the basic Catholic doctrines.

To have any chance of success, both sides knew that they would need the active support of the king, so they vied with each other to influence an often-vacillating Henry. However, the reformers under Cranmer had an advantage in having the support and active participation of the king's chief minister, Thomas Cromwell.

Cromwell and the Henrician Reformation

There is no doubt that Cromwell played a pivotal role in the Henrician Reformation. As the king's vicegerent in religious affairs, he exerted the most significant influence of any individual (with the possible exception of Thomas Cranmer) on the life of the Church. As a reflection of Cromwell's powerful influence in royal circles he was described by his enemy, Cardinal Reginald Pole (see page 125), as 'an agent of Satan sent by the devil to lure King Henry to damnation'. Denying that Cromwell held genuine evangelical convictions, Cardinal Pole claimed that he was moved instead by greed and a **Machiavellian** desire to serve the king. Indeed, Cromwell may even have agreed in part with Pole's assessment for he maintained to the end that his beliefs always took second place to his loyalty to his master, and that he would have followed whatever religion he had been instructed to. Within months of his minister's death, a regretful Henry VIII was convinced of the truth of this claim, and most historians have subsequently come to the same conclusion.

KEY TERM

Machiavellian Cleverly deceitful and unscrupulous. Named after an Italian political writer and thinker, Niccolo Machiavelli (1469–1527) of Florence.

This is not to suggest that Cromwell was without religious beliefs. Cromwell, like Cranmer, was a religious reformist who favoured some aspects of the Lutheran faith. Nor can he be accused of disinterest in religious issues because, from his letters, we know that he was. It is simply that his first priority was always to prove his unswerving loyalty to Henry. Unlike Sir Thomas More, Cromwell was prepared to carry out whatever instructions he was given by the king, even if these ran counter to either his policy objectives or his personal beliefs. Indeed, in the opinion of More, Cromwell's biggest error was in telling the king what he could do rather than what he ought to do. Nevertheless, it is clear that Cromwell sometimes took risks by pursuing a reformist agenda and passing measures through Parliament of which Henry might not necessarily approve, such as the Ten Articles (page 73).

Role and power as vicegerent

Cromwell used his authority as Henry's ecclesiastical deputy to the full. He was helped in this regard by a willing Cranmer who, as Archbishop of Canterbury and thus the leading churchman in England, brought the authority of the Church to his aid. Aware of the delicate balance that existed in Convocation between the reforming and conservative bishops, Cromwell followed a policy of divide and rule. He enlisted the help of the reformers, which included Cranmer, to devise statements on religious doctrine that could be issued in the king's name and enforced throughout the Church.

Cromwell justified his actions by declaring that he was simply following the king's instructions and that those who thought to do otherwise might be guilty of treason. Thus, Cromwell demanded that an episcopal consensus be reached so that a measure of uniformity in religious beliefs and practices could be achieved. To counter the opposition of the more militant conservatives he pursued a policy of threat and intimidation. In this way, Cromwell was able to secure a working majority in Convocation which became a useful tool in his quest to control the Church. Thus, he was able to persuade the bishops to agree to more radical measures such as the publication of a Bible in English and its distribution across the kingdom.

Cromwell issued several sets of highly detailed injunctions or orders to ensure that his measures and instructions were followed. Traditionally, injunctions had been issued either by individual bishops to deal with issues within a diocese or collectively in Convocation if the need was more national than local. Under the authority vested in him as vicegerent, Cromwell decided to bypass the episcopacy and to issue the injunctions himself. The first set of Royal Injunctions, issued in the summer of 1536, was used to enforce the Crown's doctrinal and anti-papal measures such as the following:

- erasing any reference to the Pope in religious services
- defending the royal supremacy in sermons
- removing superstitious images in churches
- encouraging the preaching of scripture
- discouraging pilgrimages.

Cromwell's greatest success: the Ten Articles

Cromwell's greatest success in securing a movement away from the existing beliefs and practices of the Church came with the passing of the Act of Ten Articles in 1536. In a clear move towards Protestantism, the central doctrine of the Catholic Church – the Seven Sacraments – was rejected, leaving only three: baptism, penance and the Eucharist. Cromwell was able to do this mainly because the king was distracted by the turmoil of his domestic life. At times of personal crisis Henry was more susceptible to Cromwell's persuasion because he wanted his chief minister to prepare a case for his divorce from Anne Boleyn. For some time the king had been reflecting on the biblical prohibitions of marriage, and having cast one wife aside using the annulment he wished to rid himself of another by divorce. Cromwell's doctrinal arguments might suggest a way of justifying his actions.

Cromwell intended to follow up the Ten Articles with a much fuller explanation of what was permissible and what was not in a revised doctrine. He planned to enlist a dedicated group of bishops and theologians who would work under his authority but follow the guidelines set out by Cranmer and Edward Foxe (see page 37). After six months' work a draft text had been completed, the details of which showed a distinct shift towards a more strongly Lutheran position.

This text was entitled *The Godly and Pious Institution of the Christian Man* (also known as *The Bishops' Book*). Cromwell ordered that a copy be given to the king.

The Bishops' Book

According to Cranmer, it was usual for Henry to rely on others to read books for him so that he tended to get his ideas second hand. However, on this occasion the king was too busy even to employ a reader so the book went unread for some months. Pressed for an opinion by Cromwell, the king agreed to its publication but only on condition that the book be clearly marked as carrying only the bishops' authority. He was willing to write a short introduction but he made plain to the readership that he had only 'taken as it were a taste of this your book'. *The Bishops' Book*, as it was popularly known, appeared in July 1537 and although it was not the definitive doctrinal statement that Cromwell had sought – there was evidence of conservative influence – he was satisfied with the results. In the opinion of historian Keith Randell, 'the publication bore all the signs of being a step in the "softening up" process that was such a typical and successful strategy of Cromwell's'. It took Henry until 1543 before he was ready to consent to the publication bearing his name, resulting in the *King's Book*.

? Study Source B. If Henry did not read the book why did he agree to have it published and distributed to every parish in England?

SOURCE B

From Henry VIII's introduction to *The Godly and Pious Institution of the Christian Man* (also called *The Bishops' Book*), published in 1537.

Hitherto we have had no time to look over your painstaking work … much less time to weigh such things as you have written. Yet, according to your petition, we have caused your said book to be printed, and will that it be conveyed into all parts of our realm, not doubting that you, being men of learning and virtue have performed in the whole work that which you have promised in the preface. We do not mislike your judgement, that you have wisely handled those places that every man may know both his whole duty towards God. Notwithstanding that we are otherwise occupied, we have taken as it were a taste of this your book, and found within it nothing that offends but regard it as being worthy of our praise and commendation.

Steps towards Protestantism

The next step in Cromwell's 'softening up' process came later in 1537 when he supported the publication of the so-called *Matthew Bible*. This English translation was the work of John Rogers, who wrote under the pseudonym 'Thomas Matthew'. Cromwell's interest in the work was first aroused by Cranmer, who sent him a copy and persuaded him to commend it to the king. Henry agreed to its publication as witnessed by the statement on the title page indicating that it was 'set forth with the king's most gracious license'. That Cromwell was able to obtain the king's permission to publish an English translation of the Bible less than a year after the execution of William Tyndale for doing the same thing, shows how far Henry had moved towards a reformist position in religion. This is not to suggest that he had embraced the Lutheran faith, for in many respects Henry remained committed to many traditional religious practices, but there were occasions when he showed some sympathy for more radical, even unorthodox beliefs.

This paved the way for the publication of Miles Coverdale's *Great Bible* in 1539. Based largely on the work of William Tyndale, this Bible was adopted as the key text for use in every parish church. Parish priests were instructed to purchase a copy of the Bible and to ensure that it was freely available for parishioners to read.

The Injunctions

In 1538 the vicegerent published his second set of Royal Injunctions. To ensure that these were not ignored, as some bishops had chosen to do to the first set in 1536, Cromwell enlisted the help of Justices of the Peace to police the process of compliance. Any bishop who refused to implement the instructions was to be reported to Cromwell. These injunctions were more specific and reformist in tone than those of 1536. Instead of merely stipulating that superstitious practices should be discouraged, they stated that objects of dubious veneration, such as the relics of saints, should be removed from churches and that people should be actively discouraged from undertaking pilgrimages. Cromwell ordered the destruction of Thomas Becket's shrine in Canterbury Cathedral to assist in this process.

Although many bishops dragged their feet in putting these policies into effect, not all did. Among the most active in implementing Cromwell's Royal Injunctions was William Barlow, Bishop of St David's. Barlow ordered that the bones of Saint David, the patron saint of Wales, should be removed from public view to discourage pilgrimage and then quietly buried. His enthusiasm for religious reform caused a rift with his clergy and he was advised, for his own safety, to stay away from his diocese. This so-called 'Protestant experiment' in St David's contrasts with the truculence displayed by Barlow's neighbour, the strongly conservative Bishop of Llandaff, George de Athequa. Although an absentee bishop, Athequa's reluctance to enforce Cromwell's injunctions in his diocese is more fully understood when we consider the fact that he had been the loyal chaplain to his fellow Spaniard, Queen Catherine.

Arguably the most significant of Cromwell's Royal Injunctions was the instruction that a register of births, marriages and deaths should be kept in every parish. The unintended consequence has been the accumulation of one of the richest sources of evidence for the study of family history.

Reversing the drift towards Protestantism

If Cromwell thought that he had secured the future direction of the nation's religion then he was mistaken. The drift towards Protestantism was brought to an abrupt end in 1539 when Parliament passed the Act of Six Articles (see page 79). This marked the beginning of a conservative ascendancy in both Church and State as the Duke of Norfolk, supported by Stephen Gardiner, Bishop of Winchester, and Cuthbert Tunstall, Bishop of Durham, sought to undermine Cromwell's reformist agenda. They were helped by the deteriorating international situation which witnessed an alliance between Francis I and Charles V. Henry feared that they might respond to Pope Paul III's call for a Catholic crusade against the recently excommunicated king of England. In addition, an ageing Henry began to think of his mortality and he was persuaded to believe that the process of religious reform had gone too far.

Protestants were horrified by the change in direction and they feared for their lives.

? Study Source C. Why did Foxe use the phrase 'The Whip with Six Strings' to describe the Act of Six Articles?

SOURCE C

From John Foxe's *Book of Martyrs*, first published in 1563. Foxe, a Protestant, was reflecting on the impact of the Act of Six Articles.

In this parliament certain articles touching religion, were decreed to the number of six, commonly called 'The Six Articles' (or, 'The Whip with Six Strings'), to be had and received among the king's subjects, on pretence of unity. But what unity thereof followed, the groaning hearts of a great number and also their cruel deaths in the days of King Henry.

The doctrine of these wicked articles in the bloody Act contained, although it be worthy of no memory amongst Christian men, but rather deserves to be buried in perpetual oblivion, yet, for that the office of history compels us to faithfully and truly comprise things done in the church.

Cranmer and the Henrician Reformation

Cranmer was widely believed by his contemporaries to be either a Lutheran or a Lutheran sympathiser. In an age when it was considered dangerous to be either, this perception of Cranmer's religious sympathies could have led to his destruction. That it did not speaks volumes about the man, for not only did he survive, he actually prospered under Henry. There is no doubt that during this period of religious uncertainty Cranmer's views, in common with others', fluctuated as the influences on him changed. He was always more of a reformist than the conservative king would have wished him to be but it did not hinder his career. Cranmer was careful to distinguish between his personal faith (which he openly declared to the king) and the royal policies he was helping to implement. Thus, he was prepared to pass judgements of **heresy** (leading to death by burning) on individuals such as John Frith and Andrew Hemet, whose beliefs were no different from his own. Some historians have accused Cranmer of hypocrisy but this is perhaps unfair as he truly believed that it was a sin to disobey the king. Furthermore, Cranmer lived in the social and political reality of the time and the course of action open to him was limited. The fate of a man of conscience like Sir Thomas More was a lesson to his contemporaries. Cranmer was a 'creature of the king', in that he owed his promotion to Henry, who also had the power to destroy him. Cranmer preached the doctrine of the divine right of kings not just out of a sense of duty but because he believed it.

Division of opinion on Cranmer

The debate about Cranmer has continued to divide historians. Although many argue that his influence on the Henrician Reformation was considerable, others are more critical. His champions point out that, as the spiritual head of the Church under Henry, Cranmer had no choice but to exercise caution in his approach to doctrinal reform. Nevertheless, his contribution to the drawing up of the Ten Articles in 1536 – the first guidelines issued to the Church of England as it became independent of Rome – shows that he actively supported Cromwell's attempts to move the theology of the Church towards Protestantism. Following this, Cranmer headed a committee of 46 bishops and theologians who published *The Godly and Pious Institution of the Christian Man* (*The Bishops' Book*) in 1537. The purpose of the work was to further the cause of reform and to promote unity by instructing parish priests and their parishioners in Church doctrine. These were no mean achievements, particularly as Cranmer had to endure difficult relationships with several bishops, especially Cuthbert Tunstall, Bishop of Durham, who objected to his position and title and argued that the Act of Supremacy did not define the role of the Archbishop of Canterbury. Gardiner (see page 122) resented Cranmer's meteoric rise to power because, prior to his appointment as Archbishop of Canterbury, he had held no position within the clerical hierarchy. Although Cranmer was an ordained priest, he was the first outsider to have been elevated to Canterbury for over a century.

Cranmer's critics

John Stokesley, John Longland and Stephen Gardiner were among Cranmer's fiercest critics. Stokesley, Bishop of London, opposed any change in the doctrines of the Church, remaining hostile to the translation of the Bible into English and clerical marriage. Stokesley was a staunch opponent of Lutheranism and very active in persecuting heretics. In this he was supported by Longland, Bishop of Lincoln, who complained to Cromwell that Cranmer's lax stewardship of the Church had led to an increase in Lutheran preachers, especially in his diocese. Gardiner's opposition was a natural by-product of his religious conservatism and leadership of the conservative faction at court. He and Cranmer publicly clashed when the latter proposed a visitation of his diocese of Winchester to which the bishop objected. Gardiner felt that this visit would serve no other purpose than to embarrass him by highlighting the failure to embrace properly the religious reforms thus far introduced to the Church.

Cranmer's critics point out that apart from the Ten Articles and *The Bishops' Book*, the archbishop did little to further the cause of reform in the Church. They claim that Cranmer's efforts were of no lasting significance because he was eclipsed by Cromwell who, as vicegerent, did more to enhance the authority of the king's spiritual jurisdiction. Cromwell's title and power reduced Cranmer to the position of a junior partner. Consequently, at best, one is left with the uncorroborated claim that his mere presence as the most senior cleric in the Church of England acted as an encouragement to those who wished to see Protestantism triumph.

That said, it must be remembered that after Cromwell's execution in 1540 it was Cranmer who emerged as one of the leading reform-minded councillors on the king's council. With the king's support, Cranmer survived the so-called 'Prebendaries' Plot' of 1543 (orchestrated and led by Gardiner) and was allowed to promote his own English Litany and *King's Prymer*. Yet, however one argues the case, it is impossible to escape the conclusion that, although Cranmer's significance in the Reformation after 1547 was very considerable, up to 1547 it was minimal in comparison to that of the men he served, Cromwell and the king.

Summary diagram: Cromwell, Cranmer and the progress of the Reformation after 1534

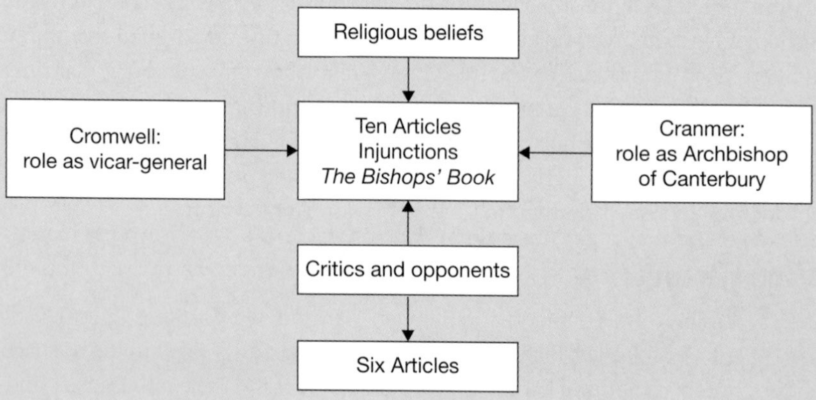

4 The state of the English Church by 1547

▶ *Was there more change than continuity in doctrine during this period?*

The first major statement of doctrine, the Act of Ten Articles, came in 1536. This Act was passed when the reformers were in the ascendancy, and introduced a number of Lutheran doctrines into the Church of England, for example belief in **consubstantiation**.

KEY TERM

Consubstantiation The belief that the wine and bread taken during the Eucharist represent the blood and body of Christ.

Three years later, the conservatives regained royal favour and the Act of Six Articles (1539) was passed to remove many of the Lutheran beliefs. Such shifts of policy meant that by 1547 the doctrines of the Church of England were a compromise and contained many inconsistencies which were unacceptable to reformers and conservatives alike.

The Act of Ten Articles

The Act was a statement of official doctrine which maintained that, like Luther, only three (baptism, the Eucharist and penance) of the seven Catholic sacraments were to be accepted. It is clear that the Ten Articles had been inspired by the **Augsburg Confession** of 1530, from which parts had been copied word for word. But, unlike the Augsburg Confession, the Ten Articles rejected justification by faith alone but instead compromised by stating that good works counted as well as faith in obtaining salvation. The Act also actively discouraged pilgrimages and visits to holy relics and shrines because they were 'superstitions' that did not help 'buy' salvation.

The articles proved controversial, so in an effort to secure some consensus Henry permitted the bishops to draw up their own statement of faith. The result was *The Bishops' Book,* which restored the 'missing' sacraments but listed them as less important because they had no scriptural foundation. The fact that *The Bishops' Book* was signed by the rival groups of clergy – reformers and conservatives – suggests that some attempt was made to heal the bitter divisions between them. However, both groups were hampered by Henry's inconsistent personal theology, which was a mixture of old and new: old in its insistence on the conservative belief in **transubstantiation** and clerical celibacy (although he tolerated Cranmer's marriage), but new in its concession to the reformers on the sacraments and superstitions.

KEY TERMS

Augsburg Confession The primary confession of faith of the Lutheran Church and one of the most important documents of the German Reformation.

Transubstantiation The belief that the bread and wine given at communion become the body and blood of Jesus Christ when they are blessed.

The Act of Six Articles

Referred to by Protestants as 'the bloody whip with six strings', the Act was a step back towards conservative Catholicism. Formally titled 'An Act Abolishing Diversity in Opinions', the Six Articles reinforced existing heresy laws and reasserted traditional Catholic doctrine as the basis of faith for the English Church. For example:

- consubstantiation was rejected and transubstantiation reintroduced
- communion was to be in 'one kind' rather than 'both kinds'
- clerical celibacy was enforced
- private masses were allowed
- confession was affirmed.

It has been suggested that the Six Articles was a 'panic measure' by a king reacting to international pressures. His excommunication by the Pope in 1538 was followed by the threat of invasion made possible by the conclusion of peace between Francis I of France and Charles V of Spain and the Empire. There is a further suggestion that the Act was inspired by Henry's declining health and increasing fear of death, which contributed to his desire to confirm his standing as a 'good Catholic'.

The doctrinal position of the Church in England by 1547

The doctrinal position of the Church in England owed much and was shaped by Henry VIII's personal religious outlook. The problem was that the king's religious beliefs were somewhat ambivalent. On the one hand, he appeared to be conservative, opposed heresy and desired uniformity but, on the other, he embraced the role of a religious reformer by rejecting pilgrimage, superstition and the monastic ideal. The Reformation took a decidedly conservative path after Cromwell's fall in 1540 but the continued influence of Cranmer as archbishop aided by the king's pro-reformist final wife, Catherine Parr (1512–48), ensured that some Lutheran principles were never completely abandoned.

Catholic doctrine in the Church of England

When Henry VIII died, the main articles of faith in the Church of England were in line with traditional Catholic orthodoxy:

- The Eucharist was clearly defined in the Catholic form of transubstantiation. The Lutheran form of consubstantiation was no longer accepted in the Church of England.
- Only the clergy were permitted to take communion with both the bread and the wine, while the laity were again restricted to taking only the sacramental bread.
- The Catholic rites of confirmation, marriage, holy orders and extreme unction had been reintroduced, alongside the previously recognised sacraments of the Eucharist, penance and baptism.
- The laity were still required to make regular confession of sins to a priest, and to seek absolution and penance.
- English clergy were no longer allowed to marry, and those who had married before 1540 had to send away their wives and families, or lose their livings.
- Although there was no specific statement on the existence of purgatory, the need for the laity to do 'good works' for their salvation had been reinstated.
- The singing of masses for the souls of the dead was held to be 'agreeable also to God's Law'. It was for this reason that the chantries, where a priest sang masses for the souls of the founder and his family, were not closed down at the same time as the monasteries.
- Paintings and statues of the saints were still allowed in the churches, although the laity was instructed not to worship them.

Many of the processions and rituals of the Catholic Church were still practised; it was maintained that they created a good religious frame of mind in those who witnessed them.

Protestant doctrines in the Church of England

Although the Church of England remained fundamentally Catholic in doctrine, it had adopted a number of Protestant practices by 1547:

- Services were still conducted in Latin, but Cranmer's prayers and responses of the Litany in English had been authorised in 1545.
- Greater importance was attached to the sermon, and the Lord's Prayer, the Creed and the Ten Commandments, all of which had to be taught in English by parents to their children.
- Similarly, the Great Bible of 1539 was the authorised English translation which replaced the Latin Bible. Moreover, the elite laity were allowed to read the Great Bible in their own homes, unlike on the Continent where often only the Catholic clergy were allowed to read and interpret the Bible.
- The practice of the Church of England with regard to some Catholic doctrines was ambiguous. Saints could be 'reverenced for their excellent virtue' and could be offered prayers, but the laity were forbidden to make pilgrimages to the shrines of saints or to offer them gifts, because it was maintained that grace, salvation and remission of sins came only from God.
- At the same time, the number of Holy Days – days on which, like Sundays, the laity were expected to attend church and not to work – had been reduced to 25.
- Finally, in sharp contrast to Catholic countries, there had been no monasteries in England since 1540, when even the larger monasteries had been closed by royal order, and their possessions had been transferred to the Crown.

Attempts between 1534 and 1546 to establish a uniform set of articles of faith for the Church of England had only succeeded in producing a patchwork of doctrines that often conflicted. Until 1547 this ramshackle structure was held together by the Henrician treason and heresy laws. Anyone breaking, or even questioning, the statutes and proclamations defining the doctrines of the Church of England was liable to confiscation of property, fines, imprisonment or execution. Moreover, the censorship laws prevented the printing, publishing or importation of books and pamphlets expressing views contrary to the doctrines of the Church of England. Among the victims of the Henrician heresy laws was **Anne Askew** (see Sources D and E).

KEY FIGURE

Anne Askew (1521–46)

Lincolnshire-born Askew was a well-educated writer and preacher who embraced the ideas and teachings of Luther. She quarrelled with her Catholic husband, whom she had been forced to marry by her family, and fled to London. She was arrested for distributing banned books and after examination was sent for trial. She was convicted of heresy and burned at the stake.

SOURCE D

From John Bale's account of the interrogation of Anne Askew prior to her conviction and execution for heresy.

Then they did put me on the rack, because I confessed no ladies or gentlemen, to be of my opinion … the Lord Chancellor and Master [Richard] Rich took pains to rack me with their own hands, till I was nearly dead. I fainted … and then they recovered me again. After that I sat two long hours arguing with the Lord Chancellor [Sir Thomas Wriothesley], upon the bare floor where he did ask me what I said about the King's Book. And I answered him that I could say nothing to it because I never saw it.

Study Source D. Why was Anne Askew considered such a serious threat by Henry VIII and his government? ?

Then he did ask me if I would deny the sacrament to be Christ's body and blood. I said yes, for the same Son of God that was born of the Virgin Mary is now glorious in heaven … and as for that you call your God is but a piece of bread. For more proof, let it lie in the box for three months and it will be mould and so turn to nothing that is good. Whereupon I am persuaded that it cannot be God.

With many flattering words, he tried to persuade me to leave my opinion … I said that I would rather die than break my faith.

SOURCE E

Is the artist of the image in Source E sympathetic or hostile to Anne Askew?

Title page from John Bale's account of Anne Askew's examination in 1546.

The impact of the Reformation on foreign relations

Prior to Wolsey's death in 1530, the most useful ally for Henry had been the Emperor Charles V. Their mutual hostility to France drew them together and, although the relationship between them was never without its problems, their alliance served both monarchs well. Thus, Henry's foreign policy had, hitherto, been dictated by political rather than religious considerations. Henry's 'power politics' was pursued with the specific aim of securing the French throne but this changed when his focus changed to obtaining a divorce from Catherine of Aragon. This shift in focus would almost inevitably sour relations between England and its former allies of Spain and the Holy Roman Empire.

Annulment comes to dominate English foreign policy

After 1530 the annulment came increasingly to dominate English foreign policy for it affected the Tudor succession. This embittered relations with Charles V because Catherine of Aragon was his aunt and he was unwilling to see a member of his family humiliated in such a public way (see page 49). It was in part Charles V's pressure on the Pope to refuse Henry's request for an annulment of his marriage that drove the king of England to reject papal headship of the Church. Henry broke with Rome not for any deeply held religious convictions but because he wanted to control the Church in England, exploit its wealth, marry Anne Boleyn and secure the succession by the birth of a son. The enactment of the royal supremacy in 1534 made Henry a schismatic for which he was excommunicated by the Pope in 1538.

The Pope followed up his excommunication of Henry by appealing to the Roman Catholic powers to invade England and depose the heretic king. Fearful of his increasing isolation and the prospect of invasion, Henry allowed himself to be persuaded by Cromwell to ally himself with the Lutheran princes of the **Schmalkaldic League** in northern Germany. To cement this alliance Henry was encouraged to marry Anne, the sister of the Duke of Cleves. It has been suggested that this realignment of English foreign policy promoted a subtle shift in Church doctrine towards a more Lutheran outlook as exemplified by the Ten Articles (1536) and *The Bishops' Book* (1537). In any event, Henry's flirtation with Continental Lutheranism was as short lived as his marriage to Anne of Cleves and it was Cromwell who paid the price with his head.

KEY TERM

Schmalkaldic League
A defensive alliance of Lutheran princes in Germany intended to defend their political and religious interests.

Fears over Franco-Scottish alliance

By 1542 mutual fears over France had restored good relations between England and the Empire. In particular, Henry VIII had seen the Franco-Scottish alliance, created by the marriage of James V and Mary of Guise in 1538, as a major threat to English security. Henry's foreign policy became increasingly belligerent during the 1540s, which has caused historians to be divided about the king's intentions at this latter stage of his reign. For example:

- It is felt by some that his main aim was to unite Britain by the conquest of Scotland.
- Others think that he was more concerned with his earlier ambition of claiming the French throne, or, at least, reconquering some of the former English territories on the Continent.

Consequently, historians have made a case either for or against Henry's conduct of foreign policy in the final stage of his reign:

- The case against Henry's conduct of foreign policy is that he failed to achieve the successes that were available to him, while squandering his wealth and endangering the financial strength of his successors by attempting to win military glory on the Continent.
- The case for Henry's conduct of foreign policy is that he succeeded in maintaining England's position as a major player at the centre of international diplomacy. He also succeeded in securing the northern frontier by defeating the Scots and in protecting Calais by capturing Boulogne.

Anglo-Imperial alliance

In 1542 an alliance was agreed by which there was to be a joint Anglo-Imperial invasion of France. This alarmed the Scots, who began to launch raids across the border into England. Henry sent a strong army under the Duke of Norfolk into Scotland, and the Scots were decisively defeated at the Battle of Solway Moss in November 1542. This Scottish reverse was followed by the death of James V in December. Mary of Guise was left as regent for the infant Mary, Queen of Scots, and was forced to make peace by the Treaty of Greenwich in 1543. Under the terms of the treaty, the Scots had to agree to a future marriage between Mary, Queen of Scots and Henry's son Edward. Mary of Guise and the Catholic party in Scotland soon rejected the marriage agreement.

In 1544 and 1545 Henry sent Edward Seymour (later to become the Duke of Somerset) to ravage the Scottish Lowlands. This did little to encourage the Scots to support the marriage proposals. At the same time, an English army had landed in France to support an invasion by Charles V. This meant that England had to fight a war on two fronts. Consequently, Seymour was given too few troops to do anything effective in Scotland, while the English army in France was too small to do more than capture the port of Boulogne. Even so, the cost of the war was enormous, and by 1546 over £2 million pounds (in modern terms, £615 million), mainly raised by the sale of monastic lands, had been spent.

Charles V withdrew from the conflict and Henry VIII, plagued by ill-health and worried about the cost of the war, was left to make peace with France. It was agreed, under the terms of the Treaty of Camp (sometimes known as the Treaty of Ardres) in June 1546, that England should hold Boulogne for eight years.

Uncertain diplomatic situation

When Henry VIII died in 1547 he left behind him a very uncertain diplomatic situation. The uneasy peace with France and Scotland was further undermined by the renewal of the Franco-Scottish alliance, which left England exposed to the danger of invasion from both north and south. England was in a precarious position, especially as the succession of the young Edward VI, a minor, could be exploited by the two main Continental powers to strengthen their own positions in their dynastic wars. Furthermore, the Catholic nations were watching with interest to see whether the religious compromise in England would survive the death of Henry VIII.

Lord Paget, England's ablest diplomat, summed up the whole position very clearly for the new Regency Council. He thought that England was not strong enough to defend Calais and Boulogne against the French. Charles V was a threat because of his support for the Catholic religion. However, he felt that it was too dangerous for England to risk assisting the Lutheran princes in Germany. Consequently, he recommended that the alliance with Charles V should be maintained, and that all efforts should be made to promote hostility between France and the Holy Roman Empire.

Summary diagram: Change and continuity in doctrine: the state of the English Church by 1547

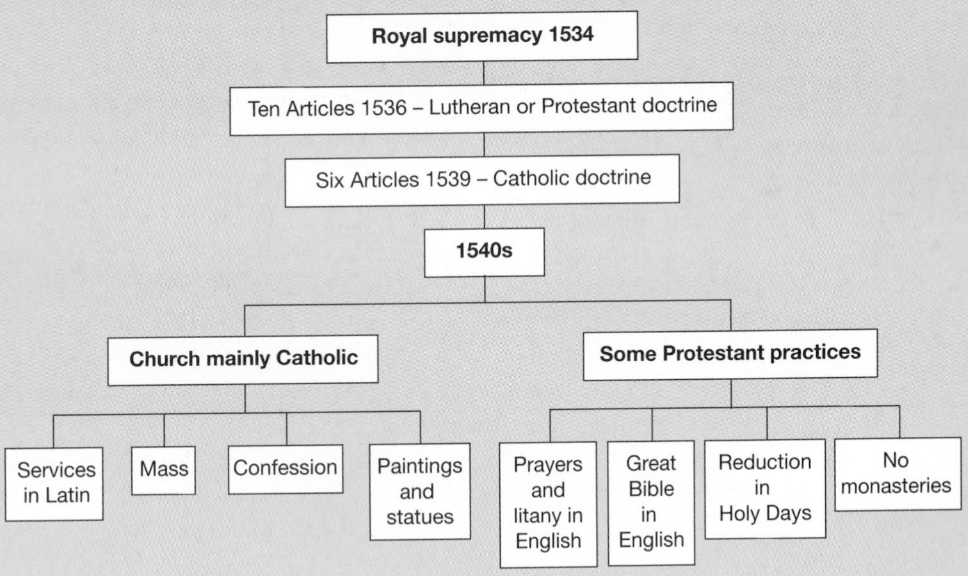

Chapter summary

The period after Henry VIII assumed the headship of the English Church witnessed significant change but also a measure of continuity in the nature of worship and the evolution of doctrine. Henry tolerated some minor changes but he remained a Catholic at heart and he was determined that England would remain conservative in religion: in effect, Catholicism without the Pope. The influence of Cromwell and Cranmer looms large in the story of the Reformation after 1534, when they steered the Church in a more Protestant direction. The dissolution of the monasteries, the passing of the more radical Act of Ten Articles and the publication of *The Bishops' Book* suggested that the reformers were winning the doctrinal battle. However, the conservatives, led by the Duke of Norfolk and Bishop Gardiner, continued the struggle to oppose religious change and influence the king. Their success may be measured by the passing of the more conservative Act of Six Articles and the fall of Cromwell. After 1540, the conservatives were in the ascendancy and although they failed to destroy Cranmer they did succeed in slowing the pace of religious reform. Some historians contend that by 1547 the Church was only 'half-reformed'.

Refresher questions

Use these questions to remind yourself of the key material covered in this chapter.

1 How significant was the compilation of the *Valor Ecclesiasticus*?
2 Why did it take two separate Acts of Parliament to dissolve the monasteries?
3 What were the short- and long-term effects of the dissolution?
4 Which had the greater impact on the dissolution of the monasteries, the *Comperta Monastica* or the *Valor Ecclesiasticus*?
5 How significant was the passing of the Act of Ten Articles?
6 Who contributed more to the Henrician Reformation: Cromwell or Cranmer?
7 What does the phrase 'Catholicism without the Pope' mean?
8 What were the most significant changes in Church doctrine?
9 Why do some historians suggest that England was only half-reformed by 1547?
10 What impact did foreign policy have on the progress of the Reformation?

Question practice

ESSAY QUESTIONS

1 'The English Church by 1547 was a Church half-reformed.' Explain why you agree or disagree with this view.
2 'The Reformation owed more to the work of Cranmer than it did to Cromwell.' Explain why you agree or disagree with this view.
3 'The dissolution of the monasteries had little to do with the king's religious conviction and everything to do with the king's greed.' Assess the validity of this view.
4 'Catholicism without the Pope best describes the religion of England at the end of Henry VIII's reign.' Assess the validity of this view.

SOURCE ANALYSIS QUESTIONS

1 With reference to Sources 1 and 2 (below), and your understanding of the historical context, which of these two sources is more valuable in explaining why the Pilgrimage of Grace occurred?
2 With reference to Sources 1, 2 and 3 below, and your understanding of the historical context, assess the value of these sources to a historian studying the nature of the threat posed by the Pilgrimage of Grace.

SOURCE 1

From Edward Hall, *The Union of the Two Noble and Illustrious Families of Lancaster and York*, published in 1542. Hall was an MP in the Reformation Parliament.

But the northern men refused to end their wicked rebellion. But, as if by a great miracle of God, the water suddenly rose to such a height and breadth, so that on the day, even when the hour of battle should have come, it was impossible for one army to get at the other.

Then a consultation was held and a pardon obtained from the King's majesty for all the leaders of this insurrection. They were promised that their petition would be presented to the King and their grievances would be gently heard and their reasonable requests granted, so that by the King's authority all things should be brought to good order and conclusion. And with this promise every man quietly departed.

SOURCE 2

From Hugh Latimer's sermon preached at St Paul's Cross in October 1537. Latimer was Bishop of Worcester.

These men in the north country, they make pretence as though they were armed in God's armour and clothed in truth and righteousness. I hear they say wear the cross and the wounds [of Christ] before and behind, and that they claim much truth to the king's grace and to the commonwealth, when, in fact, they intend nothing less. They deceive the poor ignorant people, and bring them to fight against the king, the church and the commonwealth. They rise up against the king and fight with the king, they rise up against the church and fight against the church which is the congregation of faithful men. Lo, what false pretence can the devil send amongst us! It is one of his most crafty and subtle assaults, to send his warriors forth under the badge of God, as though they were armed in righteousness and justice.

SOURCE 3

From the Pontefract Articles drawn up in December 1536 by Robert Aske, the leader of the Pilgrimage of Grace.

We humbly beseech our most dread sovereign lord that the Lady Mary may be made legitimate and the former statute [Act of Succession] be annulled in Parliament.

Touching our faith, to have the heresies of Luther, Wyclife and the works of Tyndale and other such heresies within this realm to be annulled and destroyed.

To have the supreme head reserved unto the see of Rome, as before it was accustomed.

To have the abbeys suppressed restored – houses, lands and goods.

To have the heretics and their sect to have punishment by fire.

That the privileges and rights of the Church be confirmed by act of Parliament.

Edward VI and the Protestant Reformation 1544–53

This chapter is intended to help you to understand the developing stages of the Reformation and the events connected with the changes in religion. The nature, state and authority of the Edwardian Church will be discussed, followed by an examination of the events that led to the first attempt to set up a Protestant Church. The struggle to establish a Protestant doctrine to underpin the authority of the new Edwardian Church will be discussed. These issues are examined as three main themes:

- ★ The reformists and the king
- ★ Doctrinal developments
- ★ Opposition and support

Key dates

1544 Act of Succession

1546 Henry drafted his last will

1547 Death of Henry VIII and accession of Edward VI

Edward Seymour created Duke of Somerset and Lord Protector

Cranmer issued his *Book of Homilies*

Act of Uniformity passed by Parliament

1549 Rebellion in East Anglia and the West Country

Fall of Somerset

First *Book of Common Prayer* published

1550 Emergence of John Dudley, Earl of Warwick, as the most powerful man in England

1551 John Dudley created Duke of Northumberland and Lord President of the Council

1552 Execution of the Duke of Somerset

Second *Book of Common Prayer* published

1553 Northumberland's son, Guildford, married Lady Jane Grey

Edward VI changed line of succession in favour of Lady Jane Grey

Death of Edward VI, brief reign of Lady Jane Grey and succession of Mary

Execution of Northumberland

1 The reformists and the king

▶ *How and why did the reformists triumph in the faction struggle between Protestants and Catholics?*

Impact and legacy: the decline and death of Henry VIII

Henry VIII died in January 1547. It was not a sudden event. He had been seriously ill on and off for nearly a decade. He suffered from excruciatingly painful swelling of his legs, which periodically broke out into horrible sores. After Henry's sores were discharged, paradoxically, he was brought considerable relief. Henry was massively overweight, with a waist of over 50 inches (127 cm), and other parts in proportion. This huge bulk seems to have increased the severity of the pain that he would, in any case, have suffered. Unsurprisingly, there were critical moments when both his doctors and his court had expected that their patient and monarch would soon be dead. Given his health problems, it is perhaps remarkable that Henry survived into his fifty-fifth year. Indeed, he had already outlived many of his contemporaries in an age when a person reaching 40 was thought to be entering old age rather than middle age.

Faction struggle: conservatives and reformers

There was never any doubt that Henry's successor would be his only son, Edward. However, as it was recognised that it was highly likely that Edward would still be a minor when his father died (he could not be declared 'of age' until the mid-1550s at the earliest), all interest at court centred on the arrangements to be made for the government of the realm in the years before the new king attained adult status. It was well understood that whichever faction secured the dominant position during Edward's minority would be able both to exercise enormous power and to acquire considerable wealth at the expense of the monarchy.

KEY FIGURE

Edward Seymour (c.1500–52)

Earl of Hertford and later Duke of Somerset. Ruled England as Lord Protector 1547–9. Removed from power and later executed in 1552.

The two contending factions, although they were anything but settled in their composition, were the conservatives, headed by the Duke of Norfolk, and the reformers, led by **Edward Seymour**, Earl of Hertford, who was Edward's dead mother's brother. The 'conservatives' have been so-called because they both favoured keeping the teachings and practices of the Church of England as traditional as possible and believed that the king should seek advice from his leading nobles rather than from men of common birth as had tended to happen since 1485. The most politically able of their active members was Stephen Gardiner, the Bishop of Winchester, whose plotting had been behind most of the attempts to discredit individual reformers ever since he had lost the struggle with Thomas Cromwell to win the king's favour in the early 1530s.

The reformers had been identified with Cromwell during his period of dominance. Since his fall in 1540, they had naturally been somewhat in

Contending court factions

Conservative faction members

- Thomas Howard, Duke of Norfolk and Bishop Stephen Gardiner.

Reform faction members

- Edward Seymour, Earl of Hertford and Archbishop Thomas Cranmer.

disarray. Perhaps their obvious new leader might have been Thomas Cranmer, Archbishop of Canterbury, as he had long been known to be sympathetic to their leanings towards Protestantism in religion. However, Cranmer was interested neither in politics nor in seeking greater power for himself. His competitive spirit was minimal. It was, therefore, left to Edward's relations on his mother's side to set about rebuilding the fortunes of the faction that favoured change.

The succession

Although Henry VIII's final years were marked by failing health, he managed to maintain the authority of the Crown and preserve the unity of the realm. Apart from the wars with Scotland and France, which had begun in 1542 and 1544, respectively, Henry VIII's major concern in his final years was the succession. Since 1527 he had been obsessed with the need to safeguard the dynasty by leaving a male heir to succeed him. The birth of Prince Edward in 1537 had seemed to achieve this objective. Religious differences had deepened the rift between political factions at court. Henry VIII had to tread a cautious path between the conservative Catholic and reforming Protestant parties. By 1546 the king's declining health made it clear that his son would come to the throne as a minor. To avoid any possible disputes, Henry made a final settlement of the succession in his will of 1546. This replaced the Succession Acts of 1534, 1536 and 1544, although the terms of the will were similar to the Act of 1544.

In the event of Edward dying without heirs, the succession was to pass first to Mary, the daughter of Catherine of Aragon. If Mary died without heirs her sister Elizabeth, daughter of Anne Boleyn, was to succeed. The major change to the previous settlement was that if all Henry's children were to die without heirs, the throne was to pass to his niece Frances Grey. Lady Frances was the elder daughter of Henry VIII's sister Mary from her marriage to Charles Brandon, Duke of Suffolk (Mary's first husband, King Louis XII of France, had died). This clause meant that the other possible claimant to the English throne, the infant Mary, Queen of Scots, was excluded. Mary was the descendant of Henry VIII's sister Margaret, who had married James IV of Scotland. Henry was anxious to preserve the royal supremacy, hence the inclusion of the Protestant Grey family and the exclusion of the Catholic Stuart dynasty. Although the will had replaced the earlier succession settlements, the Acts of 1534 and 1536, which had made Mary and Elizabeth illegitimate, were not repealed.

Acts of Succession	1534 – Mary out		Elizabeth in
	1536 – Elizabeth out		Any future child in
	1544 – Elizabeth and Mary out		Edward in
Will of Henry VIII	1546 – Edward first	Mary second	Elizabeth third

Figure 4.1 The Tudor family diagram on succession.

Henry's last will and testament

Henry's major concern in his will was to secure the peaceful succession of his son and safeguard the royal supremacy. By the middle of 1546 it had become clear that the surest way to achieve this, and to prevent any power struggle, was to give authority to Seymour and the reform faction. The disgrace of Howard and omission of Gardiner from the will had made the position of Seymour and his supporters more secure. Seymour's position was further strengthened by adjustments to the terms of the will right up to the time of Henry VIII's death.

The will was drafted towards the end of December 1546 but it was not authorised to be signed until a month later, when the king knew that he was about to die. The explanation that has most often been given for this sequence of events has been that the existence of the unsigned will, of which those named in it were aware, was a ploy by Henry to intimidate his leading subjects. The fact that the document was unsigned was a clear threat that if those named in it did not please him in every detail, the wording of the will would be altered to their disadvantage before it was made final.

Regency (Privy) Council

In Henry's will he specified that the country should be ruled after his death by a Regency Council, whose members were named by him and who could not subsequently be changed. It was also stated that the Council's decisions must be corporate, with no member being given greater prominence than any other. This attempt to stop the emergence of a leader, together with the fact that the Council appeared to be composed of equal numbers of 'conservatives' and 'reformers', has resulted in the claim that Henry was trying to ensure that politics remained 'frozen' in their existing state until his son was old enough to decide for himself what changes, if any, were to be made.

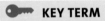

KEY TERM

Regency Council Name given to the Privy Council during the minority of Edward VI.

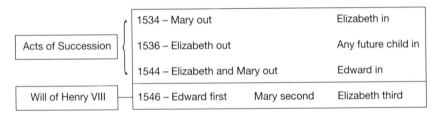

A **Regency Council** was nominated consisting of Seymour and fifteen of his most trusted allies. Members of the Council were to govern the country until Edward reached eighteen years of age. Henry had stipulated in his will that the members of the Regency Council were to have equal powers and that they should rule collectively, by majority decision. In order to secure the loyalty and co-operation of the Council, its members were to be rewarded with new titles, and lands taken from the monasteries and the Howard family. In reality, the reformists were powerful enough to dominate the Council and, if Seymour so chose, there would be little to prevent him from exercising virtually full monarchical power. On 4 February 1547, just a week after Henry's death, Seymour (now Duke of Somerset) took the title of Lord Protector. Although Henry VIII's will did not provide for the appointment of a Protector, the councillors justified their support of Seymour's action by stating that it was their collective decision 'by virtue of the authority' of the late king's wishes.

That Seymour took power, with the willing consent of thirteen of the fifteen councillors, so soon after Henry's demise suggests that he had intended to overturn the will from the moment the king's death had been confirmed.

SOURCE A

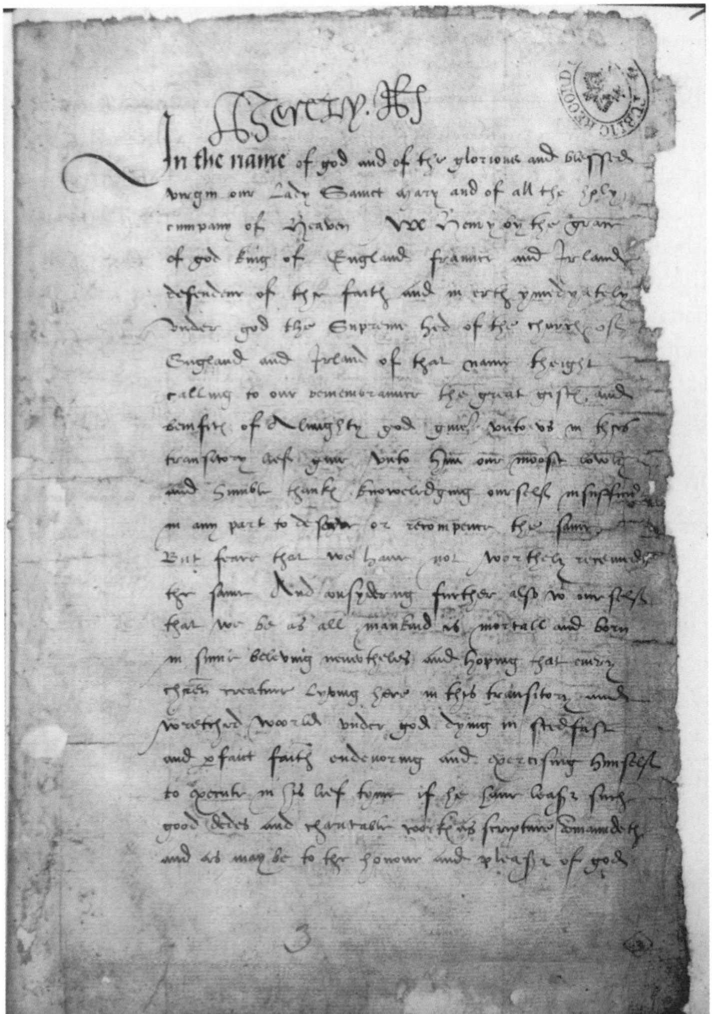

The last will and testament of Henry VIII, written in 1546.

Study Sources A and B. Why was Henry VIII's will so politically significant?

SOURCE B

Extract from the last will and testament of Henry VIII, 1546.

As to the succession of the Crown, it shall go to Prince Edward and the heirs of his body. In default, to Henry's children by his present wife, Queen Catharine, or any future wife. In default, to his daughter Mary and the heirs of her body, upon condition that she shall not marry without the written and sealed consent of a majority of the surviving members of the Privy Council appointed by him to his son Prince Edward. In default, to his daughter Elizabeth upon like condition. In default, to the heirs of the body of Lady Frances, eldest daughter of his late sister the French Queen. In default, to those of Lady Elyanore, second daughter of the said French Queen. And in default, to his right heirs. Either Mary or Elizabeth, failing to observe the conditions aforesaid, shall forfeit all right to the succession.

Aims and beliefs: Somerset's religious policy

The accession of Edward VI, who had been educated as a Protestant, raised the hopes of English reformers that there would be a swing towards more Lutheran, and possibly Calvinist, doctrines. Somerset's appointment as Lord Protector in 1547 established the reform party firmly in power, as intended under the terms of Henry VIII's will. Somerset was a moderate Protestant, but although he was devout, he had no real interest in theology. He was religiously tolerant, and favoured a cautious approach towards reform. Although he is reputed to have had Calvinistic leanings, and had exchanged letters with John Calvin, there is little evidence of such influences when he was in power.

Divisions in the Regency or Privy Council

The reformers were in the majority in the Privy Council but there was a division of opinion between the lay members on how far religious reform should be taken. This division of opinion was even more marked among the clerical members of the council. The bishops simply could not agree on a way forward so that hopes of an early consensus emerging were dashed. Although the majority of them fully supported the royal supremacy and the separation from Rome, they remained hopelessly divided on the issue of doctrinal reform:

- Nine bishops (Protestant Reformists), led by Archbishop Thomas Cranmer and Nicholas Ridley, Bishop of Rochester, supported detailed doctrinal reform.
- Ten bishops (Catholic Conservatives), led by Stephen Gardiner, Bishop of Winchester, and Edmund Bonner, Bishop of London, opposed change.
- Eight bishops (neutrals) were undecided on doctrinal issues.

With such an even balance of opinion among the bishops, Somerset and the Regency Council moved very cautiously on matters of religious reform. Seymour particularly feared Gardiner, who commanded a great deal of respect within the Church and whose influence could sway public opinion against the idea of further reform. Although Gardiner had been omitted by Henry VIII from membership of the Privy Council, as leader of the conservative faction at court, his opposition could impact on the policies being drawn up by Cranmer and the reformers. Gardiner objected to the religious changes proposed by the government both on principle and on the grounds of their being implemented during the king's minority. Because he refused to co-operate in any way with the Regency Council, Gardiner spent most of Edward VI's reign in prison.

Attitudes of the people to religious reform

The attitude towards reform outside the immediate government circle is difficult to assess:

- The ruling elites. Unlike the hard-line Gardiner, a majority of the ruling elites seem to have been in favour of (or at least, not opposed to) some measure of moderate religious reform.
- The parish clergy. In general, the parish clergy appear to have been opposed to religious change. This, it has been suggested, was largely because the English parish clergy were still relatively uneducated, and were anxious to maintain their traditional way of life without any complications.
- The lower classes. It is maintained that the same was true for the great mass of the population, who were very conservative in their outlook. Moreover, as far as they were concerned, both their popular culture, which was based on rituals and festivals associated with the farming year, and their belief in magic and superstition, all formed part of the ceremonies of the old Church.

Yet there were exceptions:

- In East Anglia, because of the settlement of large numbers of Protestant refugees from the Continent, there was considerable support for religious reform.
- In London and the larger towns, where clergy were better educated, there were very vocal minorities demanding more rapid, and more radical, religious change.

Somerset's fall from power

After less than three years as Lord Protector, Somerset was toppled from power. His autocratic leadership style had turned some councillors against him. Had he been a strong, confident leader he might have survived the coup to oust him but he was weak, incompetent and often dithered over making decisions. His failure to deal with the economic crisis, to cope with rising inflation and halt unpopular enclosures turned the ruling elites against him. His religious policy, although moderate, gained more enemies than friends in the Church. He persisted in prosecuting an unwinnable and costly war with Scotland and France and he failed to appreciate the seriousness of the rebellions of 1549. One of the main reasons why Somerset fell from power was because he would not take advice. He had a habit of making his own decisions and issuing proclamations without consulting the Council. He was simply not the right man to solve the problems inherited from Henry VIII.

The first councillors to move against Somerset were conservatives: the earls of Arundel, Southampton and Shrewsbury. By removing Somerset, the conservatives hoped to halt the Reformation. Others on the Council, too, opposed Somerset so they either actively encouraged the earls in their plan or simply acquiesced. One of those who offered the conservatives his support was **John Dudley**, Earl of Warwick (he acquired the title Duke of Northumberland in October 1551). He was a reformer but the unity and power of this conservative group meant he could do nothing in the short term.

KEY FIGURE

John Dudley (1504–53)

Earl of Warwick and later Duke of Northumberland. Ruled England as Lord President of the Council 1549–53. Removed from power and executed in 1553.

In the weeks following the arrest of Somerset in October 1549, it appeared that the conservative faction supported by Northumberland might seize power. They planned, with the help of Charles V, to make Princess Mary regent for the young Edward VI. However, neither Charles V nor Mary supported the scheme which, in any case, would not have been practical in view of Edward VI's increasing support for Protestantism. Meanwhile, Northumberland, having used the conservatives to strengthen his position on the Privy Council, then switched his allegiance to the more radical Protestant reformers. This political struggle within the Privy Council continued when Parliament met in November. Attempts by conservatives to repeal the 1549 Act of Uniformity and strengthen the power of the bishops were defeated. In December, Parliament approved measures to speed up the removal of popish images and old service books from the churches, and set up a commission to revise the procedures for the ordination of priests.

Northumberland takes power

By February 1550 Northumberland was firmly in control of the Privy Council, and the conservatives were driven out of office. To strengthen his position still further, Northumberland won support by resorting to a more collective style of government. He took a new title, Lord President of the Council, and he put the Council and its members at the heart of his decision-making.

Under Northumberland, religious reform became more radical. It is possible that the changes came about because of political infighting in the Privy Council. Northumberland knew that having turned against the conservatives he relied more than ever on the reformers on the Council for support. He also knew that the conservative faction in the Church might oppose the Protestant changes he and his reformist allies on the Council intended to introduce.

Therefore, to prevent a possible conservative backlash, Northumberland moved against the more conservative of the bishops. Gardiner, the most able of the pro-Catholics, was already imprisoned in the Tower of London. In July he was ordered by the Privy Council to agree to the doctrines of the Church of England. He refused, and was sentenced to stricter terms of confinement. Bishop Bonner of London, already imprisoned by Somerset, was retried and deprived of his diocese. He was replaced by Nicholas Ridley, then Bishop of Rochester, who was an enthusiastic reformer. During the next year active reformers were appointed as bishops of Rochester, Chichester, Norwich, Exeter and Durham. These changes cleared the way for more sweeping religious reforms. Deprived of their main spiritual leaders, the Catholic laity and clergy offered little opposition, although some pro-Catholic pamphlets were circulated.

Aims and beliefs: Northumberland's religious policy

In view of the apparent ease with which he reconverted to Catholicism before his execution in 1553, many historians do not think it likely that Northumberland was a genuine religious reformer. Other historians feel that his support for such a Protestant enthusiast as John Hooper against Cranmer and Ridley, the newly appointed Bishop of London, in the doctrinal dispute during the autumn of 1550, shows that he was interested in religious reform. Certainly, the first moves towards introducing more radical Protestantism seem to have arisen following Somerset's fall from power. To please the reformers Northumberland might have felt obliged to tread a more radical religious path. On the other hand, it has been suggested that a man of moderate beliefs would hardly have risked his position by supporting such a radical programme of religious reform that was more likely than not to provoke unrest and opposition. What is certain is that by 1553 the Church of England was nearer to being Protestant than Catholic.

SOURCE C

Study Source C. Why did the Edwardian government believe it was necessary to exile some Catholics?

Contemporary illustration showing Catholics being banished from England. The Edwardian government actively encouraged Catholics to leave the Kingdom but those that refused were exiled.

Summary diagram: The reformists and the king

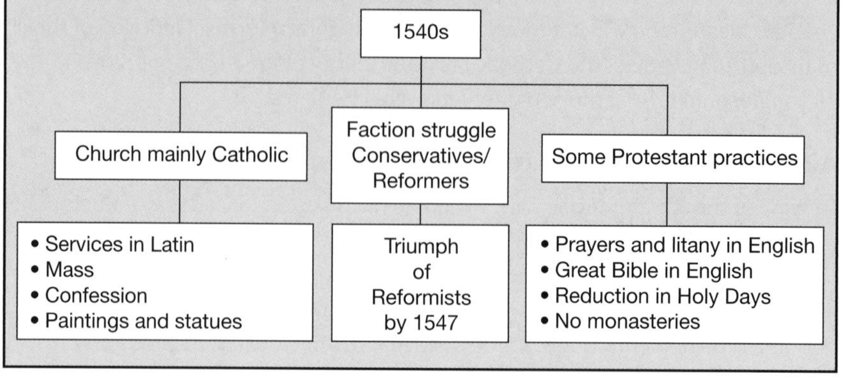

2 Doctrinal developments

▶ *How significant were the doctrinal changes introduced during Edward VI's reign?*

Cranmer and doctrinal development during the reign of Edward VI

Shortly after Henry VIII's death Cranmer issued his *Book of Homilies*, a set of official model sermons, followed by his English prayer book. Cranmer had the full backing of Protector Somerset, who encouraged a more moderate reform programme. Issued in March 1549, Cranmer's *Book of Common Prayer* has been described as his greatest achievement but it was too conservative for the reformers and too radical for the conservatives – it even provoked the Western Rebellion (see page 108). This was a rebellion of commons and some landowners in Cornwall and Devon who were protesting about the religious changes.

Following Somerset's fall from power, Cranmer set to work on a more radical edition of his prayer book which had the full support of the new leader of the government, Lord President Northumberland. Issued in 1552, the second *Book of Common Prayer* was explicitly anti-Catholic and was adapted and adopted by the Elizabethan regime to become the standard work available to an increasingly Protestant clergy.

By publishing his prayer books, Cranmer was laying the foundations of the Anglican Church. His aim was to firmly establish a Protestant Church attended by like-minded Protestant parishioners. This was no easy task. He was forced to adapt and work within the limits imposed by the belief system of two contrasting leaders – Somerset and Northumberland – while fending off the attacks of the conservative bishops and traditional parish clergy.

Somerset and the introduction of doctrinal reform

Seymour and the Privy Council decided to review the state of the Church of England, and to introduce some moderate Protestant reforms. Such a policy was opposed by the conservatives, prompted by Gardiner, who maintained that under the terms of Henry VIII's will, no religious changes could be made until Edward VI came of age at eighteen. In spite of Gardiner's vigorous opposition, royal commissioners were sent to visit all the bishoprics. They were instructed to compile a report by the autumn of 1547 on the state of the clergy and the doctrines and practices to be found in every diocese. At the same time, to help the spread of Protestant ideas, every parish was ordered to obtain a copy of Cranmer's *Book of Homilies* and a copy of Erasmus's *Paraphrases.*

In July an injunction was issued to the bishops ordering them to instruct their clergy to conduct services in English and to preach a sermon every Sunday. Furthermore, the bishops were to create libraries of Protestant literature and provide an English Bible for each parish, and to encourage the laity to read these books. Finally, the bishops were told to remove all superstitious statues and images from their churches.

Reaction of radical Protestants

These modest moves towards religious reform did not satisfy the more vocal Protestant activists. The amount of anti-Catholic protest was increased by the presence of Protestant exiles who had returned from the Continent after the death of Henry VIII. The problem for the Privy Council was that, while it did not wish to introduce reforms too quickly for fear of provoking a Catholic reaction, it was anxious not to prevent religious debate by taking repressive measures. As a result, the Henrician treason, heresy and censorship laws were not enforced and a vigorous debate over religion developed.

The more radical reformers launched a strong attack through a pamphlet campaign on both the Catholic Church and the bishops, who were accused of being self-seeking royal servants and not true pastors. Other pamphlets attacked the wealth of the Church, superstitious rituals, and in particular the Eucharist. However, there was no agreement among the protesters about the form of Protestant doctrine that should be adopted. With the government refusing to take any firm lead there was growing frustration, and some of the more radical protesters took matters into their own hands.

In London, East Anglia, Essex and Lincolnshire, where large numbers of Protestant refugees from the Continent were settling, riots broke out. These frequently included outbreaks of iconoclasm, in which stained-glass windows, statues and other superstitious images were destroyed. In some cases, gold and silver candlesticks and other church plate were seized and sold, with the money being donated to the poor. Such incidents were often provoked by extreme **millenarianists**, who wished to see a more equal society and a redistribution

KEY TERM

Millenarianists Radical thinkers who believed in social reform whereby a kingdom's wealth would be distributed equally.

of wealth to the poor. Although the Privy Council was alarmed by the violence, it refused to take any action against the demonstrators. This inaction enraged the more conservative bishops. Bishop Bonner was particularly aggressive in his protests to the government, and was imprisoned for two months.

? Study Source D. Why might the government of the Duke of Somerset not approve of the message printed in this pamphlet?

SOURCE D

From Peter Moone of Ipswich's pamphlet, *Treatise of Certain Things Abused*, 1548.

This mass as they [the priests] supposed, was alone sufficient to pacify God's wrath for our wretched misery. Free forgiveness of sins might be received at the mass was their daily doctrine. In no small time we were blinded with such popish rubbish and then making us pay for the holy consecration. Like thieves they were insatiable, they robbed soul and body without fear of God's Word, the light of our salvation.

Let us forsake all ceremonies that Scripture makes no mention and with the lively Word of God let us now be conversant. For therein shall we see what baggage we were fed, wandering in the pope's laws, forsaking Christ, heaping upon ourselves the greater damnation. These were the traditions and ceremonies maintained instead of God's true and sincere Word.

Indecision and confusion over reform

When Parliament and Convocation were summoned in November 1547, the question of religious reform was freely discussed. Both institutions were in favour of reform though disagreed on some issues such as the introduction of clerical marriage. Convocation approved but Parliament did not, so it did not pass into law. During this debate the Privy Council was still reluctant to make any decisive move towards religious reform. The reason for this was that the new regime still felt insecure, fearing that any significant doctrinal changes might provoke even more unrest and possibly lead to the fall of the government.

The two major pieces of legislation, the Chantries Act and the Treason Act, did little to resolve the doctrinal uncertainties:

- The Chantries Act. By closing the chantries this Act not only confirmed legislation already passed by Henry VIII in 1545 but went further in its confiscation of wealth and property. Although, as in 1545, the main purpose of the Act was to raise money to continue the war with France and Scotland, the reason given was that the chantries were centres of Catholic ritual and superstition.
- The Treason Act. This act effectively repealed the Henrician treason, heresy and censorship laws. This measure gave radical Protestant activists the freedom to discuss and demand doctrinal reforms. The immediate result was a renewal of the pamphlet campaign demanding that the Bible should be recognised as the only true authority for religious belief. At the same time, English translations of the writings of Luther and Calvin were being widely circulated.

In January 1548 the Privy Council issued a series of proclamations to try to calm the situation. However, the proclamations indicated no clear policy, and so only added to the confusion. The continued validity of Lent and feast days was defended. Justices of the Peace and churchwardens were ordered to enforce the existing doctrines of the Church of England, including transubstantiation. On the other hand, instructions were issued to speed up the removal of Catholic images from churches. Such indecision infuriated both reformers and conservatives alike. Finally, in September, the Council forbade all public preaching in the hope of stifling debate.

Ending the uncertainty over religious doctrine

When Parliament reassembled in November 1548, Somerset and the Council were in a stronger position after the successful campaign in Scotland. For this reason they felt secure enough to take a more positive approach to religious reform. Their objective was to end the uncertainty over religious doctrine. It was hoped that the new law, known as the First Edwardian Act of Uniformity, passed in January 1549, would achieve this.

According to the terms of the Act:

- All clergy, without exception, were ordered to use a number of Protestant practices which had been encouraged, but not enforced, during the two previous years.
- Holy communion, matins and evensong were to be conducted in English.
- The sacraments were now defined as communion, baptism, confirmation, marriage and burial.
- Cranmer adapted the old communion service by adding new prayers, so that the clergy and the laity could take both the sacramental bread and the wine.
- Clerical marriage was permitted.
- The practice of singing masses for the souls of the dead was discouraged.

It was envisaged that the cumulative effect of these terms would result in the gradual disappearance of many of the traditional Catholic rituals, many of which the Protestant reformers considered to be superstitious.

There was still no really clear statement on significant aspects of doctrine and belief, mainly because Cranmer's *Book of Common Prayer* was a mixture of Lutheran and Catholic beliefs. The government failed to clarify the following key issues:

- Nothing was said about the existence, or otherwise, of purgatory.
- Any form of the worship of saints, although not banned, was to be discouraged, while the removal of statues, paintings and other images was encouraged.
- Fast days were still to be enforced and no change was to be made in the number of Holy Days.

- The new communion service followed the order of the old Latin mass, and the officiating clergy were expected to continue to wear the traditional robes and vestments.
- Most importantly, no change was made to the doctrine of the Eucharist, which was still defined in the Catholic terms of transubstantiation.

Radical reformers refused to accept the failure of the government to substitute transubstantiation with consubstantiation. They became more vocal in their demands for the government to adopt a more Protestant definition of the sacrament of communion.

Satisfying the reformers and educating the laity

The Privy Council hoped that these cautious measures would satisfy the majority of moderate reformers, without outraging the Catholic conservatives. Although any clergy who refused to use the new service were to be liable to fines and imprisonment, no penalties were to be imposed on the laity for non-attendance. This can be interpreted as a hope by the Privy Council that it could coerce the more recalcitrant minority among the parish clergy, while not antagonising the undecided majority among the laity.

The government decided to continue with its policy of educating the laity in Protestant ideas that it had introduced in July 1547. Bishops were instructed to carry out visitations to encourage the adoption of the new services, and to test whether parishioners could recite the Lord's Prayer and the Ten Commandments in English. The effectiveness of either the legislation, or the education programme, depended on whether the bishops and ruling elites would enforce them. There was opposition in Cornwall, Devon, Dorset and Yorkshire. However, most of the country seems to have followed the lead of the aristocracy and gentry in accepting moderate Protestantism.

A swing towards more extreme Protestantism

The first move to introduce more radical Protestantism was initiated by Bishop Ridley in London, where he ordered all altars to be removed and replaced by communion tables in line with the teachings of the Calvinists and other reformed Churches. In other dioceses the destruction of altars proceeded unevenly, and depended on the attitudes of the local ruling elites and clergy. At the same time, the Parliamentary Commission's proposals to change the form of the ordination of priests were introduced, and instructions were issued to enforce the first Act of Uniformity.

The new form of ordination, which was basically Lutheran, soon caused controversy. It empowered priests to administer the sacraments and preach the gospel instead of offering 'sacrifice and [the celebration of] mass both for the living and the dead'. This change succeeded in satisfying the majority of moderate reformers. It removed the supposedly superstitious references to sacrifice, purgatory and prayers for the souls of the dead. However, it did not please some of the more extreme reformers, especially because it made no attempt to remove any of the ceremonial vestments, normally worn by bishops and priests while conducting services. These were regarded as superstitious by many of the reformed Churches, whose clergy wore plain surplices.

John Hooper, who had been invited to become Bishop of Gloucester, complained that the form of ordination was still too Catholic and started a fierce dispute with Ridley over the question of vestments. As a result he refused the offered bishopric, and in July he began a campaign of preaching against the new proposals. At first it appeared that Northumberland was sympathetic and supported Hooper, but in October he was ordered to stop preaching, and in January 1551 he was imprisoned for failing to comply. Finally, he was persuaded to compromise and was made Bishop of Gloucester, where he introduced a vigorous policy of education and reform. But he complained that both laity and clergy were slow to respond.

Northumberland and radical doctrinal change

During 1551 Northumberland consolidated his position. This cleared the way for a major overhaul of the Church of England. Cranmer was in the process of revising his prayer book, to remove the many ambiguities that had caused criticism. Further action was taken against the remaining conservative bishops. Gardiner was finally deprived of the diocese of Winchester in February, and in October reformers were appointed at Worcester and Chichester. These moves ensured that there would be a majority among the bishops to support the programme of religious changes that was being prepared.

Parliament was assembled in January 1552 and the government embarked on a comprehensive programme of reform. In order to strengthen the power of the Church of England to enforce doctrinal uniformity, a new Treason Act was passed. This made it an offence to question the royal supremacy or any of the articles of faith of the English Church. At the same time, the uncertainties over the number of Holy Days were ended by officially limiting them to 25.

In March the second Act of Uniformity was passed. Under the new Act it became an offence for both clergy and laity not to attend Church of England services, and offenders were to be fined and imprisoned. Cranmer's new *Book of Common Prayer* became the official basis for church services, and had to be used by both clergy and laity. The new prayer book was based on the scriptures, and all traces of Catholicism and the mass had been removed. The Eucharist was clearly defined in terms of consubstantiation (see page 78) being regarded as commemorative of Christ's sacrifice or the Last Supper.

Radical reformers did not approve of the new service because communicants were still expected to kneel, and they considered this to be **idolatrous**. Some historians attribute such objections to the **Calvinism** of Hooper and another extreme reformer, John Knox. It is also suggested that theirs was the influence

KEY FIGURE

John Hooper (1500–55)
A former monk who became a parish priest, he embraced the teachings and beliefs of Protestantism, which prompted him to leave for the Continent during the final decade of Henry VIII's reign. He returned to England bent on converting the people to the Protestant faith. He was appointed Bishop of Gloucester and then Worcester in Edward VI's reign but fell foul of Queen Mary. Hooper's radical writings were condemned and he was tried for heresy and executed by burning in 1555.

KEY TERMS

Idolatrous Worshipping images, such as the statue of the Virgin Mary in Catholic churches.

Calvinism Alternative Protestant faith to Lutheranism, named after John Calvin, an influential French religious reformer based in Geneva, Switzerland.

behind the instructions sent to bishops to speed up the replacement of altars by communion tables, and to stop their clergy from wearing vestments when conducting services.

Further attacks on the wealth of the Church

While these measures were being introduced, the government began a further attack on Church wealth. In 1552 a survey of the temporal wealth of the bishops and all clergy with benefices worth more than £50 a year was undertaken. The resultant report estimated that these lands had a capital value of £1,087,000 and steps were taken to transfer some of this property to the Crown.

The bishopric of Durham provides a typical example of this policy. Bishop Tunstall of Durham was arrested in October 1552 and imprisoned in the Tower of London. During his detention it was proposed that his diocese, worth nearly £4000 annually, should be divided into two parts: Durham and Newcastle:

- Durham itself would receive £1320 annually.
- The new diocese of Newcastle was to be allocated an annual income of £665.
- This left an annual surplus of £2000 from the income of the original bishopric, which was to be taken by the Crown.

In the event, this proposal never came into effect because of the death of Edward VI.

At the same time, commissioners had been sent out to draw up inventories and to begin the removal of all the gold and silver plate still held by parish churches, and to list any items illegally removed since 1547. The commissioners had only just begun their work of confiscation when the king died and the operation was brought to an end, but not before some churches had lost their medieval plate.

KEY TERM

Forty-Two Articles A list of essential doctrines drawn up by Cranmer and intended to form the basis of the new Protestant Church of England.

The Forty-Two Articles

The **Forty-Two Articles** drawn up by Archbishop Thomas Cranmer in 1553 was intended 'for the avoiding of controversy in opinions'. It was inspired, in part, by the Augsburg Confession of 1530, which set down the key articles of faith in the Lutheran Church (see page 79). It also stemmed from Cranmer's experience of meeting with a group of senior Lutheran clerics in 1538 in a conference designed to facilitate a political alliance by means of an agreement on doctrine between Henry VIII and the German protestant princes. Although the conference failed to reach a religious compromise, the detailed theological discussions did much to influence Cranmer's thinking.

The Forty-Two Articles was intended to act as a summary of Anglican doctrine under Edward VI. Cranmer intended that the articles should be short extracts that would explain and demonstrate the faith revealed in Scripture and to incorporate a balance of theology and doctrine. Completed in 1552, they were issued by Royal proclamation on 19 June 1553. It was claimed that Convocation had given its blessing to the proclamation, although this is doubtful. Following the accession of Queen Mary I and the subsequent reunion of the Church of England with the Roman Catholic Church, the Articles were never enforced.

The impact of doctrinal change on the Edwardian Church

What is certain is that the death of Edward VI and the fall of Northumberland brought this phase of the English Reformation to an abrupt end. The Forty-Two Articles, which had been drawn up to list the doctrines of the new Protestant Church of England, never became law. It is generally agreed that by 1553 the Edwardian Reformation had resulted in a Church of England that was thoroughly Protestant. There is less unity over whether its doctrines were basically Lutheran, or to what extent they were influenced by **Zwinglian**, or Calvinist ideas.

It is clear that although the doctrines of the Church of England had been revolutionised, the political and administrative structure of the Church had remained unchanged. There is equal agreement that there is insufficient evidence at present to decide whether the people of England had wholeheartedly embraced the Protestant religion. Research at a local level has so far provided

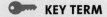

KEY TERM

Zwinglian Huldrych Zwingli was a protestant reformer as influential as Martin Luther and John Calvin. He was the leader of the reformation in Switzerland.

Figure 4.2 The inside of a Catholic (upper panel) and a Protestant (lower panel) church. How effective is this modern illustration in highlighting the visual differences between the two Christian faiths?

Thomas Cranmer

1489	Born in Nottinghamshire, the younger son of a lesser gentry family
c.1529	Became chaplain to Thomas Boleyn, Earl of Wiltshire, father of Anne
1530	Appointed English ambassador to Charles V (1530–3)
1533	Chosen by Henry VIII to succeed William Warham as Archbishop of Canterbury
1547	Took leading part in the Edwardian regime both in government and in the Church. Issued Protestant *Book of Homilies*
1549	Issued the blandly reformist first *Book of Common Prayer*
1552	Issued the more extreme second *Book of Common Prayer*
1556	Burned at the stake for withdrawing an earlier promise to accept some key Catholic doctrines

Cranmer studied at Cambridge University where he joined the 'White Horse' group, radical Protestants who met in the **White Horse Tavern** to discuss the new ideas coming from Europe such as Lutheranism. He supported Henry VIII's divorce. While in Europe on royal business he secretly married the niece of the Lutheran Church leader of Nuremberg in Germany.

Cranmer presided over Henry VIII's divorce from Catherine of Aragon, promoted the marriage with Anne Boleyn and declared Henry VIII to be head of the Church in England. He presided over Henry VIII's divorce from Anne Boleyn and promoted his marriage with Jane Seymour. He worked with Cromwell in government and in turning England towards Protestantism; for example, he was responsible for *The Bishops' Book* of 1537. He unsuccessfully opposed the conservative Act of Six Articles, he was forced to separate from his wife but refused to resign his office. He took no part in the destruction of Cromwell. He became one of the leading members of the reformist party at court. Henry VIII's support enabled him to survive conservative attempts to destroy him in the early 1540s. His contribution to religious reform during Edward's reign was the high point of his career. When Mary came to the throne he was arrested, stripped of his title as Archbishop of Canterbury and imprisoned for heresy.

Arguably, Cranmer played a greater role than any other single churchman in establishing and shaping the Church of England. He was not as timid as some historians believe but was willing to accept gradual change in the Church. He was fiercely loyal to the Crown and he proved to be an able government minister and churchman. His greatest strength lay in his refusal to support religious extremism; he advocated toleration and preached against persecution.

KEY TERM

White Horse Tavern
A meeting place in Cambridge for English Protestant reformers who discussed Lutheran ideas.

conflicting evidence. Although a majority of the landed elites and those in government circles seemed to favour moderate Protestantism, only a few of them did not find it possible to conform under Mary I.

Many of the parish clergy and a majority of the population seem to have been largely indifferent to the religious debate. Only in London, and the counties circling London and East Anglia, does there appear to have been any widespread enthusiasm for the Protestant religion. Even there, a study of the county of Essex indicates more enthusiasm among the authorities in enforcing Protestantism than among the general public in accepting it. Earlier interpretations, which indicated wild enthusiasm for either Protestantism or Catholicism, are now treated with caution. It is considered that Protestantism, if not widely opposed, received only lukewarm acceptance.

Summary diagram: Doctrinal developments

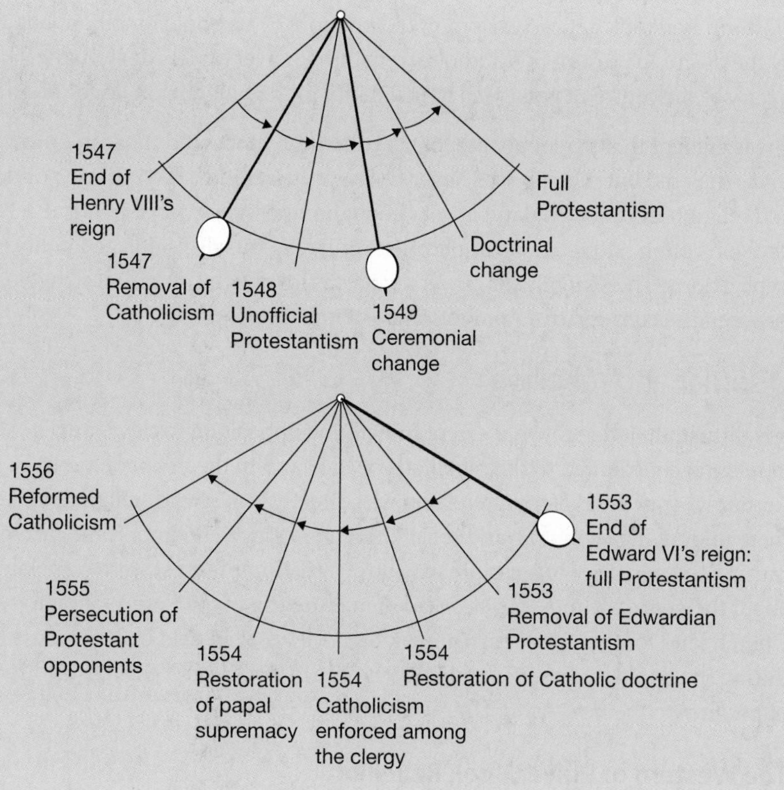

3 Opposition and support

► *Which side was stronger: the supporters or opponents of religious reform?*

Political rivalry at court

The fall of Somerset in 1549 triggered a renewed struggle for political power between the Catholic conservatives and the Protestant reformers. Some of the leading Catholic conservatives were able, briefly, to regain their positions in the Privy Council. However, once Northumberland had consolidated his position, some were expelled. Nevertheless, there was still a degree of toleration and Catholic politicians were not all excluded from government purely for religious reasons.

The power struggle between the conservatives and reformers resurfaced again in 1553 with Northumberland's attempt to change the succession. Northumberland's action was prompted not only by personal ambition, but also by the desire to prevent the Catholics regaining power under Mary Tudor. This rivalry at the centre of power led to instability in the kingdom at large.

It was evident that personal and political ambition motivated those in power to act as they did but religion was never far from their minds. To separate politics and religion in Tudor England is near enough impossible so that political decisions often had religious implications and religious decisions had political implications. The struggle for power at court mirrored the doctrinal struggle between the conservatives and reformers within the Church.

Disorder and rebellion

It is difficult to judge to what extent underlying opposition to the changes in religion contributed to the rebellions of 1549 and to the fall of Somerset. Certainly, only the Western Rebellion was directly linked with religion, and even there underlying economic and social discontent played an important part in causing the uprising. To a certain extent the rebels in the west were complaining about the gentry, whom they accused of making use of the Reformation to seize Church land for their own enrichment. Such views were held in other areas during the popular uprisings of 1549, but only in the West Country was direct opposition to the new Act of Uniformity the central issue.

The Western or Prayer Book Rebellion

The popular discontent began in Cornwall in 1549 when the Cornish people, fearing that the Act of Uniformity was going to be imposed on them, rose in rebellion and set up an armed camp at Bodmin. Because of the hostility expressed by the rebels towards landlords, only six of the more Catholic local gentry joined the uprising. However, the West Country elites were very unwilling to take any action against the rebellion on behalf of the government. The main leaders of the rebels were local clergy, and it was they who began to draw up a series of articles listing demands to stop changes in religion.

In Devon there was an independent uprising at Sampford Courtenay. By 20 June the Devon and Cornish rebels had joined forces at Crediton, and three days later they set up an armed camp at Clyst St Mary. Local negotiations broke down, and the rebels began to blockade the nearby town of Exeter with an army of 6000 men. Lord Russell, who had been sent to crush the rebellion, was hampered by a shortage of troops and a lack of local gentry support. Crucially, the rebels were led by a prominent local gentleman, Humphrey Arundell, who was a skilled tactician and an able commander. As a result, it was not until August that the rebels were finally defeated.

SOURCE E

From the manifesto drawn up by the Western rebels and presented to the king, 1549.

First, we will have the council and holy decrees of our forefathers observed, kept and performed, and whosoever shall say against them we will hold them as heretics.

Item, we will have the laws of our Sovereign Lord King Henry VIII concerning the Six Articles to be in use again as in his time they were.

Item, we will have the sacrament hang over the high altar and there to be worshipped as it was once. They that do not consent we will have them die like heretics against the holy Catholic faith.

Item, we will have holy bread and holy water made every Sunday. Images to be set up in every church and all other ancient ceremonies used before by our mother the holy Church.

Item, we will not receive the new service because it is like a Christmas game, but we will have our old service of Matins, Mass, Evensong and processions in Latin not in English. And so we the Cornishmen, whereof many of us understand no English, utterly refuse this new English.

Item, we will have every preacher and every priest pray specially by name for the souls in purgatory as our forefathers did.

Study Source E. Why would Protector Somerset and King Edward VI find it impossible to compromise with the rebels' demands?

The demands of the rebels

Some of the demands put forward in the final set of articles drawn up by the rebels clearly illustrate their religious conservatism and other grievances felt in the West Country. For example, they wanted:

- to end the changes that they claimed were taking place in baptism and confirmation
- to restore the Act of Six Articles
- to restore the Latin mass and images
- to restore old traditions such as holy bread and water
- to restore the concepts of transubstantiation and purgatory
- the return of Cardinal Pole from exile and for him to have a seat on the king's ruling council.

The government clearly saw these articles as ultra-conservative demands for a return to Catholicism and they were rejected by Cranmer, who was particularly enraged by such insubordination.

Assessing the Western Rebellion

In his book *The Western Rebellion*, published in 1994, historian Philip Caraman claims that the Western (or Prayer Book) Rebellion was 'the most formidable opposition to the reformation that England saw'. Historians agree that the rebels showed little knowledge of either Protestant or Catholic doctrines, but suggest that such ignorance in the West Country probably reflected similar confusion among the great mass of the population. Whether this is true or not, these demands do show that, in the West Country at least, many of the laity were still strongly attached to the familiar traditions of the old Church.

Although religion is acknowledged to be a key cause of the rebellion, some historians have drawn attention to the social and economic causes. For example, in his book *The History of England – A Study in Political Evolution* (1912), A.F. Pollard suggested that social tension lay at the heart of the rebellion and there is evidence to suggest that the rebels considered the gentry to be their enemies. Even the leader of the royal army, Lord Russell, referred to the unfair exploitation of the commons by the local gentry and nobility, who, he claimed, were taxing and raising rents excessively. The rebels were particularly angry at the new sheep tax, which they wanted withdrawn. However, because they failed to mention this in their list of final demands, historians tended to ignore the social and economic grievances in favour of the religious. This is no longer the case because, as Nicholas Fellows has suggested in his book *Disorder and Rebellion in Tudor England* (2002), it is possible to make a link 'between the rebels' religious grievances and their attack upon the gentry: it was after all the gentry who had gained from the Reformation'.

The Kett Rebellion 1549

East Anglia was the most densely populated and highly industrialised part of the country. Norwich was the second largest town after London, and was a major textile centre. The causes of the rebellion were symptomatic of the confused nature of discontent against the economic changes. The rising was triggered by unrest over enclosures, high rents and unsympathetic local landlords like Sir John Flowerdew. Flowerdew was a lawyer who had bought up Church property in the area.

Flowerdew was also in dispute with a local **yeoman**, **Robert Kett**, over land. Kett was a tanner and small landowner who had enclosed much common land. Flowerdew tried to turn the rioters against him but Kett turned the tables by offering to act as spokesman for the rioters. In fact, Kett showed more organisational skill and decisive leadership than is usually found in the leaders of peasant risings. He quickly gathered an army of 16,000 men, set up camp for six weeks on Mousehold Heath and, in July, was able to capture Norwich. The rebellion is notable for the discipline which Kett imposed, electing a governing council and maintaining law and order. Every gentleman that the rebels could arrest was tried before Kett and his council at the 'Tree of Reformation'.

Like the other popular uprising in the West Country, the rebellion was eventually crushed when John Dudley, Earl of Warwick (later the Duke of Northumberland), was sent to take command of the Marquis of Northampton's army of 14,000 men. Northampton had succeeded in taking Norwich but had

KEY TERM

Yeoman Class of richer peasants, just below the gentry, who either owned or rented their land.

KEY FIGURE

Robert Kett (1492–1549)

A prosperous and educated Norfolk farmer who led the rebellion against enclosures and high rents.

been forced to abandon it after only a day. Unlike Northampton, Warwick was able to bring the rebels to battle at Dussindale, just outside the city, where nearly 4000 rebels and royal troops were killed. Kett was captured and eventually hanged for **sedition**.

KEY TERMS

Sedition Speaking or acting against the government by inciting protest or rebellion.

Bondmen Medieval peasants who lived and worked on their lord's manor.

The demands of the rebels

The rebels drew up a list of 29 articles covering a range of topics. Among their demands were the following:

- landowners to stop enclosing common land
- rents to be reduced to the levels they were under Henry VII
- rivers to be open to all for fishing and that fishermen be allowed to keep a greater share of the profits from sea fishing
- all **bondmen** be given their freedom, 'for God made everyone free with his precious blood shedding'
- corrupt local officials 'who have offended the commons' be punished 'where it has been proved by the complaints of the poor'
- incompetent priests to be removed from their churches, particularly those who were 'unable to preach and set forth the word of God to their parishioners'.

Assessing the Kett Rebellion

Unlike the West Country rebels who seemed to wish for religion to be returned to the good old days of Henry VIII, the Norfolk insurgents supported the Protestant religious changes. Kett encouraged Protestant ministers to preach to the rebels on Mousehold Heath and to use the new prayer book.

Although enclosure has, in the past, been cited as the primary cause of the rebellion, in truth it was just one among many agricultural demands made by the rebels. Indeed, apart from local incidents such as at Wymondham and Attleborough, there had been relatively few enclosures in Norfolk during the previous 50 years. Similarly, the requests that bondmen or serfs should be made free seems to be going back to past struggles, because there is no evidence that there were many unfree tenants in sixteenth-century Norfolk.

The major demands were for commons to be kept open and free for husbandmen to graze their livestock, and that rents should not be increased excessively. The Norfolk rebels appeared to yearn for the favourable economic conditions that existed under Henry VII. This does seem to support the notion that the major cause of the popular unrest in 1549 was the harsh economic conditions that prevailed in that year.

Lady Jane Grey and the succession crisis

By 1552 Northumberland seemed to be firmly in control. Even the rapid swing towards Calvinism in the Church of England did not appear to be provoking any serious opposition. However, his power depended on the support of Edward VI. By the end of the year the king's health was obviously deteriorating quickly, and the problem of the succession became a central issue once again. In accordance with Henry VIII's will, Mary was to succeed if Edward died childless. Mary's strong Catholic sympathies made her unpopular with the reform party and with Edward himself. Moreover, it was feared that Mary might renounce the royal supremacy.

To prevent a return to Catholicism, and to retain power, Northumberland, with the full support of the king, planned to change the succession. As the Succession Acts of 1534 and 1536 (see pages 91–2) making Mary and Elizabeth illegitimate had not been repealed, it was decided to disinherit them in favour of the Suffolk branch of the family. Frances, Duchess of Suffolk, was excluded as her age made it unlikely that she would have male heirs and her eldest daughter, Lady Jane Grey, was chosen to succeed. To secure his own position Northumberland married his eldest son, Guildford Dudley, to Jane in May 1553.

Unfortunately for Northumberland, Edward VI died in July before the plans for the seizure of power could be completed. Jane Grey was proclaimed queen by Northumberland and the Council in London, while Mary proclaimed herself queen at Framlingham Castle in Suffolk. Northumberland's mistakes were two-fold:

- he failed to arrest Mary and keep her in custody
- he underestimated the amount of support for Mary in the country.

On 14 July he marched into Suffolk with an army of 2000 men, but his troops deserted him. The Privy Council in London hastily changed sides and proclaimed Mary as queen. Northumberland was arrested in Cambridge, tried, and executed on 22 August in spite of his renunciation of Protestantism (see page 131).

Assessing Lady Jane Grey and the succession crisis

The ease with which Mary upheld her right to the throne showed the growing stability of the State and the nation. A potential political crisis had been avoided because the majority of the nation supported the rule of law and rightful succession. The direct line of descent was still considered legitimate in spite of Acts of Parliament to the contrary. A period of dynastic weakness and minority rule had passed without the country dissolving into civil war. Two Acts were passed, one in 1553 and another in 1554, to resolve the constitutional position. This legislation was designed to confirm Mary Tudor's legitimacy, and to establish the right of female monarchs to rule in England. However, no attempt was made to make Elizabeth legitimate, although she was recognised as Mary's heir in the event of her dying childless.

The strength of the reformed religion

Under Edward VI, England and Wales became officially Protestant. The chantries had been dissolved and the new prayer books had changed the order of service and the nature of worship in the parish church. Church services were now in English (even in Welsh-speaking Wales), the mass had been replaced by communion, communion tables replaced altars, and church plate and vestments were removed. Priests were free to marry and confession was abolished.

Outwardly the Church was transformed but inwardly the people might not have been enthusiastically Protestant. Declaring Protestantism to be the state religion did not necessarily mean that the king's subjects embraced the new faith. The Acts of Uniformity may have compelled people to conform but many may still have retained an affection for the old faith. In northern England the influence of the Reformation at grassroots level was quite limited by 1553. Certainly in Lancashire the population remained more solidly Catholic after the Reformation than in any other part of England.

SOURCE F

From Christopher Haigh, *Reformation and Resistance in Tudor Lancashire*, Cambridge University Press, 2008, p. 178.

For geographical, social and economic, as well as religious reasons, orthodox Catholicism in the county was at its high-point immediately before the Reformation, so that the history of religious change in Lancashire in the sixteenth century is not the conventional one of Protestant triumph and Catholic failure. The Henrician Reformation was met by resistance and rebellion, while the Edwardian reforms were inadequately enforced and made little impact, though a handful of radical preachers made a few gains in one corner of the county. The Marian regime was able to revitalize the old religion.

According to Source F, why did Lancashire's reaction to religious reform differ so radically from other counties in England?

It seems that the Reformation had made virtually no impact in Lancashire and research suggests that elsewhere in England reformed ideas had strongly influenced only a small minority of the lower classes by 1553. Being largely illiterate, the lower classes would need time to become accustomed to the new ideas. The merits of doctrinal changes such as the denial of the Real Presence or the sacramental value of holy orders were beyond the competence of many people to understand, let alone debate. The majority of parishioners were indifferent to the finer points of clerical theology and would be prepared to acquiesce in whatever the government decided, partly through fear of the consequences of opposition but mainly through blind loyalty to the monarch. The consequence was that the changes left many of the lower classes confused or uncommitted to the newly introduced practices and rituals.

The acid test of the strength of the reformed religion came with the accession of Mary in 1553. A devout Roman Catholic, Mary immediately reversed the religious changes and she did so without any significant resistance. The majority of historians believe that the bulk of people reluctantly acquiesced in the religious changes rather than welcomed them and that the Catholic religion was still widely popular by 1553. The old faith, with its familiar services, ceremonies, vestments and shrines that had been removed in 1552–3, was willingly embraced. The strength of the reformed religion was more apparent than real.

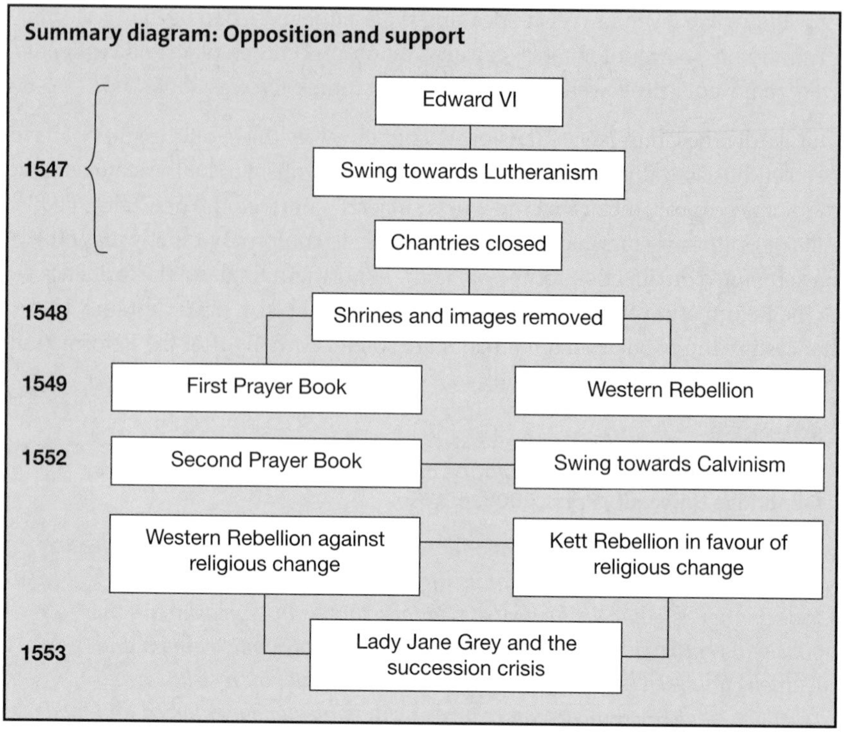

Chapter summary

The accession of a minor to the throne was a cause of some anxiety. This is why the Act of Succession and Henry VIII's will were so influential. The Lord Protectorship of the Duke of Somerset proved divisive owing to his autocratic style of government. By means of the Act of Uniformity, Somerset introduced a moderate form of Protestantism which not only sought an end to the 'popish mass' but was the first attempt to set up a Protestant Church. The six years of Edward's reign witnessed the struggle to establish a Protestant doctrine to underpin the authority of the new Church. Guided by Archbishop Cranmer, the period witnessed the triumph of the Reformists at court, who welcomed his *Book of Homilies* and first *Book of Common Prayer*. The Western and Kett rebellions brought about the downfall of Somerset but did not halt the progress of the Protestant Reformation. Under the Duke of Northumberland, the pace of religious reform quickened. Doctrinal developments led to the publication of the more radical second *Book of Common Prayer*. The combination of prayer book, Bible translation and chantry dissolution contributed to establishing the reformed religion, although its strength was tested during Mary's reign.

Refresher questions

Use these questions to remind yourself of the key material covered in this chapter.

1 Why has Henry VIII's legacy been debated by historians?
2 Why was Edward's succession such a problem and how was it resolved?
3 Why was Somerset cautious about introducing religious reform?
4 How did the Edwardian government deal with Catholic opposition to the religious changes?
5 Why were the chantries dissolved?
6 What caused the Western and Kett rebellions?
7 Why were two versions of the *Book of Common Prayer* published?
8 How significant was Cranmer's contribution to the Edwardian Reformation?
9 Why did Northumberland try to alter the succession on Edward's death?
10 Did Northumberland succeed in turning England into a Protestant nation?

Question practice

ESSAY QUESTIONS

1 How far might England be described as a Protestant nation by 1553?
2 'The driving force for religious reform in the reign of Edward VI was not Somerset or Northumberland but Thomas Cranmer.' Assess the validity of this view.
3 To what extent did Henry VIII bequeath a Church in crisis to Edward VI?
4 'Religion played little, if any, part in the rebellions of 1549.' Assess the validity of this view.

SOURCE ANALYSIS QUESTION

1 With reference to Sources 1, 2 and 3 below, and your understanding of the historical context, assess the value of these sources to a historian studying the causes of the rebellions in 1549.

SOURCE 1

From William Paget's letter of 7 July 1549 to Lord Protector Somerset. Paget was a senior member of the King's Council who advised the Lord Protector and the young King Edward.

I told your grace the truth and was not believed. The king's subjects are out of all discipline, out of obedience, caring neither for protector nor king. And what is the cause? Your own softness, your intention to be good to the poor. Consider, I beseech you most humbly, that society in a realm is maintained by means of religion and law. The use of the old religion is forbidden by a law, and the use of the new is not yet embraced by eleven out of twelve parts of the realm. As for the law, the foot takes on him the part of the head, and the common people are behaving like a king. I know in this matter that every man of the Council has not liked the way in which you have dealt with the rebellious commons and they had wished you had acted otherwise.

SOURCE 2

From Lord Protector Somerset's letter of 27 July 1549 to Lord Russell, commander-in-chief of the royal army sent to deal with the Western rebels.

You have declared that is has been difficult to recruit men to serve in the king's army in Somerset due to the evil inclination of the people and that there are among them many who speak openly using traitorous words against the king and in favour of the rebels. Treat them not as you would good and loyal citizens of the king. You shall hang two to three of them and cause them to be publicly executed as traitors. Sharpe justice must be used against those traitors so that others may learn the consequences of their actions in opposing the king. Send to us news of your dealings with these traitorous rebels so that we may inform his Majesty of your success in this venture.

SOURCE 3

From Matteo Dandolo's letter to the Senate of Venice of 20 July 1549. The Venetian ambassador was writing to his government to report on the rebellions and the English government's response.

There is news of major risings against the government of his grace the Duke of Somerset in England, and that the King has retreated to a strong castle outside London. The cause of this unrest is the common land, as the great landowners occupy the pastures of the poor people. The rebels also require the return of the Mass, together with the religion as it stood on the death of Henry VIII. The government, wishing to apply a swift and ruthless remedy, put upwards of five hundred persons to the sword, sparing neither women nor children. They hope by this action to crush any who might be inclined to oppose or challenge the government of his grace, the Duke of Somerset, who does rule the kingdom on behalf of the young King.

Mary and the Catholic Counter-Reformation 1553–8

This chapter is intended to help you to understand the next stage in the Reformation and the events connected with the changes in religion introduced by Mary. The nature, state and authority of the Roman Catholic Marian Church will be discussed, followed by an examination of the events that led to the Counter-Reformation and the attempt to turn back the clock to the period prior to the Henrician Reformation. These issues are examined as three key themes:

★ The restoration of the 'true faith'

★ Reformation and persecution

★ A crisis in religion? Opposition and conformity

Key dates

1553	Succession of Mary I
	Execution of the Duke of Northumberland
	Catholic mass reintroduced
1554	Wyatt Rebellion
	Execution of Lady Jane Grey and Guildford Dudley
	Marriage of Mary I and Philip of Spain
1554	Cardinal Pole returned to England as papal legate
	England and Rome reconciled
	Reintroduction of the heresy laws
1555	Bishops Ridley and Latimer burned at the stake
1556	Archbishop Cranmer burned at the stake
1558	Death of Mary and Cardinal Pole

1 The restoration of the 'true faith'

▶ *How successful was Mary in restoring the Catholic faith?*

Restoring the rightful succession

Mary (1516–58), the daughter of Catherine of Aragon, was 37 years old when she came to the throne. During Edward VI's reign she had resisted Protestant reform just as strongly as she had under her father. While Somerset was in power she had been allowed to follow her Catholic religion in private, and she had remained on good terms with the Protector and Edward. With the swing towards Calvinism under Northumberland, increasing pressure had been put on Mary to abandon Catholicism and to conform to the latest doctrines of the Church of England.

During this difficult period she had received constant support and advice from her Habsburg cousin, Emperor Charles V. It was fear of the Habsburgs that had prevented the reformers taking extreme measures against her. Mary was a proud woman, who resented the pressures put on her and was embittered by the treatment of her mother. This caused her to distrust her English councillors when she became queen, and instead, rely heavily on advice from the imperial ambassador, **Simon Renard**.

When Mary proclaimed herself queen on 11 July 1553, even Renard and Charles V had thought it a futile gesture. Yet when she entered London at the end of the month she was greeted with enormous enthusiasm. The reason why Mary enjoyed such enthusiastic support, even from among her Protestant subjects, was expressed by Sir Nicholas Throckmorton (*c.*1515–71):

> *And though I liked not the religion*
> *Which all her life Queen Mary had professed*
> *Yet in my mind that wicked notion*
> *Right heirs for to displace, I did detest.*

Political prisoners such as the Duke of Norfolk and Stephen Gardiner were released. Following the advice of Charles V, she showed leniency towards her opponents. Only Northumberland and two of his closest confederates were executed. Although some members of Northumberland's Council, like Sir William Cecil, were imprisoned, others, such as Sir **William Paget**, were allowed to join the new Privy Council. Throckmorton expressed what many of his contemporaries believed, that Mary 'stood for the true religion' and that, as a devout Catholic, she would insist that England return to the Church of Rome. At the same time, Mary was convinced that the kingdom's safety depended on a close alliance with the Habsburgs. Consequently, her policy rested on the achievement of these two aims:

- the restoration of England's links with Rome
- the conclusion of an alliance with the Habsburg Emperor, Charles V.

Until 1555 this strategy appeared to be prospering, but thereafter Mary's popularity steadily declined and, at her death in 1558, the strategy had unravelled.

Mary: character and personality

The cause of this unpopularity has generally been attributed to Mary's own character. Renard's assessment of the queen in 1555, following his dismissal from office, that she was 'good, easily influenced, inexpert in worldly matters and a novice all round' was scarcely a flattering tribute. Elizabethan propagandists later were eager to depict Mary as a weak and unsuccessful

KEY FIGURES

Simon Renard (1513–73)

As the French-born Spanish ambassador to England, Renard exercised considerable influence over Mary I, to the point where some believe he was virtually directing English affairs until his dismissal from office in 1555. He arranged Mary's marriage to Philip of Spain but the latter did not like or trust Renard because he was not Spanish.

William Paget (1505–63)

One of the most able and influential men in the governments of Henry VIII, Edward VI and Mary. He was a friend of Gardiner and was trusted by both Somerset and Mary, who employed him in her government, as did Elizabeth later. He was made Baron Paget in 1549.

pro-Spanish monarch in order to highlight the achievements of their own queen. Protestant reformers reviled her as a cruel tyrant trying to enforce Catholicism through torture and burnings. This has produced a popular picture of 'Bloody Mary': a stubborn, arrogant, Catholic bigot, who burned Protestants and lost Calais to the French because of her infatuation with Philip of Spain.

In a modified form, this has been the view of many historians, but recently there have been attempts to revise this critical appraisal. It has been pointed out that she showed skill and resolution in defeating Northumberland's attempted ***coup d'état***. Mary has also been criticised for indecision in the negotiations over the restoration of Catholicism to England and her marriage to Philip of Spain. However, this, it has been suggested, was in fact masterly political inactivity and pretended weakness, designed to win greater concessions from the papacy and the Habsburgs, similar tactics to those that her half sister Elizabeth used so successfully.

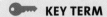

KEY TERM

Coup d'état The French term for a sudden and illegal seizure of a government.

SOURCE A

A portrait of Mary Tudor painted in 1544, when she was 28 years old. The text in the background reads: 'Anno domini 1544 – In the year of our Lord, Lady Mary daughter to the most Virtuous prince King Henry the Eighth. The age of XXVIII (28) years'.

Study Source A. What does this portrait reveal about the relationship between Mary and her father Henry VIII?

Indeed, it is suggested that Mary had the broad support of the majority of the people until 1555. The problem was not the weakness of Mary's character and policies, but her failure to produce an heir to consolidate her position. This, the outbreak of war with France and the declining economic position, were the real causes of Mary's growing unpopularity.

The religious situation in 1553

In 1553 no one in England doubted that Mary, after her twenty years of resistance to the royal supremacy for the sake of her religion, would restore Roman Catholicism. There is good evidence to suggest that it was just as much Edward VI's wish to preserve Protestantism, as Northumberland's personal ambition, that led to the attempt to exclude Mary from the throne. Mary and her Catholic supporters saw the failure of the scheme as a miracle, and she was determined to restore England to the authority of Rome as quickly as possible. What Mary failed to realise was that her initial popularity sprang not from a desire for a return to the Roman Catholic Church, but from a dislike of Northumberland, and respect for the legitimate succession.

Mary's main supporters in England and abroad urged caution. Both Charles V and Pope Julius III (1550–5) warned her not to risk her throne by acting too rashly. Cardinal Reginald Pole, appointed as papal legate to restore England to the authority of Rome, stayed in the Netherlands for a year before coming to England. Whether this was because Charles V refused to allow the Cardinal to leave until the planned marriage between Philip and Mary had come to fruition, or whether it reflected Pole's natural caution about returning to his native land and a possibly hostile reception, is difficult to decide. Even Gardiner, Mary's most trusted English advisor, who had consistently resisted reform, was unenthusiastic about returning to papal authority.

? Study Source B. Why might this declaration have served to confuse rather than clarify the nature of Mary's religious policy?

SOURCE B

From the Royal Proclamation issued by Mary I in August 1553. This proclamation set out Mary's religious policy.

Her Majesty will observe the Catholic religion she has professed all her life, and desires that all her subjects would quietly follow suit. However she will not compel any to this until further decisions are made. She commands her subjects to live together in Christian charity, avoiding the new and devilish terms of papist and heretic, and trying to live peaceful Christian lives. Any man who stirs up the people to disorder will be severely punished. Printers have published books and ballads written in English which discuss controversial religious teachings. Let nobody do so in future without the Queen's permission.

So I accept myself bound on my behalf to show such example as may encourage and maintain well those persons doing their Christian duty.

Mary singularly failed to realise the political implications of restoring Roman Catholicism to England. A return to papal authority would mean an end to the royal supremacy, which was strongly supported by the ruling and landed elites. Even the most ardent of the leading conservatives had been firm in their allegiance to the Crown and the Tudor State. It is agreed by most historians that the major causes of Mary's widespread unpopularity by the end of her reign, apart from the religious persecution, were the return to papal authority and the Spanish marriage. Most of the population regarded this as interference by foreigners and an affront to English nationalism.

The restoration of Anglo-Catholicism

In 1553 there was no doubting Mary's popularity and the ruling elites rallied to her support. The aristocracy and gentry were initially prepared to conform to Mary's religious views, and the bulk of the population followed their example. But some 800 strongly committed Protestant gentry, clergy and members of the middle orders left the country and spent the remainder of the reign on the Continent. Such an escape was less easy for the **lower orders**, and most of the 274 Protestant activists executed during Mary's reign came from this group. At the beginning of the reign even the most zealous of **urban radicals** were not prepared to go against the mainstream of public opinion, and waited to see what would happen. Certainly, when Mary, using the royal prerogative, suspended the second Act of Uniformity and restored the mass, there was no public outcry.

Mary's relationship with Parliament

This lack of religious opposition was apparent when Parliament met in October 1553. Admittedly, the arrest and imprisonment of Cranmer (see page 106), John Hooper (see page 103) and **Nicholas Ridley**, along with other leading Protestant bishops, removed the major source of opposition in the House of Lords. After a lively, but not hostile debate, the first step towards removing all traces of Protestantism from the Church of England was achieved with the passing of the first Statute of Repeal. This Act swept away all the religious legislation approved by Parliament during the reign of Edward VI, and the doctrine of the Church of England was restored to what it had been in 1547 under the Act of the Six Articles. Thus, the mass, clerical celibacy and ritual worship were reinstated.

Although Mary had succeeded in re-establishing the Anglo-Catholicism of her father, her advisers had managed to persuade her into some caution. There had been no attempt to question the royal supremacy, or to discuss the issue of the Church lands which had been sold to the laity. Both these issues were likely to provoke a more heated debate.

When Parliament reassembled it refused to repeal the Act of Supremacy, despite Mary's insistence. Mary responded to Parliament's refusal to repeal the Act of Supremacy by rejecting the title of Supreme Head of the English Church. Opposition to Mary's proposed marriage to Philip II of Spain and the

KEY TERMS

Lower orders The social class representing the mass of the population that occupied a position below the upper classes of nobility and gentry.

Urban radicals Educated artisans, tradesmen and merchants who had embraced the teachings and ideas of Protestantism.

KEY FIGURE

Nicholas Ridley (1502–55)

Radical Protestant cleric and martyr who served as Bishop of London. He tried and failed to persuade Mary to accept the new Protestant faith. His support for Queen Jane made him an enemy of Mary. On her accession he was dismissed from office, tried for treason and heresy, and executed.

consequent rebellion meant that further religious legislation was postponed until the spring of 1554. In the meantime Mary issued royal injunctions ordering the following:

- removal of married clergy from office
- the suppression of heresy
- the restoration of Holy Days and attendant ceremonies
- the ordination of clergy who had been ordained under the **English Ordinal**.

KEY TERM

English Ordinal The process by which priests were appointed and consecrated. This ceremony was to be conducted in English rather than in Latin.

Gardiner's conflict with Paget

Gardiner, anxious to regain royal favour after his opposition to Mary's marriage, tried to quicken the pace at which Protestantism was removed by beginning a methodical purge of married clergy. He demanded that all married clergy should give up their wives and families, or lose their livings. The authorities

Stephen Gardiner

c.1483	Born in Bury St Edmunds to John Gardiner, a prosperous cloth merchant
1530–4	Principal secretary to Henry VIII
1532	Appointed Bishop of Winchester
1535–8	Ambassador to France
1539	Promoted Act of Six Articles
1548	Forced out of government and imprisoned in the Tower of London for opposing Somerset
1553	Appointed Lord Chancellor
1555	Died

Gardiner was educated at Cambridge University and became a doctor of civil law. He continued his studies and was awarded a doctorate in canon law. His legal expertise in common law and ecclesiastical law provided a firm foundation for future promotion. In 1521 he was appointed tutor to the Duke of Norfolk's son. His first significant appointment to public office came in 1524 when he became secretary to Lord Chancellor Wolsey (see page 22), Henry VIII's chief minister.

Gardiner supported Henry VIII over the divorce and approved of the royal supremacy but he disagreed with the religious changes proposed by Cromwell. Because of his opposition to Cromwell he fell out of favour with the king. He got his revenge later when he took part in the destruction of Cromwell. Together with the Duke of Norfolk, he led the conservative faction at court. Back in royal favour, he became one of Henry VIII's leading ministers between 1542 and the king's death in 1547. In Edward's reign he fell foul of the new Protestant regime; he was imprisoned and stripped of his title of Bishop of Winchester. In 1553 he was restored to all his offices and titles by Mary, who appointed him Lord Chancellor. He presided over the wedding of Philip and Mary.

Gardiner was a talented government minister, and respected thinker and theologian. His opposition to Somerset in the final years of Henry VIII's reign ensured his downfall after the king's death. Although Somerset was prepared to work with Gardiner, the two could not agree on the religious direction the Edwardian government should take. In spite of his strong Catholic beliefs, he tried to save the leaders of the reformist party, Cranmer and Northumberland, from execution. The accession of Mary rescued his career and although he had supported the break with Rome in 1534 he was willing to restore the Pope as head of the Church in 1554. He led the Catholic Counter-Reformation and promoted conservative legislation in Parliament. He served out the remainder of his life as a trusted adviser to the Crown.

largely complied with these instructions, and some 800 parish clergy (almost a quarter) were so deprived. Although some fled abroad, the majority were found employment elsewhere in the country. The government made no provision for the wives and children of deprived clerics and many were forced to seek charity or to rely on the support of family. Gardiner also persuaded Parliament to support the queen's injunction by passing into law a bill to reintroduce the heresy laws. He was successfully opposed by Sir William Paget, who feared that such a measure might provoke further disorder.

Paget was a formidable enemy. He was trusted by Henry VIII and the Duke of Somerset but not by Northumberland. His support of Mary earned her trust and gratitude and his handling of the marriage negotiations won the admiration of Philip of Spain. However, his opposition to what he regarded as extreme religious legislation drawn up by Gardiner, his one-time friend and with whom he quarrelled quite violently, led to his losing his leading place in Mary's government.

Thwarted by Paget, Gardiner proceeded to turn his attention to senior Protestant clergy. The bishops of Gloucester, Hereford, Lincoln and Rochester and the Archbishop of York were deprived of their bishoprics, and were replaced by committed Catholics. In March 1554 the bishops were instructed to enforce all the religious legislation of the final year of Henry VIII's reign. Apart from ensuring a return to 'the old order of the Church, in the Latin tongue', these injunctions demanded that all married clergy should give up their wives and families or lose their livings. Around 800 parish priests were deprived of their livings.

Summary diagram: The restoration of the 'true faith'

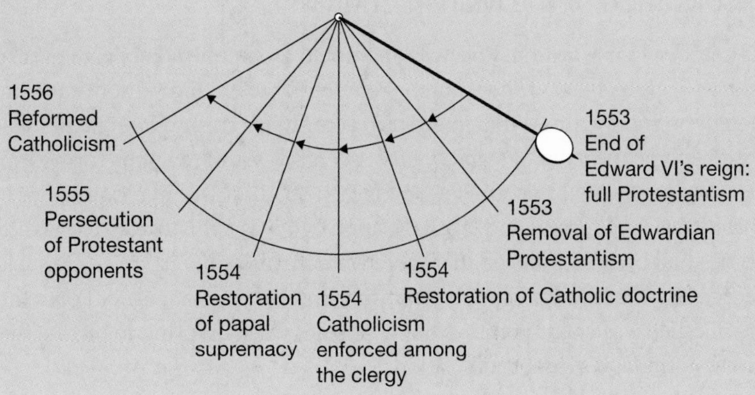

2 Reformation and persecution

▶ *Why did Mary follow a policy of religious persecution?*

Restoration of papal authority

Cardinal Pole finally arrived in England in November 1554, after a delay of some months, and this marked the next decisive stage in the restoration of Roman Catholicism and papal authority. Parliament met in the same month and passed the second Statute of Repeal. This Act ended the royal supremacy, and returned England to papal authority by repealing all the religious legislation of the reign of Henry VIII back to the time of the break with Rome.

For Mary to achieve her aim of sweeping away all anti-papal legislation she had to come to a compromise with the landed elites. In fact, Parliament's threatened refusal to restore papal primacy in England unless the queen agreed to let confiscated Church wealth (mainly monastic and chantry property) remain in the hands of its new lay owners, angered Mary. Nevertheless, in spite of her anger, careful provision was made in the Act to protect the property rights of all those who had bought Church land since 1536. This demonstrates that Mary had no choice but to recognise the authority of Parliament over matters of religion. It meant that she had to abandon her plans for a full-scale restoration of the monasteries. Instead, she had to be content with merely returning the monastic lands, worth £60,000 a year and still held by the Crown, to those religious orders who were persuaded to return to England. Clearly, there were limits to the restoration of religion intended by Mary, who was constrained to work within them.

Consolidation of the Marian Church

In December 1555 Cardinal Pole was appointed as Archbishop of Canterbury. In his new role as head of the Church, Pole set out to eradicate Protestantism, although he soon realised that in order to accomplish this mission he first had to restore some measure of stability after twenty years of religious turmoil. It is widely considered that, in view of his lack of administrative experience and ability, such a formal and legalistic approach was a mistake. Ecclesiastical revenues had been so reduced that there were insufficient resources available to reorganise the Marian Church effectively. Indeed, a great part of Pole's three years in office was spent in the virtually hopeless task of trying to restore the Church of England's financial position.

Pole's attempts to reorganise and reconcile the Church of England to Rome were not helped by the death of Pope Julius III in 1555. The new Pope, Paul IV, disliked Pole and hated the Spanish Habsburgs. He stripped Pole of his title of legate and replaced him with Friar William Peto. However, Mary refused to recognise the appointment. The Pope then ordered Pole to return to Rome to

Reginald Pole

1500	Born in Stourton Castle in Staffordshire to Sir Richard Pole, a senior official in the household of Prince Arthur
1527	Became Dean of Exeter Cathedral
1530	Became Dean of Windsor but refused the king's offer of the Archbishopric of York
1537	Summoned to Rome by the Pope, who made him a cardinal and papal legate to England
1549	Narrowly failed to get elected Pope
1554	Returned to England as papal legate and helped return the Church to Rome
1555	Succeeded Cranmer as Archbishop of Canterbury
1558	Died on the same day as Mary I

Pole was born a younger son of Sir Richard Pole and Margaret, Countess of Salisbury. He was educated at Oxford University where he received his degree in divinity. He continued his studies on the Continent between 1521 and 1530, including two years in Paris. His mother was executed in 1541.

Pole was a dedicated Catholic who risked his life, and the lives of his family, to oppose Henry VIII's break with Rome. He criticised in print Henry VIII's supremacy of the Church in England. Henry VIII was furious and had his mother and brother arrested, charged with treason and executed. In the immediate aftermath of the death of Henry VIII he failed to persuade Somerset to return England to the Roman Church. He spent most of his life abroad and was out of touch with the feelings and attitudes of his fellow English when he returned in 1554. On his return to England he was invited to address Parliament, where he assured the audience that he came 'to reconcyle, not to condemne, … not to destroy but to build, … not to compel but to call agayne'.

Pole's impact on English religious thinking was limited and he failed to turn the clock back to the 1520s. His restoration of the Pope as head of the English Church lasted only three years and it did not survive his death. His greatest achievement was to maintain an English presence at the papal court.

answer charges of heresy. With Mary's backing, Pole refused to comply, and continued his work in England as Archbishop of Canterbury, but the papacy would not recognise his authority. This further hindered his work because he could not appoint bishops, and by 1558, seven dioceses were vacant. Such quarrels, and the blatant papal intervention in English affairs, did little to convince anyone except the most zealous Catholics of the wisdom of returning to the authority of Rome.

Certainly, such events did not help the government in its task of winning the hearts and minds of the English to the Roman Catholic faith. Pole's hopes that the re-establishment of the old religion would lead to wholehearted acceptance of Roman Catholicism were not to be realised. Pole was fully in favour of the educational programme which was being adopted on the Continent. He appointed capable and active bishops, all of whom subsequently refused to serve in the Elizabethan Protestant Church of England.

The Twelve Decrees

In 1555 the Westminster synod approved the passing of the Twelve Decrees that included the establishment of seminaries in every diocese for the training of priests, but shortage of money limited the programme to a single creation at

York. This meant that the majority of the parish clergy remained too uneducated, and lacking in evangelical zeal, for the new laws to have any immediate impact on the laity. Mary's death in November 1558 came too soon for Catholic reform to have had any lasting effect. That is not to say that if Mary had lived longer, Catholicism would not have gained wider support than the significant minority, who clung to their faith even after the establishment of the Elizabethan Church.

Religious persecution

Parliament's approval of the restoration of the old heresy laws marked the beginning of religious persecution. The extract in Source C suggests that at the beginning of her reign Mary was prepared to be tolerant.

? Study Source C. How true a reflection of Mary's religious beliefs and intentions is this statement?

SOURCE C

Extract of a Royal Proclamation issued by Queen Mary in 1553.

Touching the punishment of heretics, we thinketh it ought to be done without rashness … and [the people] not to be condemned without just oration. And especially within London I would wish none to be burnt without some of the Council's presence and – both there and everywhere – good sermons [preached] at the same.

The first Protestant was burned at the stake for heresy on 4 February 1555, and Hooper suffered a similar fate five days later in his own city of Gloucester. In October, Ridley and Hugh Latimer, the former Bishop of Worcester, were likewise executed at Oxford (see Source D), where they were followed by Cranmer in March 1556 (see Source E). The death of Gardiner in November 1555 had removed a trusted and restraining influence, and thereafter the regime became more repressive. Although Gardiner had started the persecution on the grounds that some executions would frighten the Protestant extremists into submission, he was too astute a politician to fail to see that the policy was not working. Far from cowing the Protestants, he realised that the executions were hardening the opposition to Mary and encouraging the colonies of English exiles on the Continent. He counselled caution, but his advice was ignored.

After Gardiner's death, Mary and Pole felt that it was their sacred duty to stamp out heresy, and stepped up the level of persecution. Pole was so confident of success that he declined the offer of Jesuit missionaries to help infuse the English laity with enthusiasm for the 'old faith'. In the long term this proved to be a mistake because there was no attempt to win over the doubters, there was only fear. It has been estimated that the 274 religious executions carried out during the final three years of Mary's reign exceeded the number recorded in any Catholic country on the Continent over the same period, even though it was much less than in some other periods. This modifies the claim by some historians that the Marian regime was more moderate than those on the Continent.

SOURCE D

Report of the burning of Hugh Latimer, Bishop of Worcester, and Nicholas Ridley, Bishop of London, contained in *Acts and Monuments*, popularly known as Foxe's *Book of Martyrs*, published by John Foxe in 1563.

Then they brought a faggot kindled with fire, and laid the same down at Dr. Ridley's feet. To whom Master Latimer spoke in this manner 'Be of good comfort, Master Ridley, and play the man. We shall this day light such a candle, by God's grace, in England, as I trust shall never be put out'.

Study Source D. What do you think Latimer meant by this quotation?

SOURCE E

The martyrdom of Cranmer (1556), from John Foxe's *Book of Martyrs* (published in 1563).

How is Cranmer depicted in Source E? In your opinion, was Foxe a Catholic or a Protestant author?

SOURCE F

Report by Simon Renard to King Philip, February 1555.

Sire,

The people of London are murmuring about the cruel enforcement of the recent acts of parliament on heresy which has now begun, as shown publicly when a certain Rogers was burnt yesterday. Some of the onlookers wept, others prayed to God to give them strength … others gathered the ashes and bones … yet others did threaten the bishops. The haste in which the bishops have proceeded in this matter may well cause a revolt. I do not think it well that your Majesty should allow further executions to take place unless the reasons are strong. Tell the bishops that they are not to proceed without having first consulted you and the Queen. Your Majesty will also consider that the Lady Elizabeth has her supporters and that there are Englishmen who do not love foreigners.

Read Source F. What does the source reveal about the dangers of the Marian persecution?

Popular reactions against religious persecution

Gardiner's unheeded warnings were soon justified, and Mary's popularity waned rapidly. There was widespread revulsion in the south-east of England at the persecution, and to many people Catholicism became firmly linked with dislike of Rome and Spain. According to historian David Loades, writing in his biography entitled *Mary Tudor: A Life* (1989), 'it was during Mary's reign that Catholicism first began to be seen as something foreign' whereas Protestantism was gradually acquiring the status of being more 'English, even patriotic'. The terror associated with the policy of 'turn or burn' not only made for a bad press but tarnished the image of 'caring' Catholicism. It was a godsend for Protestant propagandists who were able to demonise the queen and attack the tyrannical nature of her rule. Thus, the myth of 'Bloody Mary' was born.

Many local authorities either ignored or tried to avoid enforcing the unpopular legislation. The number of people fleeing abroad increased (over 800 had fled during the reign), reinforcing the groups of English exiles living in centres of Lutheranism and Calvinism on the Continent. They became the nucleus of an active and well-informed opposition, which began to flood England with anti-Catholic books and pamphlets. The effectiveness of this campaign is shown in the proclamations issued by the Privy Council in 1558, ordering the death penalty by martial law for anyone found with heretical or seditious literature. In truth, government censorship was not rigorous enough to stop the importation and circulation of illicit Protestant literature. If before 1555 the English people were generally undecided about religion, the Marian repression succeeded in creating a core of highly committed English Protestants.

The Marian government lost the propaganda war because it was ill-equipped to deal with it. Historian Robert Tittler (1983) has pointed out that one of the major weaknesses of the Counter-Reformation was the fact that Mary's government 'neglected to mount a sustained propaganda campaign'. Whereas Henry VIII and Cromwell had conducted a massive propaganda exercise (see pages 33–4) to help 'sell' the Henrician Reformation, Mary believed this was unnecessary as the people were, at heart, genuine Catholics who required no such motivation to embrace the 'true faith'. Consequently, as Tittler stated, 'Mary's regime concentrated on the suppression of opposition voices rather than the projection of its own.'

Summary diagram: Reformation and persecution

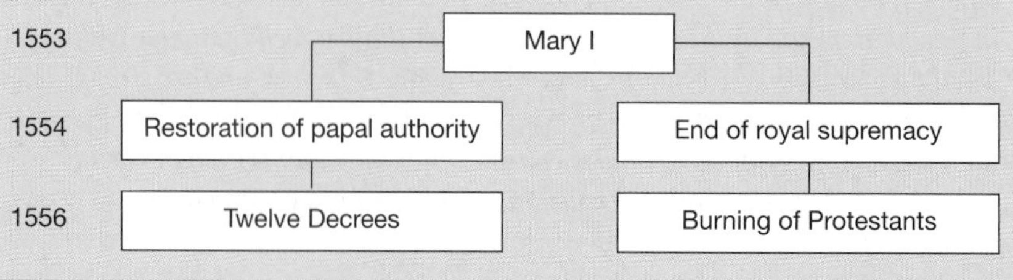

3 A crisis in religion? Opposition and conformity

▶ *How serious was the crisis in religion during Mary's reign?*

Potential crisis: the Spanish marriage

Mary's political inexperience and stubbornness are shown in the first major issue of her reign: the royal marriage. This had the potential to turn into a political crisis which had major implications for Mary's desire for religious reform. The Privy Council was divided on the matter. There were two realistic candidates for Mary's hand:

- Edward Courtenay, Earl of Devon, who was favoured by Gardiner
- Philip of Spain, who was supported by Paget.

Courtenay was a descendant of the Plantagenet kings and such a marriage would have strengthened the Tudor dynasty, but Mary favoured a closer link with the Habsburgs through Philip. It was not until 27 October that Mary raised the matter in Council, and then only to announce that she was going to marry Philip. This disconcerted Gardiner, who was blamed by Mary for the petition from the House of Commons in November asking her to marry within the realm. Mary disregarded all opposition to her plans.

On 7 December a marriage treaty, drafted by Mary, Paget, Gardiner and Renard, was presented to the Council. It was ratified at the beginning of January 1554. Mary had achieved her objective of forming a closer alliance with the Habsburgs. The terms of the treaty were very favourable to England. Philip was to have no regal power in England, no foreign appointments were to be made to the Privy Council, and England was not to be involved in, or pay towards the cost of any of Philip's wars. If the marriage was childless, the succession was to pass to Elizabeth.

In spite of these safeguards, Mary's popularity began to ebb, as many people still thought that England would be drawn into Philip's wars and become a mere province of the Habsburg Empire. The objections to the marriage were mainly political but Mary's reasons for the union with Philip were largely religious. She wanted the powerful, prestigious and devoutly Catholic Philip to assist her in her religious mission to re-Catholicise England. In the final analysis it must be remembered that Mary was herself half Spanish.

By the end of January 1554, anti-Spanish feelings led to rebellion. The rebellion was led by Sir James Croft, Sir Peter Carew and Sir Thomas Wyatt. These men had all held important offices at court under both Henry VIII and Edward VI. Although they had supported Mary's accession, they feared that the growing Spanish influence would endanger their own careers.

Actual crisis: Wyatt's Rebellion

Sir Thomas Wyatt was a member of a wealthy and well-connected gentry family from Kent. He succeeded to the family estates on the death of his father, also called Sir Thomas, in 1542. Sir Thomas Wyatt senior had been a courtier and diplomat, and his son was expected to follow suit. He became friendly with the influential Henry Howard, Earl of Surrey, who acted as his patron. Wyatt fought in France under Surrey in 1543–4 and in 1545 he was promoted to the English council governing English-controlled Boulogne. Unfortunately for Wyatt, his career suffered a setback in 1546 when Surrey fell into disfavour with Henry VIII and was later executed. As a committed Protestant, Wyatt found favour with the Edwardian regime, which he defended in 1549 when riots broke out in Kent. He was trusted by Northumberland, who appointed him to represent the English government in negotiations with the French in 1550.

Wyatt served the Edwardian regime loyally but he declared his support for Mary when Jane Grey was proclaimed queen. Wyatt's initial support for Mary soon evaporated when he heard of the Spanish marriage. As an MP he became involved in the opposition to the proposed marriage in Parliament but his hopes of persuading the queen to reject the marriage failed.

Conspiracy and rebellion

Unlike the rebellions of 1549, Wyatt's Rebellion of 1554 was a political conspiracy among the ruling elites, and there was little popular support. The conspirators planned to marry Elizabeth to Edward Courtenay, Earl of Devon, who Mary had rejected as an unsuitable match.

Simultaneous rebellions in the West Country (Carew), the Welsh borderland (Croft), the Midlands (Suffolk, father of Lady Jane Grey) and Kent (Wyatt) were to be supported by a French fleet. The plan failed because the inept Courtenay disclosed the scheme to his patron, Gardiner, before the conspirators were ready. In any case, Carew, Croft and the Duke of Suffolk bungled the uprisings. Wyatt succeeded in raising 3000 men in Kent, and this caused real fear in the government because the rebels were so close to London, the capital. The situation was made worse because a number of royal troops sent to crush the revolt under the command of the aged Duke of Norfolk deserted to the rebels. Realising the danger, the Privy Council desperately tried to raise fresh forces to protect London.

Failure of Wyatt's Rebellion

An overcautious Wyatt failed to press home his advantage and although he led his motley troops with some dash, his delay in marching on London gave Mary the time she needed to see to the capital's defence. In refusing to flee her capital, Mary's courage impressed those whom she called on to support her regime. By the time Wyatt arrived at the gates of the city the revolt was doomed to fail. Repulsed at London Bridge and the Tower, Wyatt crossed the Thames at Kingston, but found Ludgate closed and his troops began deserting in droves.

Wyatt surrendered and the revolt was crushed. Paget suggested leniency for the rebels for fear of provoking further revolts. Fewer than a hundred executions took place among the commons and most were pardoned. As for the rebel elite, apart from Wyatt and Suffolk, only Jane Grey and her husband Guildford Dudley were executed. Croft was tried and imprisoned but he was pardoned and released after nine months in the Tower. Carew fled to France but returned in 1556 on promise of a pardon. Both Elizabeth and Courtenay were interrogated and imprisoned but were later released.

The Wyatt Rebellion came as close as any to overthrowing the monarchy. According to historian Paul Thomas, writing in *Authority and Disorder in Tudor Times 1485–1603* (1999): 'Mary's new regime was pushing its luck, not so much with a policy of Catholic restoration, as with the Spanish marriage and the provocation of those members of the Court elite who either felt excluded or feared imminent exclusion.'

Frustrated and increasingly desperate, men like Wyatt felt compelled to act in a way that had only two possible outcomes: failure would result in their own death while success would almost inevitably lead to the death of the monarch. In the opinion of historian Diarmaid MacCulloch, writing in *Tudor Rebellions* (2008), the fact that the Wyatt Rebellion failed demonstrates 'the bankruptcy of rebellion as a way of solving political crises'.

SOURCE G

From Sir Nicholas Throckmorton's evidence given at his trial for treason in 1554. He made no effort to conceal his distaste for the queen's marriage but he denied that there was anything treasonable about this.

I did see the whole realm was against it [the marriage] and although I counselled caution and urged restraint on those who would do mischief, it is I who is brought here before you. My lords, in no wise am I guilty of treason because it was no treason, nor no procurement of treason, to talk against the coming hither of the Spaniards.

Study Source G. Throckmorton (see page 118) was found not guilty and was acquitted of all charges. Why do you think he was spared while Wyatt (see below) was executed?

War with France and the loss of Calais

In 1557 Mary declared war on France. She did so not out of any justifiable grievance but on account of her alliance with Spain. As the conflict between Spain and France intensified, Philip put pressure on Mary to join him in making war on the French. Some royal councillors advocated against war for the following reasons:

- Mary and Philip had promised that their marriage would not result in England being dragged into Spain's Continental conflicts.
- War would damage an already fragile English economy by disrupting trade.

- War might lead to the revival of the Franco-Scottish alliance, thus threatening England's northern border.
- The safety and security of Calais would be put in danger.

Mary ignored her councillors' advice and allied herself with Philip.

? Study Source H. After declaring war on France why did Mary permit Frenchmen 40 days to leave England?

SOURCE H

Mary's declaration of war, issued on 7 June 1557.

All Englishmen to regard Henry, the French King, and his vassals as public enemies of this kingdom and to harm them wherever possible, abstaining from trading or any other business with them. We have seen fit to allow his subjects and merchants forty days to leave this kingdom with such property as the law permits them to export.

In spite of some minor successes, the war went badly for Mary. A Scottish invasion was repulsed and the city of St Quentin was captured by Anglo-Spanish forces but French power proved too strong. Defeat and retreat led to the fall of Calais, the last English possession in Continental Europe. As the merchants had feared, trade was disrupted and the economy suffered. Of greater concern to Mary was the possibility that by making war on the French she might risk conflict with the papacy. The Franco-Papal alliance against Spain would be likely to extend to England if Mary dared join her husband in war. Having worked so hard to repair England's relations with the papacy and to restore papal power over the English Church, Mary could not face the prospect of a new schism. In the event, Mary was spared this embarrassment when a serious rift developed in Franco-Papal relations.

Religion and the Church of England under Mary

To assess the state of religion and the Church in England at the end of Mary's reign in 1558 is just as difficult as it is to measure the advance of Protestantism by its beginning in 1553. It is almost impossible to decide to what extent the bulk of the population had any particular leanings towards either the Protestant or the Catholic faith. While it is easy to trace the changing pattern of official doctrine in the Church of England through the acts and statutes passed in Parliament, it is a much greater problem to determine what the general public thought about religion. At present, the consensus among historians is that the ruling elites accepted the principle of the royal supremacy and were prepared to conform to whichever form of religion was favoured by the monarch. Although the lower orders are generally considered to have had a conservative affection for the traditional forms of worship, it is thought that they were prepared to follow the lead of the local elites. It is also fair to say that a sizeable proportion of the population – the doubters – may still have been undecided about religion. Whether the religious legislation passed in Parliament was put into effect very much depended on the attitudes of the local elites, and to a lesser extent those of the parish authorities.

Arguably, although there were small minorities of committed Protestants and Catholics, neither religion seems to have had a strong hold in England when Mary I died. When Elizabeth I came to the throne the country was willing to return to a form of moderate Protestantism. However, during her reign deeper religious divisions began to appear, and the unity of the Church of England came to an end.

Summary diagram: A crisis in religion? Opposition and conformity

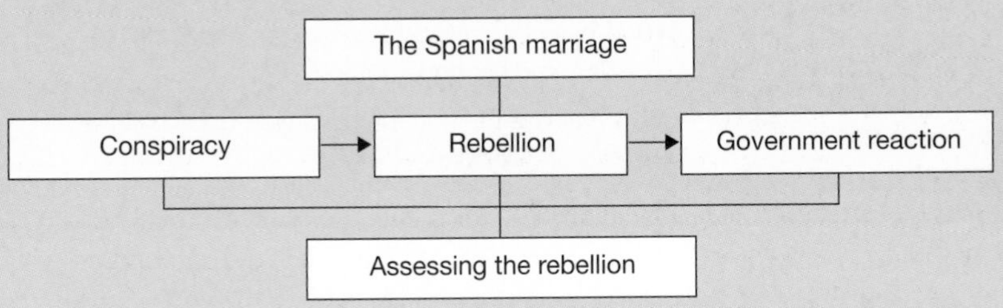

Chapter summary

The accession of Mary witnessed the re-establishment of the Roman Catholic faith in England. As a devout Catholic, Mary was determined to erase the Protestant reforms introduced to the Church by her half-brother Edward VI. She restored the Pope as head of the Church, reintroduced the Catholic mass and re-established the heresy laws. Adopting the tactics of the European Counter-Reformation, Mary set about returning the people to the 'true faith'. She was aided in her mission by Cardinal Pole, who returned from exile as papal legate and was appointed Archbishop of Canterbury. For those who opposed her, she resorted to fear and persecution, which resulted in the public burnings of nearly 300 people. Among the victims was the former Archbishop of Canterbury and architect of the Protestant reformation, Thomas Cranmer. The harsh treatment of Protestants proved counter-productive since distinguished clerics such as bishops Ridley and Latimer became martyrs. As the first female monarch to rule England, Mary faced a unique situation since her male-dominated court expected her to marry. However, the Spanish marriage, with Philip of Spain, proved controversial and provoked men such as Sir Thomas Wyatt to rebel. Her reign proved too short to establish Roman Catholicism firmly.

Refresher questions

Use these questions to remind yourself of the key material covered in this chapter.

1. What problems did Mary face when she became queen?
2. Why did Mary restore Roman Catholicism?
3. How popular were Mary's religious changes?
4. Why did Mary follow a policy of religious persecution?
5. How significant was Gardiner's contribution to religious change during Mary's reign?
6. Why was Cranmer executed?
7. What impact did Pole have on the religious changes introduced during Mary's reign?
8. Why was the Spanish marriage so important for Mary?
9. What caused the Wyatt Rebellion?
10. Why was the Wyatt Rebellion so dangerous to Mary and her government?
11. What was the state of the English Church at the end of Mary's reign?

Question practice

ESSAY QUESTIONS

1. 'Mary's marriage to Philip of Spain did more harm than good to the cause of religious reform.' Assess the validity of this view.
2. To what extent did the re-establishment of Catholicism in England owe more to the work of Gardiner than it did to Pole?
3. 'The restoration of the Pope as head of the English Church encouraged more opposition than support for Mary's attempts to re-Catholicise England.' Assess the validity of this view.
4. 'The Marian Counter-Reformation was a failure and the persecutions and burnings prove it.' Assess the validity of this view.

SOURCE ANALYSIS QUESTION

1. With reference to Sources 1, 2 and 3 below, and your understanding of the historical context, assess the value of these sources to a historian studying the effectiveness of the Marian Counter-Reformation.

SOURCE 1

From the Royal Proclamation issued by Mary I in August 1553. This proclamation set out Mary's religious policy.

Her Majesty will observe the Catholic religion she has professed all her life, and desires that all her subjects would quietly follow suit. However she will not compel any to this until further decisions are made. She commands her subjects to live together in Christian charity, avoiding the new and devilish terms of papist and heretic, and trying to live peaceful Christian lives. Any man who stirs up the people to disorder will be severely punished. Printers have published books and ballads written in English which discuss controversial religious teachings. Let nobody do so in future without the Queen's permission.

So I accept myself bound on my behalf to show such example as may encourage and maintain well those persons doing their Christian duty.

SOURCE 2

From a report sent by Simon Renard, the Spanish ambassador, to his master, King Philip of Spain, in February 1555.

The people of this town of London are murmuring about the cruel enforcement of the recent acts of Parliament against heresy which has now begun, as shown publicly when a certain Rogers was burnt yesterday. Some of the onlookers wept. Others prayed to God to give them strength, persistence, and patience to bear the pain and not to convert back to Catholicism. Others gathered the ashes and bones and wrapped them up in paper to preserve them. Yet others threatened the bishops. The haste with which the bishops have proceeded in this matter may well cause a revolt. If the people got the upper hand, not only would the cause of religion be again menaced, but the persons of your Majesty and the Queen might be in peril.

SOURCE 3

From John Foxe's book *Acts and Monuments*, published in 1563. Foxe was a Protestant writer who described here the execution of Agnes Potter and Joan Trunchfield.

These two advocates and sufferers for the pure gospel of Jesus Christ, lived in the town of Ipswich. Being apprehended on information of heresy, they were brought before the bishop of Norwich, who examined them concerning their religion in general and their faith in the real presence of Christ in the sacrament of the altar in particular. With respect to the latter they both delivered their opinion, that in the sacrament of the Lord's supper there was represented the memorial only of Christ's death and passion, saying that according to the scriptures he was ascended up into heaven and sat on the right hand of God the Father, and therefore his body could not really be in the sacrament.

A few days later, they were examined by the bishop when both of them still continuing steadfast in the profession of their faith, sentence was pronounced against them as heretics, and they were delivered over to the secular power.

On the day appointed for their execution, which was in the month of March 1556, they were both led to the stake and burnt, in the town of Ipswich. Their courage and conviction was admired by the multitude who saw them suffer.

Elizabeth and the settlement of religion 1547–70

This chapter is intended to help you to understand how the religious changes in Edward's reign paved the way for the Elizabethan Anglican Church. It also examines the means by which Elizabeth attempted to settle the issue of religion by establishing an Anglican Church acceptable to moderate Protestants and Catholics. The nature, state and authority of the Elizabethan Church will be discussed, followed by an examination of the events that led to the first successful attempt to set up a Protestant Anglican Church. These issues are examined as three key themes:

★ The Elizabethan religious settlement

★ Establishing the Anglican Church

★ The end of the settlement

The key debate on *page 141* of this chapter asks the question: Why did the Elizabethan religious settlement take the form that it did and would it last?

Key dates

1547	Accession of Edward VI and the first attempt to set up an English Protestant Church
1549	The first *Book of Common Prayer*
1552	The second *Book of Common Prayer*
1553	Cranmer's Forty-Two Articles and the end of the Protestant experiment
1558	Accession of Elizabeth I
1559	Religious settlement: Acts of Supremacy and Uniformity passed
1559	Matthew Parker appointed Archbishop of Canterbury
1563	Parker drew up the Thirty-Nine Articles
1566	Parker's *Advertisements* and the Vestiarian Controversy
1568	Mary, Queen of Scots, sought refuge in England
1569–70	Rising of the northern earls
1570	Pope excommunicated Elizabeth

1 The Elizabethan religious settlement

▶ *How significant was the religious settlement?*

Elizabeth's accession

After a turbulent five-year reign, Mary succumbed to cancer and died in November 1558. At her funeral service, John White, Bishop of Winchester, eulogised Mary: 'She was a king's daughter; she was a king's sister; she was a king's wife. She was a queen, and by the same title a king also.' Despite determined opposition, she was the first woman to rule England and, for a short time, she enjoyed popular support. However, her increasingly harsh rule and bloody persecution, added to the unpopularity of her Spanish marriage, turned many people against her. She died in the middle of an unpopular war with France that witnessed the loss of Calais and with a treasury that was all but bankrupt. Many did not mourn her passing.

Mary was succeeded as queen of England by her 25-year-old half-sister Elizabeth. Given the political, religious and economic problems she had inherited from Mary, Elizabeth was well aware that the enthusiasm and popular support that accompanied her accession could evaporate overnight. She was determined to learn from the errors made by her predecessors and, in an effort not to repeat them, she quickly identified those issues that required careful attention.

Elizabeth realised that the main danger areas were religion and faction. She inherited a kingdom divided and confused in its religion and in its politics. In order to avoid faction and religious tension, Elizabeth moved swiftly to settle both. There was no purge of Marian politicians, eleven of whom were appointed by Elizabeth to serve on her Privy Council. To these, the new queen added seven new appointments to create a balanced Council of eighteen members. Two of the most prominent casualties of the new reign were Sir William Paget and Mary's Lord Chancellor, Archbishop Heath, both of whom were dismissed from the Council.

Religious background

Elizabeth adopted a cautious approach, such as when she informed the Spanish ambassador that she intended to restore the form of religion as practised in the final years of her father's reign. Not fully understanding what the queen meant by this statement, the ambassador chose to think that she intended to adopt a more conservative approach to religion: something similar to post-supremacy Catholicism with trace elements of Protestantism. In leaving the ambassador to reach his own conclusion, Elizabeth aimed to avoid confrontation. In reality, her aim was to establish an Anglican Church that was essentially Protestant but with some elements of Catholicism. Elizabeth hoped her subjects too might make up their own minds rather than confront the Crown with their grievances, both real and imagined.

The question of whether the England inherited by Elizabeth was more Catholic than Protestant, or the other way around, is hotly debated. Indeed, the argument is unlikely to be resolved because the issue is complex and the evidence contradictory. There were probably as many enthusiastic and committed Catholics as Protestants in England but given the years of change and confusion, the majority of the people were possibly more inclined to be religiously indifferent. If the law compelled them to go to church, habit or fear rather than conviction impelled them to attend its services.

In such volatile circumstances, the majority of the population were ripe for conversion to either faith, which is why the settlement of religion was thrashed out in Elizabeth's first Parliament. Meeting within eight weeks of her accession, between January and April 1559, Parliament enacted what historians have labelled the '**Elizabethan religious settlement**'. The legislation set out the following:

- it reconfirmed the royal supremacy
- it set out the way in which the Church was to be run
- it established the content and conduct of services in every parish church.

Although the settlement included an Act of Uniformity that restored the Edwardian prayer book of 1552, the government hoped that by being deliberately vague on some aspects of doctrine the legislation would appeal to Protestants and Catholics alike.

KEY TERMS

Elizabethan religious settlement Phrase used by historians to describe the organisation, ritual and teaching of the Church of England as enforced by Acts of Parliament.

Puritans Protestants who wished to reform the Anglican Church by eradicating all trace of Catholicism and Catholic practices.

Religious divisions

There is no doubt that the revolutionary upheavals in religious worship and doctrine had a transforming effect on the mental and material worlds of the population of Tudor England and Wales. As historian Susan Doran has said, in her book *England and Europe 1485–1603* (1986), Elizabeth 'inherited a realm ill at ease with itself. The religious persecution of her sister, Mary, had divided communities and traumatised English Protestants and their sympathisers.' The confusion and concern experienced by the majority of Elizabeth's subjects was not lost on the new queen, who sought to calm their fears by pursuing a non-aggressive religious policy. There was no doubt that when Elizabeth ascended the throne she would adopt some form of Protestantism, but in doing so she had to avoid alienating her Catholic subjects. Equally, Elizabeth had to take care not to upset the radical reformers, many of whom had returned from exile in Europe filled with evangelical zeal and **puritan** conviction.

Some form of compromise was likely, but would it be enough to satisfy Protestants and Catholics at home, let alone impress a sceptical Pope Pius V and the Spanish king (Philip II) abroad? Historian William Sheils (*The English*

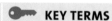

Reformation 1530–1570, 1989) believes that Elizabeth managed to do just that by framing a settlement or *via media* (middle way) that not only seemed to satisfy all parties but also laid the foundations of the Anglican Church. However, for those radical religious groups who were on the fringes of the religious community and who remained unreconciled to the Elizabethan Church, opposition became the only option available. These relatively small extremist groups evolved into the **recusants** and puritans of Elizabeth's later reign.

KEY TERM

Recusants Catholics who refused to conform to the State religion and refused to attend church services.

SOURCE A

From the Venetian ambassador's letter to the Senate of Venice, December 1558. The ambassador was writing to his government to report on the state of the kingdom in the weeks after Elizabeth acceded to the throne.

Queen Elizabeth often promised to continue the Catholic religion. But on Christmas Day, Her Majesty told the Bishop that he was not to elevate the host during mass. He replied that this was the only way he knew, so Her Majesty rose and departed. On the same day, two individuals, a mechanic and a cobbler, followed by a very great mob, entered by force into the church of St. Augustine, breaking the locks of the doors. Both leaped into the pulpit and preached uttering rude jokes about the blessed Queen Mary and Cardinal Pole. Queen Elizabeth forbade such preaching for fear of provoking riots. The Queen is fearful of tumults and uprisings which is why she proceeds with caution. She has no wish to follow the path taken by her late sister.

Study Source A. What impression of the new queen of England would the Venetian government have formed as a result of this report? ?

The Elizabethan religious settlement

To heal the division in the religious lives of her subjects, Elizabeth embarked on a policy of reconciliation embodied in the Elizabethan religious settlement. In the opinion of Denys Cook, writing in *Sixteenth-century England 1450–1600* (1980), Elizabeth's settlement 'halted the English church somewhere between "Rome and Geneva" though nearer to the latter than the queen wished'. In his opinion, Elizabeth was a conservative at heart who wished to avoid adopting the more radical religious doctrine associated with John Calvin's Geneva brand of Protestantism (see pages 103–4). By the same token, she wished to avoid retaining those elements of Catholic worship that she and her Protestant subjects most objected to. The task confronting the queen and her Privy Council was fraught with danger and it was to Parliament that they turned to secure the nation's compliance in whatever legislation they thought fit for the purpose. In the opinion of Peter Servini (*The English Reformation*, 1997), the problem to be resolved was 'what form of Protestantism would be imposed. Would it be the doctrinally conservative supremacy of Henry VIII or the "full Protestantism" of Edward VI? Nor need it end there.'

Parliamentary legislation

The two key pieces of parliamentary legislation on which the religious settlement was founded were the Act of Supremacy and the Act of Uniformity. Drawn up by the queen in conjunction with her ministers and the Archbishop of Canterbury, Matthew Parker, the settlement of 1559 was intended to clarify, regulate and stabilise religion in the kingdom.

The terms of the settlement were worked out in the queen's first Parliament, which sat from January to April 1559. The passing in Parliament of the Act of Supremacy abolished papal authority in England and restored the monarch as head of the Church. In a clever piece of politicking Elizabeth opted to use the title 'Supreme Governor' of the Church rather than that – 'Supreme Head' – used by her father, Henry VIII, in the hope that it might:

- please those of her subjects who objected to a woman as 'head' of the Church
- not offend the Pope by suggesting that the issue was open to interpretation
- satisfy both Protestants and Catholics by suggesting the possibility of a compromise.

The new title did not diminish Elizabeth's power over the Church because the legal clauses in the Act ensured that she would have the same ecclesiastical authority as her father and brother. Mindful of her duty to God and to her people, and seeking a political compromise, Elizabeth was determined that the settlement should appeal to as wide a range of opinion as possible.

Supremacy, uniformity and the royal injunctions

The Act of Supremacy and the Act of Uniformity, together with the royal injunctions used to enforce them, brought about the following:

- they severed the kingdom from Rome by substituting royal for papal supremacy in the Church
- they gave the Anglican Church its prayer book and made the kingdom uniformly Protestant.

These seem to suggest that Elizabeth had adopted the 'full Protestantism' of Edward VI but this was not the case. Whereas the religious settlement did adopt the more radical second *Book of Common Prayer* of 1552 (see pages 98–9), according to historian John McGurk (*The Tudor Monarchies, 1485–1603*, 1999): 'on the question of the Real Presence; the 1552 Prayer Book which implied that Communion was a symbolic commemorative act was supplemented by words from the 1549 Book which suggested Christ's Body was really present in the Eucharist'.

KEY TERM

Black Rubric A set of instructions issued to the clergy on the order of service in church ceremonies.

By careful manipulation of the text together with amendments such as the so-called '**Black Rubric**', the prayer book was capable of either a Catholic or Protestant interpretation. For example, the Black Rubric permitted the priest to decide if parishioners taking communion should do so standing, sitting or kneeling. It may have been a minor concession, but it was important because it gave the impression that the Crown was prepared to be moderate and flexible.

In the final analysis, enough of the old Church remained – bishops, the wearing of clerical vestments and certain aspects of ritual in worship – to keep Catholics happy. On the other hand, the innovations in religion – adoption of the Edwardian prayer book, restoration of the supremacy and rejection of the mass – were sufficient to satisfy Protestants. In the opinion of historian Conrad Russell (*The Crisis of Parliaments, 1603–1660*, 1971), the Elizabethan Church 'looked Catholic but sounded Protestant'.

Summary diagram: The Elizabethan religious settlement

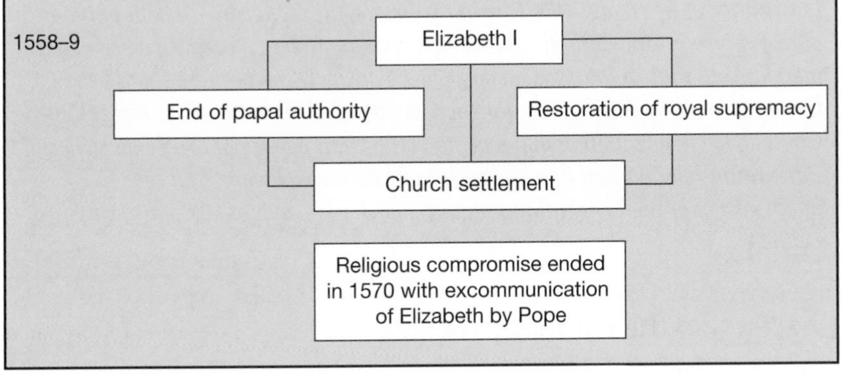

2 Key debate

▶ *Why did the Elizabethan religious settlement take the form that it did and would it last?*

The religious settlement of 1559 has provoked considerable disagreement among historians on the issue of why it took the form that it did. What factors influenced the framing of the settlement and how long would it last? The established view of the settlement is that it was an unpopular compromise between Elizabeth and her reformist supporters in the Commons and their conservative opponents in the Lords. This compromise was forced on Elizabeth by the pressure exerted by the conservative Catholics. Thus, the settlement was less Protestant and more Catholic than she would have wished. Unfortunately, it satisfied neither side and was thought unlikely to last. Critics of this view, however, challenged it as being either too simplistic or mistaken. The following sub-sections indicate some of the major contributions to the debate that has evolved in three distinct stages over a century.

The established view

Writing in 1904, W.H. Frere provided the historical analysis that first set out the established interpretation of events. Elizabeth and her chief minister, Sir **William Cecil**, were manipulated and manoeuvred by the competing religious factions at court into a compromise that was doomed to failure because neither side got what it wanted.

KEY FIGURE

William Cecil (1520–98)

Secretary of State in Northumberland's regime but retired from politics during the reign of Mary. Elizabeth appointed him her chief minister in 1558 and he led the government until his death.

EXTRACT 1

From W.H. Frere, *The English Church in the Reigns of Elizabeth I and James I, 1558–1625*, Macmillan, 1904, p. 51.

Uncertainty reigned. Even when the religious policy of the government – that is, of the queen and Cecil – had been defined and imposed by the two great Acts of parliament and the royal visitation, there was little visible prospect of permanence; indeed this policy seemed to have less chance of ultimate victory than either of its rivals – the Marian policy or the Genevan. To both of these parties a protestant Catholicism seemed contemptible; ... because it seemed a mere hybrid that could have no posterity. For the Marian there could be no Catholicism without the pope; for the Genevan a Protestantism which retained Catholic doctrine and worship was no better than popery: a brief experience of Edwardian religion had brought each to its own conclusion, and the modification of the Edwardian religion, which was now put forward, satisfied neither.

Challenging the established view

Half a century later, Frere's interpretation was challenged by Sir John Neale, arguably the most authoritative of Elizabethan parliamentary scholars. Neale contended that a cautious and conservative queen was manoeuvred against her will into adopting a more Protestant settlement by an organised group of radical MPs. In his opinion, this '**Puritan Choir**' of Protestant politicians in the Commons ensured that the moderate, possibly, interim, settlement envisaged by Elizabeth was abandoned.

KEY TERM

Puritan Choir Coined by historian Sir John Neale to describe what he perceived to be an organised Puritan political group in the House of Commons.

EXTRACT 2

From J.E. Neale, *Elizabeth I and Her Parliaments 1559–1581*, Jonathan Cape, 1953, pp. 82–4.

The main structure of the Elizabethan religious settlement was now determined. In giving way to the Protestant divines Elizabeth had been wise. Thereby she had obtained as conservative and comprehensive a Church as was possible.

The compromise of 1559 of course created its own difficulties ... Doubtless she detested Puritanism the more for having wrested so much from her in this Parliament.

The fascinating element in this story is that the criticism, the anger, the bitterness of the radicals, were not focused on the Queen. They fought the forces of darkness about her at Court, but she was to them a child of light. To read their praise of Elizabeth, when we know that she was their main obstacle, is both surprising and pathetic.

The revisionist view

Norman Jones, writing in 1982, dismissed Neale's claim that there was an organised Puritan faction in the 1559 Parliament. Not only was there no 'Puritan Choir' but the compromise settlement was exactly what Elizabeth had intended from the beginning. The queen resisted the pressure exerted by both radical reformists in the Commons and conservative Catholics in the Lords and implemented a settlement, with its carefully contrived vagueness, that was intended to be temporary until such time as she felt able to enact a more robust religious framework.

EXTRACT 3

From N.L. Jones, *Faith by Statute, Parliament and the Settlement of Religion, 1559*, Royal Historical Society, 1982, pp. 186, 189.

This study began by asking whether the Elizabethan Settlement resulted from a compromise between a Puritan House of Commons and their conservative Queen, or if it was formed in a struggle between the Catholics and Elizabeth.

The creation of the Settlement was not a simple process. It was a difficult political manoeuvre which might have ended in disaster. The Queen played her role well, handling dissenters and foreign enemies with great care, compromising with all sides, and doing the possible without demanding the impossible. In this she was aided by a kind fate (or the Protestants' God) which disarmed her opponents and covered her mistakes. Perhaps the greatest miracle of the entire episode was that Elizabeth obtained what she sought without either abandoning most of it or causing a civil war. After considering the welter of political problems surrounding the change in religion, one cannot help but admire the political sagacity [sound judgement] and sheer luck that brought that faith back to England.

How significant are the differences in the historical interpretations given in Extracts 1–3 regarding the making of the religious settlement?

3 Establishing the Anglican Church

► *What steps were taken to establish the Anglican Church?*

Elizabeth's religious beliefs and aims

The religious outlook of the monarch was a vital consideration because the supreme head or governor had the power to urge, encourage, coerce or enforce changes in Church doctrine and liturgy. Thus, the beliefs, patterns, forms and actions through which public worship was conducted, were determined by the Crown. This had been a major factor in shaping the Henrician, Edwardian and Marian religious settlements. The majority of people had acquiesced in these contrasting religious arrangements mainly out of loyalty to the monarch. However, Elizabeth was different in so far as she was careful never to express her personal religious beliefs and tended to hide her true intentions. That Elizabeth reportedly refused to 'make windows into men's souls' and suggested that 'there is only one Jesus Christ and all the rest is a dispute over trifles' serves to underline the ambiguity of her position. This has made it difficult for historians to understand properly Elizabeth's religious convictions.

Nevertheless, as the living symbol of her father's break with Rome it was thought likely that Elizabeth would move the Church in a Protestant direction. That said, it may be deduced more from what she did than from what she said that she was essentially conservative, cautious and reluctant to innovate. For example, by disliking images, pictures and 'Romish relics' in churches and by forbidding the **elevation of the host** in the church service, she was expressing a Protestant view of religion. On the other hand, by opposing married clergy, retaining bishops and encouraging the wearing of vestments she was appealing to Catholic tastes.

KEY TERM

Elevation of the host The host is the bread consecrated by the priest which Catholics believe to be the body of Christ. By raising the host the priest is signalling the transformation of the bread to the body. This is enshrined in the concept of transubstantiation.

Injunctions, visitations and the consolidation of the settlement

Elizabeth's dominant place in British history is assured by the establishment and defence of the 1559 settlement – the English prayer book and the Thirty-Nine Articles of Religion – which remains the basis of the Church of England today.

Susan Doran, writing in 1986, is in no doubt that the founder of the Anglican Church was Elizabeth and that its origins can be traced back to the settlement of 1559. However, some historians disagree with this, stating that the foundations of the Anglican Church were laid in the reign of Edward VI. There is a great deal of truth in this latter assertion since the Elizabethan Church was based on an amended version of the second Edwardian prayer book.

In 1559 a set of royal injunctions was issued by the Crown with a view to establishing the pattern of worship that must be followed in Church. Although it was largely Protestant in character, some Catholic practices were retained. The following list gives some idea of the terms of the injunctions:

- Catholic-style religious processions and pilgrimages were banned.
- Monuments associated with miracles were removed.
- Recusants (those who refused to attend the services of the Anglican Church) were to be reported to the authorities.
- Clergy were to teach the royal supremacy.

Whereas these points would have satisfied most Protestants, the following terms would not:

- Churches were allowed to keep some of the more popular religious images.
- Protestant preaching was restricted to those who obtained a licence issued by the authorities.

- Parishioners were required to bow their heads at the name of Jesus and kneel at prayer.
- Clergy were required to wear distinctive clerical dress.

The majority of both Catholics and Protestants would have found the following points acceptable:

- Each parish was required to obtain a copy of the Bible in English and a copy of Erasmus's (see page 12) ***Paraphrases* of the Gospels**.
- Clergymen were allowed to marry but only with the permission of their bishop and two justices of the peace.

To ensure that the terms of the injunctions were being enforced, a series of **visitations** (see pages 12–13) was ordered to be carried out. Acting on the instructions of individual bishops, the visitors had the power to question the parish clergy about their beliefs and to punish those who refused to abide by the terms of the Acts of Supremacy and Uniformity and the royal injunctions. Between 1559 and 1564 some 300 parish clergy either resigned or were ejected from their livings.

KEY TERM

***Paraphrases* of the Gospels** Rewritings of the Gospels with commentaries by Erasmus.

The Thirty-Nine Articles 1563

In 1563 Convocation (see page 39) met to discuss and clarify the doctrinal position of the Anglican Church. Led by Archbishop Parker and working on the authority of Queen Elizabeth, the clergy decided to adopt a revised version of Cranmer's Forty-Two Articles (see page 104). The articles served to define the doctrine of the Church of England as it related to Calvinist doctrine and

SOURCE B

From the Thirty-Nine Articles as agreed and drawn up by Convocation in 1563.

Article I: Of Faith in the Holy Trinity
There is but one living and true God, everlasting, without body, parts, or passions; of infinite power, wisdom, and goodness; the Maker, and Preserver of all things both visible and invisible. And in unity of this Godhead there be three Persons, of one substance, power, and eternity; the Father, the Son, and the Holy Ghost.

Article VI: Of the Sufficiency of the Holy Scriptures for Salvation
Holy Scripture contains all things necessary to salvation: so that whatsoever is not read therein, nor may be proved thereby, is not to be required of any man, that it should be believed as an article of the Faith, or be thought necessary to salvation.

Article XXII: Of Purgatory
The Romish Doctrine concerning Purgatory, Pardons, Worshipping, and Adoration as well of Images as of Relics, and also invocation of Saints, is a fond thing vainly invented, and grounded upon no warranty of Scripture, but rather repugnant to the Word of God.

Study Source B. Why would devout Roman Catholics accept Article I but reject Articles VI and XXII?

Roman Catholic practice. The Articles avoided a direct attack on Catholic belief but Article 17 sanctioned the Protestant belief in **predestination**. The Thirty-Nine Articles were given the force of statute law by Parliament and became the fundamental confession of faith of the Anglican Church. The significance of the Thirty-Nine Articles is that it underlined the fact that due to the religious settlement the Church was now a State Church under the domination of the Crown.

The Vestiarian controversy

The Vestiarian controversy (or vestments controversy) has its roots in the Convocation of 1563. It was concerned with the question of whether clerical vestments – declared to be 'popish' by some clerics – were theologically important. The debate was first initiated by the Protestant martyr Bishop John Hooper's (see page 103) rejection of clerical vestments in the Church of England under Edward VI. The issue of clerical dress was revived under Elizabeth I when a group of clergymen began actively to resist Archbishop Matthew Parker's drive for unconditional conformity to the terms set out in the settlement. Parker was responding to pressure from the queen, who demanded that he used his

KEY TERMS

Predestination Belief that a person's life has been mapped out by God before birth and cannot be changed.

Burgess A member of the ruling council of a town.

Matthew Parker

1504	Born in Norwich to William Parker, a **burgess** and merchant in the city
1527	Ordained a priest
1535	Appointed chaplain to Anne Boleyn
1544	Master of Corpus Christi College, Cambridge
1552	Appointed Dean of Lincoln Cathedral
1554	Deprived of his clerical posts by Mary I
1559	Appointed Archbishop of Canterbury
1563	Revised Cranmer's Forty-Two Articles of Religion; reduced to 39
1575	Died

Parker was born the eldest son of William Parker and Alice Monins, who may have been related by marriage to Thomas Cranmer. He was educated at Cambridge University where he received his degree in divinity. While at university he came under the influence of religious reformers associated with the White Horse Tavern group.

Parker was a dedicated reformer who supported Henry VIII's break with Rome. He became chaplain to Anne Boleyn and was entrusted with the care of her daughter Elizabeth. He was later appointed chaplain to Henry VIII. Shortly after Henry VIII's death, he abandoned his clerical vow of celibacy and took a wife. As a committed Protestant he supported both Cranmer and, during the reign of Edward VI, the Duke of Northumberland. He went into hiding during Mary's reign.

Parker's impact on English religious thinking was significant and his contribution to the cause of Protestantism is embodied in the Thirty-Nine Articles which established the core doctrine of the Elizabethan Anglican Church. His *Advertisements* of 1566 provoked the Vestiarian controversy and helped fuel debate about the wearing of vestments and the validity of episcopacy as an institution.

authority to ensure that the clergy did not deviate from the rites and practices set out in the settlement and subsequent injunctions. Elizabeth was herself responding to information that some senior clergy were circumventing or ignoring the regulations imposed by the Crown in 1559. The bishops responsible for 'turning a blind eye' to clergy who had refused to wear the vestments did so out of frustration at their failure in Parliament and Convocation in 1563 to secure revision of the *Book of Common Prayer*.

In 1566, to settle the matter and to make clear what was expected of the clergy in terms of doctrine, prayer, sacraments and clerical dress, Parker published his ***Advertisements***. This provoked intense debate on the validity of vestments because, as some clerics pointed out, the scriptures had nothing to say on the matter. Others argued that the matter of clerical dress was one of only minor significance and that, in any case, the queen, as Supreme Head of the Church, had the right to impose such regulations. In an effort to stifle unrest, Parker adopted the idea of ***adiaphora***, or 'things indifferent', which stated that some religious practices may not have been welcomed but they were unlikely to affect a person's salvation.

KEY TERMS

Advertisements Published by Archbishop Parker to assist parish priests in the performance of their duties in church services, such as instructions on the wearing of vestments, the administration of common prayers and the holy sacraments.

Adiaphora From the Greek meaning a tolerance of conduct or belief not specifically mentioned or forbidden in the scriptures.

SOURCE C

From Brett Usher, *William Cecil and Episcopacy, 1559–1577*, Ashgate Publishing, 2003, p. 128. According to Usher, too much has been made of the Vestiarian controversy by historians.

[The controversy] scarcely rippled beyond the boundaries of what is now Greater London – the two universities and the diocese of Durham excepted. Repercussions in Durham resulted in the arraignment [criminal charging] of six leading clerics, including Dean Whittingham, Chancellor Robert Swift, and Archdeacon John Pilkington. Two canons, Thomas Lever and William Birche, were deprived in 1567.

Study Source C. Why have some historians attached so much importance to the Vestiarian controversy?

Summary diagram: Establishing the Anglican Church

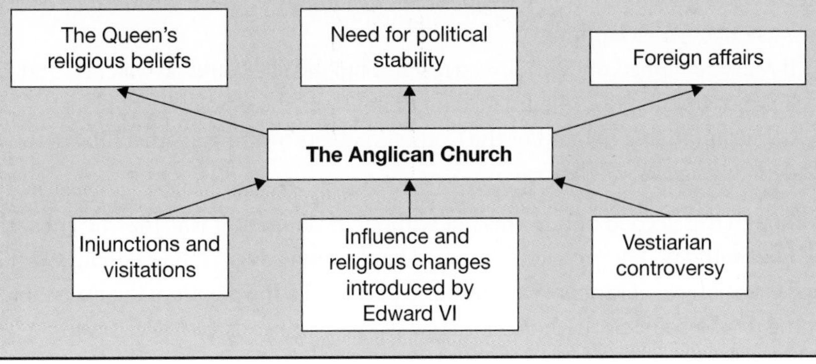

4 The end of the settlement

▶ *To what extent did the religious settlement provoke opposition at home and abroad?*

Mary, Queen of Scots

Mary Stuart was directly descended from Henry VII and, as such, was Elizabeth's closest living relative. In the opinion of historian M. Levine, writing in 2004, Mary was Henry Tudor's 'only living descendant whose lineage could not be challenged with a charge of bastardy by alleging a doubtful marriage'. Elizabeth was reluctant to recognise her cousin as her heir because she might yet marry and have a son of her own. Mary was viewed with suspicion because she was a Roman Catholic with strong ties to France. So long as she remained in Scotland she could be largely ignored by both Elizabeth and her leading councillors.

This changed in 1568 when Mary was forced to abdicate her throne and flee south to England in search of shelter and protection. Mary's rule in Scotland had been a disaster and her arrival on English soil began a political crisis that would not be resolved for nearly twenty years. She was considered a dangerous threat to Elizabeth and the Tudor regime because English Catholics, who distrusted Elizabeth and opposed her Protestant reform of the Church, saw Mary as a realistic candidate for the English Crown. In 1569 a group of northern Catholic nobles, led by the Earl of Northumberland, rose in rebellion. They failed in their aim to put Mary on the throne but the shock of rebellion frightened Elizabeth and her ministers.

Elizabeth faced a number of options on what to do with Mary. She could either release her or keep her prisoner in England:

- If Mary was released, Elizabeth could either send her back to Scotland or help her get to France. The dangers posed to England by a civil war in Scotland and/or a French-led military expedition in support of Mary meant that release was not a realistic option.
- If Mary remained under house arrest in England she could be watched and her movements controlled. The danger here was the possibility of plots being laid to free her and/or the Catholic powers' uniting against Elizabeth demanding Mary's freedom.

Although this second option was not without its dangers, it was the one chosen by Elizabeth and her ministers. Some of her leading advisers, Sir William Cecil and especially Sir **Francis Walsingham**, preferred a third option: the execution of the troublesome Scottish queen. They worked for nearly two decades to achieve their aim.

KEY FIGURE

Francis Walsingham (1530–90)

Politician and statesman who served in Elizabeth's government as her Secretary of State. He was responsible for her safety and security and was largely responsible for the execution of Mary, Queen of Scots.

The danger posed by Mary's imprisonment increased year on year:

- In 1570 the Pope excommunicated Elizabeth and issued a pardon to all English Catholics who dared rebel against the heretic queen of England.
- In 1571 the Ridolfi Plot was discovered, which involved the Duke of Norfolk. Norfolk planned to marry Mary Stuart and raise the standard of rebellion in collaboration with Spain. Norfolk was executed in 1572.
- In 1583 (Throckmorton), 1585 (Parry) and again in 1586 (Babington) a series of plots to free Mary and remove Elizabeth from the throne was discovered and put down. The plotters were executed.

It was not until 1587 that Elizabeth reluctantly agreed to the execution of Mary, Queen of Scots. She did so only on account of evidence presented to her that revealed her cousin's involvement in the **Babington Plot** (1586). With her death, it was hoped that the crisis surrounding Mary would be ended. However, it proved to be the excuse Philip of Spain needed to launch his **Armada** against England in 1588. The failure of the Armada finally put paid to the Mary, Queen of Scots affair.

KEY TERMS

Babington Plot A conspiracy led by Sir Anthony Babington to assassinate Elizabeth and replace her with Mary, Queen of Scots.

Armada An invasion fleet sent by Philip of Spain which intended to land an army in southern England and then conquer the country.

The rising of the northern earls

The Northern Rebellion used to be seen as a religious rising but that has been questioned. The rebel leaders, the earls of Northumberland and Westmorland, had genuine religious concerns but their rebellion was mainly about politics and the succession. The roots of the rebellion can be found in the politics and faction of the day and the arrival on English soil of the fugitive Mary, Queen of Scots, which provided a focus for the discontented northern nobility.

Politics and faction

The first few years of Elizabeth's reign witnessed a period of political unity. This was the time when the regime was being established. Sir William Cecil enjoyed a close working relationship with Elizabeth, who relied on him for advice. This gave Cecil unrivalled political prominence at court and made him a target for rival factions. As Elizabeth's chief minister, Cecil was responsible for co-ordinating the implementation of most policy decisions at home and abroad. In some respects, Cecil's position can be compared to that of Thomas Cromwell (see pages 32–3): both were powerful at court, both had the confidence of the monarch and both were talented and imaginative ministers.

Like Cromwell, Cecil, too, had rivals at court but, unlike Cromwell, they were never outright enemies determined to cause his death. Faction fighting at the Court of Elizabeth did not become a serious issue until later in her reign when England went to war with Spain in the mid-1580s. Self-interest and short-term aims often pushed rival factions together. Cecil and Leicester sometimes found themselves on the same side and even when they were enemies neither wished to see the other executed, only 'cowed' or 'retired'.

Cecil's rivals included the following:

- Robert Dudley, Earl of Leicester. The son of the former Lord President, the Duke of Northumberland, executed by Mary in 1553. He was a Protestant and a firm favourite of Queen Elizabeth. He was appointed to the Privy Council in 1562 and created Earl of Leicester in 1564. Their relationship was so close that there was talk of them marrying but this never happened. Elizabeth's emotional attachment to Leicester gave him personal access to the queen, which posed a serious threat to Cecil.
- Thomas Radcliffe, Earl of Sussex. A talented soldier and administrator. On his return from governing Ireland in 1565, he was appointed to the Privy Council. He was neutral in religion, counting both Catholics and Protestants among his friends and associates. Sussex was an independent who tended to oppose Leicester and support Cecil.
- Thomas Howard, Duke of Norfolk. A religious conservative who leaned towards Catholicism. He was ambitious, arrogant but politically incompetent. He tended to side with Sussex but his lack of courage and honesty made him few friends.

The Northern Rebellion

The conspiracy that led to the Northern Rebellion is complex and consists of two overlapping but disconnected strands.

First strand

A plot was hatched at court by the Sussex and Leicester factions whereby the Duke of Norfolk would be encouraged to marry Mary, Queen of Scots. Part of the arrangement was to be the elimination of Cecil as a political force. He would be replaced by pro-Catholic sympathisers and the traditional friendship with Spain, in the person of Philip II, would be renewed.

The plot failed when rumours of the Norfolk–Mary marriage plan reached the queen. Leicester confessed his part in the affair while Norfolk panicked and left court without permission. Racked by indecision, Norfolk spent the best part of six weeks on his country estate at Kenninghall, Norfolk. While Elizabeth feared he might rebel, Mary actively encouraged it. Norfolk's supporters in the north, his brother-in-law, Charles Neville, Earl of Westmorland, and Thomas Percy, Earl of Northumberland, waited to see what he would do. Westmorland was fully prepared to rise in support of Norfolk but Northumberland was unwilling to 'hazard myself for the marriage'. Eventually, Norfolk broke down under the strain: he wrote to Westmorland advising him not to rebel, after which he submitted to Elizabeth. Norfolk was promptly put in the Tower.

Second strand

The second strand of the conspiracy involved the pro-Catholic earls of Northumberland and Westmorland. The earls, along with Lord Dacre, had been sidelined by the Elizabethan regime, which did not fully trust them. Aware of the lingering sympathy for Catholicism that existed in the north, Elizabeth opted to put men she trusted in positions of authority in the region:

- The queen's cousin, Lord Hunsdon, was put in charge of Berwick and half of the border region.
- The Earl of Sussex was appointed President of the Council of the North in York.
- James Pilkington, an enthusiastic Protestant, was appointed Bishop of Durham.

Resentment at being passed over for offices which they considered to be traditionally theirs by right turned to outright anger by Pilkington's aggressive evangelical style. News of the failure of the Norfolk–Mary marriage plan, together with the duke's imprisonment, added to their frustration. They felt they had no choice but to lead a rebellion against a hostile, uncaring and, as far as their grievances were concerned, increasingly deaf Protestant regime.

In order to attract as much support as possible, the earls issued a proclamation stating that the reason for their rebellion was to resist the 'new-found religion and heresy'. The pro-Catholic gentry and peasantry flocked to join what they saw as a religious crusade. In all, some 6000 joined the rebellion: a fair number but nowhere near as many as the earls had hoped. Apart from the capture of Durham and the restoration of the mass in the cathedral there, the rebel army did no more than march to and from Bramham Moor near York.

When news arrived that a royal army of 10,000 men was marching north to meet them, the earls panicked, disbanded their army and fled over the border to Scotland. A rebellion which had begun on 9 November ended without a major confrontation on 16 December 1569. All was not over, for, within a few days, Lord Dacre rose in rebellion with 3000 men, but he was defeated in battle early in January 1570. The Northern Rebellion was over. The government was ruthless in its pursuit of the rebel leaders. Westmoreland escaped abroad but Northumberland was captured and executed. Norfolk was eventually tried for treason and executed in 1572.

Assessing the Northern Rebellion

In the opinion of most historians the rebellion failed because of poor leadership: it was incoherent and aimless. As Nicholas Fellows said (2001), the earls did not 'cut a dash; instead their image is one of reluctant rebels, driven into rebellion out of despair, rather than with an iron will'.

There is no agreement on the causes of the rebellion. Writing in the 1930s, Sir John Neale saw the rebellion purely in terms of the failed Norfolk–Mary marriage. In his opinion the one led directly to the other. In contrast, recent revisionist studies, such as that by David Marcombe (*The Last Principality: Politics, Religion and Society in the Bishopric of Durham, 1494–1660*, 1987), have tended to see the rebellion as a distinctly northern phenomenon. To Marcombe the rising was part of a regional crisis in which dissatisfied conservative northern gentry and nobility reluctantly rebelled out of frustration and anger at:

- their treatment by southerners planted in the area to run their affairs
- their exclusion from office and power
- the treatment of the Catholic faith.

According to J.J. Scarisbrick (*The Jesuits and the Catholic Reformation*, 1988), the rebellion 'revealed to the government with shocking clarity how lamentably the new regime had failed to take root in the north-east'. The rebellion spurred the government into action by ordering the rigorous enforcement of the Act of Uniformity and by insisting on regular and thorough visitations. Most visitations went ahead without incident but when the Bishop of Chester's visitation of Lancashire in 1571 proved ineffective owing to local hostility, a special visitation organised by the Archbishop of Canterbury was dispatched to deal with the county. With the full weight of the law and the authority of the spiritual head of the Church behind it, this visitation proved more effective.

? Study Source D. How does the experience of Lancashire differ from the general historical picture of how the settlement was received in the kingdom?

SOURCE D

From Christopher Haigh, *Reformation and Resistance in Tudor Lancashire*, Cambridge University Press, 2008, back cover.

In this significant corner of the realm, the Marian regime was able to revitalize the old religion, and the Elizabethan Settlement encountered widespread opposition. Catholic practices could not be excluded from the established Church, and Catholic recusancy developed earlier and on a wider scale than in any other area of England.

The defeat of the northern earls represented a turning point for the Elizabethan regime. The regime and the largely Protestant religious settlement it had established by Act of Parliament had survived its first test and would never be seriously challenged again.

Excommunication

In April 1570, following the defeat of the Northern Rebellion, the Pope excommunicated Elizabeth.

? How did the Pope justify his excommunication of Elizabeth in Source E?

SOURCE E

From the Papal Bull of Excommunication, *Regnans in Excelsis*, 1570. Here, the Pope accuses Elizabeth. A Papal Bull was a legal document or charter issued by the Pope which was authenticated by a lead seal called a *bulla*.

... having seized the crown and monstrously usurped the place of the supreme head of the Church in all England, together with the chief authority and jurisdiction belonging to it and turning this same kingdom, which had already been restored to the catholic faith and to good fruits, to a miserable ruin.

In a move calculated to cause her maximum damage, Pope Pius V made treason unavoidable for all true Catholics. The publication of the Bull was a declaration of war because English Catholics were encouraged to rebel against the heretic queen of England. Popes would be expected to uphold the law, discourage rebellion and abide by the notion of the Great Chain of Being (see pages 6–7), but not in this instance. Pius believed that loyal Catholics had a duty to forcefully replace a heretic queen, for which he offered them the comfort of a papal pardon.

The settlement: success or failure?

If the settlement had been designed simply to avoid religious conflict and possible civil war (as happened in France) then it was a success. It lasted almost intact for some ten years, until 1570, during which time the Church had the opportunity to establish itself, evolve and refine its clerical and doctrinal position. As early as 1563 Archbishop Parker, working through Convocation, adopted a revised version of Cranmer's Forty-Two Articles (see page 104), the Thirty-Nine Articles.

In political terms, the settlement may also be considered a success. Elizabeth had succeeded in establishing a State Church under the domination of the Crown. This meant that religious opposition to the settlement would be regarded in the same way as political opposition to the State. The laws of treason could be applied to stamp out opposition. This fact, allied to a misunderstanding of the queen's role in the Church, caused some Continental Catholic critics to describe the Church of England as a mere parliamentary religion devoid of any truly spiritual conviction. This was unfair and untrue since Elizabeth had, from the beginning, ensured that the bishops would retain their responsibility for the administration and supervision of the Church and its clergy.

In religious terms, the settlement had mixed success. It largely succeeded in establishing a broad-based national Church, which excluded as few people as practicable. Until at least 1570, the settlement made conformity as easy as possible without provoking opposition or disagreement. In theological terms, the Thirty-Nine Articles was widely accepted and remained at the doctrinal heart of the Church. On the other hand, the settlement failed not only to attract the Puritans but to harness their evangelical enthusiasm. Devout Catholics were likewise marginalised, which encouraged non-conformity and opposition to the Anglican Church.

The settlement after 1570

Shortly before his death, Archbishop Parker confided to Cecil his concern over the permanence of the religious settlement. His chief concerns were two-fold:

- the threat posed to the queen by the Catholic Mary, Queen of Scots
- the threat posed to the Anglican Church by the Puritans, whom he considered almost as dangerous as the Catholics.

Study Source F. How significant was Pope Pius's excommunication of Elizabeth?

SOURCE F

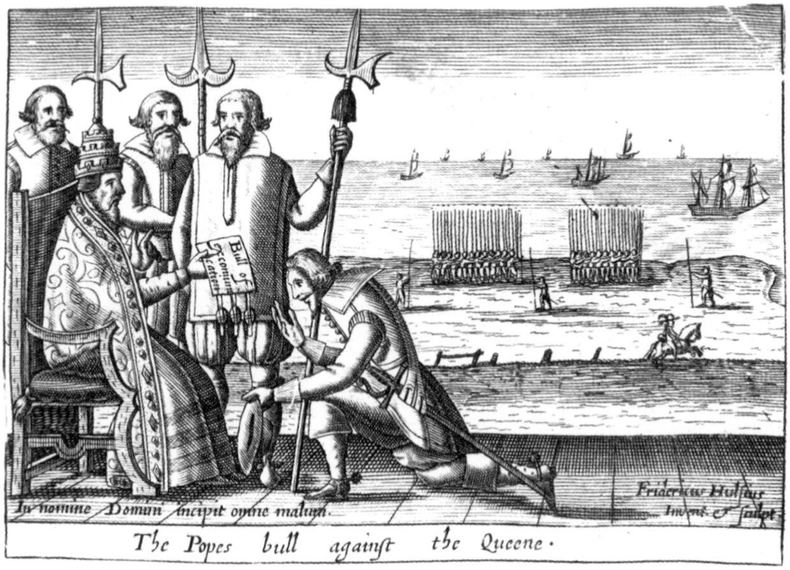

Bull of excommunication
In nomine Domini incipit omne malum.
Fridericus Hulsius Invent. et sculpt.
The Popes bull againſt the Queene.

A contemporary image of Pope Pius V issuing the Bull of excommunication against Elizabeth in 1570.

Study Source G. Which posed the greater threat to the Anglican Church: Catholicism or Puritanism?

SOURCE G

From a letter sent by Archbishop Parker to Sir William Cecil, Lord Burghley, 1572.

If only that desperate person [Mary Stuart] were away, as by justice soon it might be, the queen's majesty's good subjects would be in better hope, and the papists' daily expectations vanquished.

The comfort that these puritans have, and their continuance, is marvellous [the queen is] almost alone to be offended with the puritans, whose government in conclusion will undo her and all others who depend on her.

A disillusioned Parker died in 1575 'apprehensive', according to historian Claire Cross, 'of what the future might hold for Elizabeth and her church'.

Why did the religious settlement survive, according to Source H?

SOURCE H

From Claire Cross, *The Elizabethan Religious Settlement*, Headstart History Publishing, 1992, p. 36.

He ought to have had more confidence in the queen's determination [to rule] and in Cecil's support for the royal supremacy and for uniformity in religion. The partnership between the supreme governor and her chief minister lasted a further twenty years and largely through their efforts … the religious settlement survived without substantial change until the Civil War.

Summary diagram: The end of the settlement

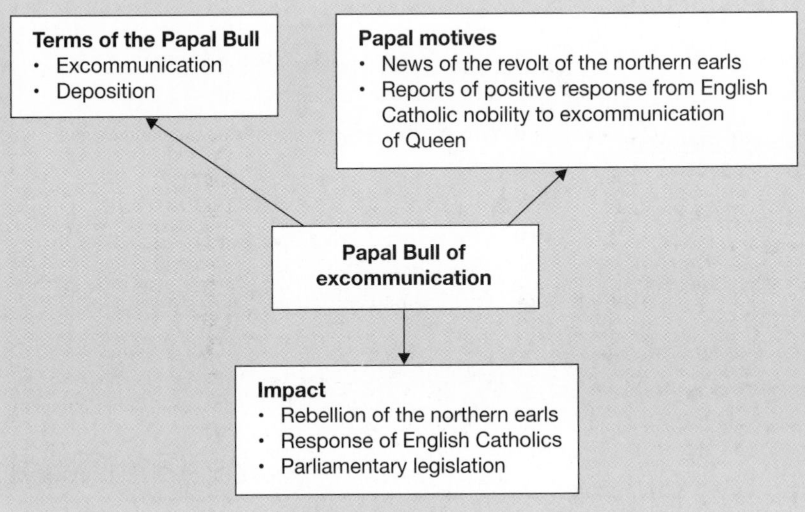

Chapter summary

The accession of Elizabeth paved the way for further religious reform. Elizabeth was helped in this respect by the work carried out during the reign of her half brother Edward. Edward VI laid the foundations of the Anglican Church, enabling Elizabeth to complete the structure. It was generally accepted that, as a Protestant, she would never accept the Roman Catholicism of her sister and that the Church would be reformed. What contemporaries did not know was how far she was prepared to take the reform process. The queen faced pressure from radical Protestants and devout Catholics and externally from the papacy and the Catholic powers. Elizabeth attempted to settle the potentially divisive issue of religion by establishing an Anglican Church acceptable to moderate Protestants and Catholics. By pursuing a policy of moderation and toleration Elizabeth hoped to satisfy both sides of the religious divide by establishing the religious settlement. With the aid of Parliament the settlement was passed into law by way of the Acts of Supremacy and Uniformity which were supplemented by royal injunctions. The process of reform was carried on by means of the Thirty-Nine Articles and Archbishop Parker's publication of his *Advertisements*. In spite of some problems such as the Vestiarian controversy, the settlement succeeded in maintaining peace until the arrival of Mary, Queen of Scots. Mary provoked the rising of the northern earls, which led to Elizabeth's excommunication by the Pope.

Refresher questions

Use these questions to remind yourself of the key material covered in this chapter.

1 What does the evidence reveal about Elizabeth's personal religious beliefs?
2 Why did the passing of the Acts of Supremacy and Uniformity prove so contentious?
3 Why do historians continue to debate the religious settlement?
4 How significant were the Thirty-Nine Articles?
5 What caused the Vestiarian controversy?
6 What role did the queen play in shaping religious reform after 1559?
7 How significant was Archbishop Parker's contribution to religious reform?
8 Why did the religious consensus break down in 1569?
9 What caused the rising of the northern earls?
10 What impact did rebellion have on Elizabethan religious policy?
11 Why did the Pope excommunicate Elizabeth?
12 Had the Anglican Church been firmly established by 1570?

Question practice

ESSAY QUESTIONS

1 'The religious settlement of 1559 settled nothing and the rising of the northern earls proves it.' Assess the validity of this view.
2 'The Anglican Church owed its establishment not to Elizabeth's religious settlement of 1559 but to the fear generated by the arrival in England in 1568 of Mary, Queen of Scots.' Assess the validity of this view.
3 To what extent did Mary I bequeath a Church in crisis to Elizabeth I?
4 How seriously did the Pope's excommunication of Elizabeth threaten the queen and her kingdom?

SOURCE ANALYSIS QUESTION

1 With reference to Sources 1, 2 and 3 below, and your understanding of the historical context, assess the value of these sources to a historian studying the Elizabethan religious settlement.

SOURCE 1

From the Venetian ambassador's letter to the Senate of Venice in December 1558. The ambassador was writing to his government to report on the kingdom in the weeks after Elizabeth assumed the Crown.

Queen Elizabeth often promised to continue the Catholic religion. But on Christmas Day, Her Majesty told the Bishop that he was not to elevate the host during mass. He replied that this was the only way he knew, so Her Majesty rose and departed. On the same day, two individuals, a mechanic and a cobbler, followed by a very great mob, entered by force into the church of St. Augustine, breaking the locks of the doors. Both leaped into the pulpit and preached uttering rude jokes about the blessed Queen Mary and Cardinal Pole. Queen Elizabeth forbade such preaching for fear of provoking riots. The Queen is fearful of tumults and uprisings which is why she proceeds with caution. She has no wish to follow the path taken by her late sister.

SOURCE 2

From the preamble and oath contained in the Act of Supremacy passed by Parliament in April 1559.

All and every archbishop, bishop, and all and every ecclesiastical person and all and every temporal judge, justice, mayor, and other lay or temporal officer and minister, and every other person having your Highness' fees or wages shall make an oath according to the tenor and effect hereafter following, that is to say:

I _______ do utterly testify and declare that in my conscience that the Queen's Highness is the only supreme governor of this realm and of all other her Highness' dominions and countries, as well in all spiritual or ecclesiastical things and that no foreign prince, person, prelate, state or potentate hath or ought to have any jurisdiction, power, superiority, pre-eminence or authority ecclesiastical or spiritual within this realm, and therefore I do utterly renounce and forsake all foreign jurisdictions and do promise that from henceforth I shall bear faith and true allegiance to the Queen's Highness, her heirs and lawful successors, and to my power shall assist and defend all jurisdictions and privileges granted or belonging to the Queen united and annexed to the imperial crown of this realm. So help me God and by the contents of this Book [Bible].

SOURCE 3

From a visitation report sent to the chief minister, Sir William Cecil, in 1564. The report was compiled by a royal official instructed to carry out a visitation of the diocese of Lincoln. The official was expected to visit and assess the quality of religious worship in selected parish churches.

Some say their priests conduct the service in the chancel, others say in the body of the church; some say the same in a seat made in the church, some in the pulpit with their faces to the people. Some priests keep precisely to the order of the Prayer Book but others do not. Some do intermeddle with the psalms reciting them in metre. Some wear the surplice but others who conduct services do so without the surplice. The communion table standeth in the body of the church in some places but in others it standeth in the chancel. In some churches the administration of the Communion is done by priests with surplice and cap, some with surplice alone but others with none. Some parishioners receive communion kneeling, others standing, others sitting. Some priests baptize in a font, some in a basin. Some priests make the sign of the cross, others sign not.

AQA A level History

Essay guidance

At both AS and A level for AQA Component 2: Depth Study: Religious Conflict and the Church in England, *c*.1529–1570, you will need to answer an essay question in the exam. Each essay question is marked out of 25:

- for the AS exam, Section B: answer **one** essay question from a choice of two
- for the A level exam, Section B: answer **two** essay questions from a choice of three.

There are several question stems which all have the same basic requirement: to analyse and reach a conclusion, based on the evidence you provide.

The AS questions often give a quotation and then ask whether you agree or disagree with this view. Almost inevitably, your answer will be a mixture of both. It is the same task as for A level – just phrased differently in the question. Detailed essays are more likely to do well than vague or generalised essays, especially in the Depth Studies of Paper 2.

The AQA mark scheme is essentially the same for AS and the full A level (see the AQA website, www.aqa.org.uk). Both emphasise the need to analyse and evaluate the key features related to the periods studied. The key feature of the highest level is sustained analysis: analysis that unites the whole of the essay.

Writing an essay: general skills

- *Focus and structure.* Be sure what the question is asking and plan what the paragraphs should be about.
- *Focused introduction to the essay.* Be sure that the introductory sentence relates directly to the focus of the question and that each paragraph highlights the structure of the answer.
- *Use detail.* Make sure that you show detailed knowledge – but only as part of an explanation being made in relation to the question. No knowledge should be standalone; it should be used in context.
- *Explanatory analysis and evaluation.* Consider what words and phrases to use in an answer to strengthen the explanation.
- *Argument and counter-argument.* Think of how arguments can be balanced so as to give contrasting views.
- *Resolution.* Think how best to 'resolve' contradictory arguments.
- *Relative significance and evaluation.* Think how best to reach a judgement when trying to assess the relative importance of various factors, and their possible interrelationship.

Planning an essay

Practice question 1

To what extent was Henry VIII's desire for wealth mainly responsible for the dissolution of the monasteries in the years between 1536 and 1540?

This question requires you to analyse the reasons why Henry VIII closed the monasteries between 1536 and 1540. You must discuss:

- The extent to which the king's desire for wealth provided the motivation for the dissolution (your primary focus).
- Other factors that contributed to the dissolution (your secondary focus).

A clear structure makes for a much more effective essay and is crucial for achieving the highest marks. You need three or four paragraphs to structure this question effectively. In each paragraph you will deal with one factor. One of these *must* be the factor in the question.

A very basic plan for this question might look like this:

- Paragraph 1: 'desire for wealth' as the prime motive for the dissolution together with the

influence of Henry VIII and the manipulation of Cromwell. The money could be used to fund Henry's Continental adventures and dreams of glory on the battlefield.
- Paragraph 2: the impulse for the reform of the Church. Support for the monastic ideal was waning and questions were raised about the ability of the monasteries to maintain the high ascetic ideals of their founders. This view underpinned humanist questioning of the monastic vocation.
- Paragraph 3: fear of monastic opposition to Henry's marriage and assumption of power over the Church as Supreme Head. Despite the requirement to swear the oath of loyalty to Henry VIII, it was believed that the monasteries remained loyal to the Pope. The presence of the abbots in the House of Lords contributed to the continuation of the concept of two powers which challenged the imperial idea.

It is a good idea to cover the factor named in the question first, so that you don't run out of time and forget to do it. Then cover the others in what you think is their order of importance, or in the order that appears logical in terms of the sequence of paragraphs.

The introduction

Maintaining focus is vital. One way to do this from the beginning of your essay is to use the words in the question to help write your argument. The first sentence of question 1, for example, could look like this:

Henry VIII dissolved the monasteries because he was motivated by a desire to acquire their wealth, but there were other factors which help explain why they were closed.

This opening sentence provides a clear focus on the demands of the question.

Focus throughout the essay

Structuring your essay well will help with keeping the focus of your essay on the question. To maintain a focus on the wording in question 1, you could begin your first main paragraph with 'desire for wealth'.

The desire for wealth was one very important factor in motivating Henry VIII to close the monasteries.

- This sentence begins with a clear point that refers to the primary focus of the question (the dissolution of the monasteries) while linking it to a factor (the desire for wealth).
- You could then have a paragraph for each of your other factors.
- It will be important to make sure that each paragraph focuses on analysis and includes relevant details that are used as part of the argument.
- You may wish to number your factors. This helps to make your structure clear and helps you to maintain focus.

Deploying detail

As well as focus and structure, your essay will be judged on the extent to which it includes accurate detail. There are several different kinds of evidence you could use that might be described as detailed. These include correct dates, names of relevant people, statistics and events. For example, for question 1 you could use terms such as *Valor Ecclesiasticus* and *Comperta Monastica*. You can also make your essays more detailed by using the correct technical vocabulary.

Analysis and explanation

'Analysis' covers a variety of high-level skills including explanation and evaluation; in essence, it means breaking down something complex into smaller parts. A clear structure which breaks down a complex question into a series of paragraphs is the first step towards writing an analytical essay. The purpose of explanation is to provide evidence for why something happened, or why something is true or false. An explanatory statement requires two parts: a *claim* and a *justification*.

For example, for question 1, you might want to argue that one important reason was the king's need for money and a desire to fund his militaristic foreign policy. Once you have made your point, and supported it with relevant detail, you can then explain how this answers the question. For example, you could conclude your paragraph like this:

*Clearly, the evidence suggests that the primary motivation for the dissolution of the monasteries was Henry VIII's need for money to fund his war against the French***[1]***. This is because his desire for personal glory on the battlefield allied to his ambition to secure the Crown of France outweighed any concern he might have had for the impact and consequences of monastic dissolution***[2]***. For Henry, the dissolution of the monasteries was a means to an end***[3]***.*

1 The first part of this sentence is the claim while the second part justifies the claim.
2 'Because' is a very important word to use when writing an explanation, as it shows the relationship between the claim and the justification.
3 The justification.

Evaluation

Evaluation means considering the importance of two or more different factors, weighing them against each other, and reaching a judgement. This is a good skill to use at the end of an essay because the conclusion should reach a judgement which answers the question. Your conclusion to question 1 might read as follows:

Clearly, the Crown was in financial difficulties. Henry VIII had spent his father's inheritance on wars with France and was considerably poorer than his rivals. The failure of the Amicable Grant in 1525 demonstrated Henry's difficulties in raising money through taxing his subjects. However, Henry wanted to strengthen his coastal defences and invade France but had insufficient funds. The Valor Ecclesiasticus preceded Henry's attack on the Monasteries. The Valor demonstrated the extensive wealth of the monasteries in terms of both land and movable goods. Therefore, this encouraged Henry to proceed with the dissolution.

Words like 'however' and 'therefore' are helpful to contrast the importance of the different factors.

Complex essay writing: argument and counter-argument

Essays that develop a good argument are more likely to reach the highest levels. This is because argumentative essays are much more likely to develop sustained analysis. As you know, your essays are judged on the extent to which they analyse.

After setting up an argument in your introduction, you should develop it throughout the essay. One way of doing this is to adopt an argument–counter-argument structure. A counter-argument is one that disagrees with the main argument of the essay. This is a good way of evaluating the importance of the different factors that you discuss. Essays of this type will develop an argument in one paragraph and then set out an opposing argument in another paragraph. Sometimes this will include juxtaposing the differing views of historians on a topic.

Good essays will analyse the key issues. They will probably have a clear piece of analysis at the end of each paragraph. While this analysis might be good, it will generally relate only to the issue discussed in that paragraph.

Excellent essays will be analytical throughout. As well as the analysis of each factor discussed above, there will be an overall analysis. This will run throughout the essay and can be achieved through developing a clear, relevant and coherent argument.

A good way of achieving sustained analysis is to consider which factor is most important.

Here is an example of an introduction that sets out an argument for question 1:

*Arguably, the most important reason why Henry VIII dissolved the monasteries was because he needed money to pursue his dream of the conquest of France and the acquisition of the French Crown***[1]***. The pressure from 'heretical ministers' and the landowning elite was used* *by Cromwell to persuade the king to take the decision to proceed with the dissolution of the monasteries*[2]. *The wealth uncovered by the Valor Ecclesiasticus encouraged Cromwell to manufacture a reason to close the monasteries and he engineered the means by which this could be accomplished*[3].

1 The introduction begins with a claim.
2 The introduction continues with another reason.
3 The introduction concludes with the outline of an argument of the most important reason.

- This introduction focuses on the question and sets out the key factors that the essay will develop.
- It introduces an argument about which factor was most significant.
- However, it also sets out an argument that can then be developed throughout each paragraph, and is rounded off with an overall judgement in the conclusion.

Complex essay writing: resolution and relative significance

Having written an essay that explains argument and counter-arguments, you should then resolve the tension between the argument and the counter-argument in your conclusion. It is important that the writing is precise and summarises the arguments made in the main body of the essay. You need to reach a supported overall judgement. One very appropriate way to do this is by evaluating the relative significance of different factors, in the light of valid criteria. Relative significance means how important one factor is compared to another.

The best essays will always make a judgement about which was most important based on valid criteria. These can be very simple, and will depend on the topic and the exact question.

The following criteria are often useful:

- Duration: which factor was important for the longest amount of time?
- Scope: which factor affected the most people?
- Effectiveness: which factor achieved most?
- Impact: which factor led to the most fundamental change?

As an example, you could compare the factors in terms of their duration and their impact. A conclusion that follows this advice should be capable of reaching a high level (if written, in full, with appropriate details) because it reaches an overall judgement that is supported through evaluating the relative significance of different factors in the light of valid criteria.

Having written an introduction and the main body of an essay for question 1, a concluding paragraph that aims to meet the exacting criteria for reaching a complex judgement could look like this:

It is clear that the reasons why Henry VIII closed the monasteries are complex with several interrelated factors. The king's greed and desire for wealth, the influence of Lutheranism and the impulse for reform all conspired to provide the Tudor government with an opportunity to close the monasteries and seize their assets. Cromwell's contribution to the dissolution should not be overlooked for he masterminded the process. Cromwell's careful manipulation of the king into believing that the money raised from the dissolution could be used to fund a war against the French appealed to Henry. Equally important was Henry's belief that he was master in his own house and that as Supreme Head of the Church he had a right to 'reform' the Church, even if this involved complete closure of the monasteries. It was becoming clear that by the early sixteenth century support for the monastic ideal was waning and Henry could claim that he was merely responding to those humanist reformers who questioned the ability of the monasteries to maintain the high ascetic ideals of their founders.

Sources guidance

Whether you are taking the AS exam or the full A level exam for AQA Component 2: Depth Study: Religious Conflict and the Church in England, *c.*1529–1570, Section A presents you with sources and a question which involves evaluation of their utility or value.

AS exam	A level exam
Section A: answer question 1, based on two primary sources. (25 marks)	Section A: answer question 1, based on three primary sources. (30 marks)
Question focus: with reference to these sources and your understanding of the historical context, which of these two sources is more valuable in explaining … ?	Question focus: with reference to these sources and your understanding of the historical context, assess the value of these three sources to a historian studying …

Sources and sample questions

Study the sources. They are all concerned with the Western and Kett rebellions in the summer of 1549.

SOURCE 1

Adapted from William Paget's letter of 7 July 1549 to Lord Protector Somerset. Paget was a senior member of the King's Council who advised the Lord Protector and the young King Edward.

I told your grace the truth and was not believed. The king's subjects are out of all discipline, out of obedience, caring neither for protector nor king. And what is the cause? Your own softness, your intention to be good to the poor. Consider, I beseech you most humbly, that society in a realm is maintained by means of religion and law. The use of the old religion is forbidden by a law, and the use of the new is not yet embraced by eleven out of twelve parts of the realm. As for the law, the foot takes on him the part of the head, and the common people are behaving like a king. I know in this matter that every man of the Council has not liked the way in which you have dealt with the rebellious commons and they had wished you had acted otherwise.

SOURCE 2

Adapted from Matteo Dandolo's letter of 20 July 1549 to the Senate of Venice. The Venetian ambassador was writing to his government to report on the rebellions and the English government's response.

There is news of major risings against the government of his grace the Duke of Somerset in England, and that the King has retreated to a strong castle outside London. The cause of this unrest is the common land, as the great landowners occupy the pastures of the poor people. The rebels also require the return of the Mass, together with the religion as it stood on the death of Henry VIII. The government, wishing to apply a swift and ruthless remedy, put upwards of five hundred persons to the sword, sparing neither women nor children.

SOURCE 3

Adapted from Lord Protector Somerset's letter of 27 July 1549 to Lord Russell, commander-in-chief of the royal army sent to deal with the Western rebels.

You have declared that it has been difficult to recruit men to serve in the king's army in Somerset due the evil inclination of the people and that there are among them many who speak openly using traitorous words against the king and in favour of the rebels. You shall hang two to three of them and cause them to be publicly executed as traitors. Sharp justice must be used against those traitors so that others may learn the consequences of their actions in opposing the king.

AS style question

With reference to Sources 1 and 2, and your understanding of the historical context, which of these two sources is more valuable in explaining why the rebellions had broken out in 1549?

A level style question

With reference to Sources 1, 2 and 3, and your understanding of the historical context, assess the value of these sources to a historian studying the causes of the rebellions in 1549.

AS mark scheme

See the AQA website (www.aqa.org.uk) for the full mark schemes. This summary of the AS mark scheme shows how it rewards analysis and evaluation of the source material within the historical context.

Level 1	Describing the source content or offering generic phrases.
Level 2	Some relevant but limited comments on the value of one source or some limited comment on both sources.
Level 3	Some relevant comments on the value of the sources and some explicit reference to the issue identified in the question.
Level 4	Relevant well-supported comments on the value and a supported conclusion, but with limited judgement.
Level 5	Very good understanding of the value in relation to the issue identified. Sources evaluated thoroughly and with a well-substantiated conclusion related to which is more valuable.

A level mark scheme

This summary of the A level mark scheme shows how it is similar for the AS, but covers three sources. Also the wording of the question means there is no explicit requirement to decide which of the three sources is the most valuable. Concentrate instead on a very thorough analysis of the content and evaluation of the provenance of each source, using contextual knowledge.

Level 1	Some limited comment on the value of at least one source.
Level 2	Some limited comments on the value of the sources or on content or provenance, or comments on all three sources but no reference to the value of the sources.
Level 3	Some understanding of all three sources in relation to both content and provenance, with some historical context; but analysis limited.
Level 4	Good understanding of all three sources in relation to content, provenance and historical context to give a balanced argument on their value for the purpose specified in the question.
Level 5	As Level 4, but with a substantiated judgement.

Working towards an answer

It is important that knowledge is used to show an understanding of the relationship between the sources and the issue raised in the question. Answers should be concerned with the following:

- provenance
- arguments used (and you can agree/disagree)
- tone and emphasis of the sources.

The sources

The two or three sources used each time will be contemporary – probably of varying types (for example, diaries, newspaper accounts, government reports). The sources will all be on the same broad topic area. Each source will have value and your task is to evaluate how much value in terms of its content and its provenance.

You will need to assess the *value of the content* by using your own knowledge. Is the information accurate? Is it giving only part of the evidence and ignoring other aspects? Is the tone of the writing significant?

You will need to evaluate the *provenance* of the source by considering who wrote it, and when, where and why. What was its purpose? Was it produced to express an opinion; to record facts; to influence the opinion of others? Even if it was intended to be accurate, the writer may have been biased – either deliberately or unconsciously. The writer, for example, might have only known part of the situation and reached a judgement solely based on that.

Here is a guide to analysing the provenance, content and tone for Sources 1, 2 and 3.

Analysing the sources

To answer the question effectively, you need to read the sources carefully and pull out the relevant points as well as add your own knowledge. You must remember to keep the focus on the question at all times.

Source 1 (page 162)

Provenance:

- The source is from William Paget's letter of 7 July 1549 to Lord Protector Somerset. He will have a particular view on how the leader of the government has handled the rebellion.
- It will therefore be a private letter addressing that particular person about his handling of the rebellion.

Content and argument:

- The source argues that Lord Protector Somerset has failed to heed good advice on how to deal with the rebels.
- The people are confused, restless and angry: the fault of the government in failing to deal with their concerns.
- The Lord Protector must listen to the advice and concerns of the members of the King's Council.

Tone and emphasis:

- The tone is assertive. Writing on behalf of the King's Council, Paget is demanding action by Somerset to deal ruthlessly with the rebels.

Own knowledge:

- Use your own knowledge to agree/disagree with the source, for example: details about why the people were restless and angry and why Somerset's social and economic policies had confused the common people, or evidence relating to why Paget thought that Somerset was incompetent and how this had contributed to the popular unrest in the kingdom.

Source 2 (page 162)

Provenance:

- The source is from an eyewitness seeing the events unfolding in England.
- It is written by a foreigner, the Venetian ambassador, who is reporting on the seriousness of the rebellions affecting the kingdom.

Content and argument:

- The source outlines the economic and religious causes of the rebellions.
- The ruthless treatment of some rebels has not deterred the rebels, who gain in strength and confidence.

Tone and emphasis:

- The writer is seriously concerned about the outcome of the rebellions. The king has had to seek safety in a castle outside the capital city.

Own knowledge:

- Use your own knowledge to agree/disagree with the source, for example: detailed knowledge about the situation across the kingdom, such as the size and scale of the rebellions, their locations and potential threat to the security of the kingdom, or knowledge about why some military commanders were seemingly reluctant to act brutally against the rebels.

Source 3 (page 163)

Provenance:

- The source is from a letter written by Lord Protector Somerset to Lord Russell, the commander of the royal forces sent against the rebels.
- It provides a contemporary account of what Somerset thought at the time.

Content and argument:

- The author of the source demands that the common people who are openly hostile towards the government must be punished to set an example to others.
- Those who might favour rebellion may increase in numbers and confidence because of Russell's incompetence and lack of effective leadership.

Tone and emphasis:

- The tone shows signs of fear that if the protests and the unrest continue the rebellion may spread across the kingdom.

Own knowledge:

- Use your own knowledge to agree/disagree with the source, for example: evidence about the apparent inability of the military commander (Russell) to deal with the rebels, or the attitude of the people towards both the government and the rebels.

Answering AS questions

You have an hour to answer the question. It is important that you spend at least one-quarter of the time reading and planning your answer. Generally, when writing an answer, you need to check that you are remaining focused on the issue identified in the question and are relating this to the sources and your knowledge.

- You might decide to write a paragraph on each 'strand' (that is, provenance, content and tone), comparing the two sources, and then write a short concluding paragraph with an explained judgement on which source is more valuable.
- For writing about content, you may find it helpful to adopt a comparative approach, for example when the evidence in one source is contradicted or questioned by the evidence in another source.

At AS level you are asked to provide a judgement on which is more valuable. Make sure that this is based on clear arguments with strong evidence, and not on general assertions.

Planning and writing your answer

- Think how you can best plan an answer.
- Plan in terms of the headings above, perhaps combining 'provenance' with 'tone and emphasis', and compare the two sources.

As an example, here is a comparison of Sources 1 and 2 in terms of provenance, and tone and emphasis:

The two sources have different viewpoints. In terms of their provenance, Source 1 is very one-sided as it is critical of Somerset's leadership. The viewpoint is based on the desire to avoid any blame for the rebellions that have broken out in England.

Source 2 is more measured in its analysis; however, it is taken from a confidential report sent by the Venetian ambassador to his government in Venice. The ambassador was a foreigner who may not have been in full possession of the facts.

Then compare the *content and argument* of each source, by using your knowledge. For example:

Source 1 is arguing for a change of policy by the Lord Protector. The situation with the Kett and Western rebellions was critical at the time; the government was becoming increasingly unpopular because it appeared to be indifferent to the plight of the poor, and the King's Council had no confidence in the leadership of Lord Protector Somerset.

Source 2, however, focuses on the anger which had become commonplace in the kingdom, especially when 16,000 rebels led by Robert Kett marched on the city of Norwich to demand changes in government policy. This source blames the landowners for taking and enclosing the land of the poor. The government is also blamed for pursuing an unpopular religious reform programme. The government's ruthless reaction to the rebellions had the potential to exacerbate the situation.

Which is *more valuable*? This can be judged in terms of which is likely to be more valuable in terms of where the source came from; or in terms of the accuracy of its content. However, remember the focus of the question – in this case, why the rebellions had broken out.

With these sources, you could argue that Source 1 is the more valuable because it was written by a senior government minister who was closer to the actual events connected to the rebellions than Source 2, and it gives a real sense of the urgency in the heart of the government. Source 2 is more limited because its author was a foreigner who had to rely on second-hand reports and gossip for information.

Then check the following:

- Have you covered the 'provenance' and 'content' strands?
- Have you included sufficient knowledge to show understanding of the historical context?

Answering A level questions

The same general points for answering AS questions (see 'Answering AS questions') apply to A level questions, although of course here there are three sources and you need to assess the value of each of the three, rather than choose which is most valuable. Make sure that you remain focused on the question and that when you use your knowledge it is used to substantiate (add to) an argument relating to the content or provenance of the source.

If you are answering the A level question with Sources 1, 2 and 3 above:

- Keep the different 'strands' explained above in your mind when working out how best to plan an answer.
- Follow the guidance about 'provenance' and 'content' (see the first two points of the AS guidance).
- Here you are *not* asked to explain which is the most valuable of the three sources. You can deal with each of the three sources in turn if you wish.
- However, you can build in comparisons if it is helpful, but it is not essential. It will depend to some extent on the three sources.
- You need to include sufficient knowledge to show understanding of the historical context. This might encourage cross-referencing of the content of the three sources, mixed with your own knowledge.
- Each paragraph needs to show clarity of argument in terms of the issue identified by the question.

Glossary of terms

Adiaphora From the Greek meaning a tolerance of conduct or belief not specifically mentioned or forbidden in the scriptures.

Advertisements Published by Archbishop Parker to assist parish priests in the performance of their duties in church services, such as instructions on the wearing of vestments, the administration of common prayers and the holy sacraments.

Annates Money equivalent to about one-third of the annual income paid to the Pope by all new holders of senior posts within the Church in England and Wales.

Armada An invasion fleet sent by Philip of Spain which intended to land an army in southern England and then conquer the country.

Augsburg Confession The primary confession of faith of the Lutheran Church and one of the most important documents of the German Reformation.

Babington Plot A conspiracy led by Sir Anthony Babington to assassinate Elizabeth and replace her with Mary, Queen of Scots.

Benefit of clergy An arrangement whereby any person charged in one of the king's courts could claim to be immune from prosecution if he was in holy orders.

Black Rubric A set of instructions issued to the clergy on the order of service in church ceremonies.

Bondmen Medieval peasants who lived and worked on their lord's manor.

Burgess A member of the ruling council of a town.

Calvinism Alternative Protestant faith to Lutheranism, named after John Calvin, an influential French religious reformer based in Geneva, Switzerland.

Canon law Church laws that were administered in Church courts.

Cardinal Senior cleric in the Catholic Church.

Clerks and clerics Clerks were involved in the administration of a diocese while clerics were responsible for spiritual matters.

Common law Secular laws applying to the general population and administered in the king's courts.

Comperta Monastica A book compiled by Cromwell's agents which contained lists of transgressions and abuses admitted by monks and nuns.

Consubstantiation The belief that the wine and bread taken during the Eucharist represent the blood and body of Christ.

Continental humanism Return to the study of the original classical texts and to the teaching of the humanities as the basis of civilised life. The movement began in fifteenth-century Italy and spread throughout Europe owing to the inspired leadership of intellectuals and scholars.

Convocation Church equivalent of Parliament where clerics meet in two houses to discuss and transact Church affairs.

Coup d'état The French term for a sudden and illegal seizure of a government.

Cure of souls God-given authority to safeguard the salvation of men as part of Christ's mission on earth.

Dissolving The dissolution or closure of the monasteries.

Doctrine The rules, principles and teachings of a belief system, in this case, the Church.

Elevation of the host The host is the bread consecrated by the priest which Catholics believe to be the body of Christ. By raising the host the priest is signalling the transformation of the bread to the body. This is enshrined in the concept of transubstantiation.

Elizabethan religious settlement Phrase used by historians to describe the organisation, ritual and teaching of the Church of England as enforced by Acts of Parliament.

English Ordinal The process by which priests were appointed and consecrated. This ceremony was to be conducted in English rather than in Latin.

Erastianism Justification of a State-controlled Church, expounded by Thomas Erastus.

Eucharist Also known as Holy Communion, a Catholic sacrament in which the bread and wine are taken in the belief that the body and blood of Christ are contained within.

Ex officio Office holders who enjoy certain rights and privileges associated with or attached to their office.

Excommunicate To expel a person from the Church and deny them a Christian burial in consecrated ground, with the result that their souls would suffer everlasting torment in purgatory.

Faction Political groups working against each other at the royal court and in government.

Forty-Two Articles A list of essential doctrines drawn up by Cranmer and intended to form the basis of the new Protestant Church of England.

Guild Religious or community group that provided its poorest members with assistance and charity.

Heresy Criticism or denial of the Church and its teachings.

Iconoclasm Deliberate destruction of religious icons and other Church symbols in either community-inspired or State-organised attacks.

Idolatrous Worshipping images, such as the statue of the Virgin Mary in Catholic churches.

Laity The main body of Church members who do not belong to the clergy but are part of the wider community.

Legatine powers Authority delegated by the Pope.

Legatus a latere A position normally awarded for a specific purpose so that a representative with full papal powers could be present at a decision-making occasion far distant from Rome.

Lollards Followers of John Wycliffe (d.1384), a university-trained philosopher and theologian whose unorthodox religious and social doctrines in some ways anticipated those of the sixteenth-century Protestant reformers.

Lords temporal The nobility who sat in the House of Lords.

Lower orders The social class representing the mass of the population that occupied a position below the upper classes of nobility and gentry.

Machiavellian Cleverly deceitful and unscrupulous. Named after an Italian political writer and thinker, Niccolo Machiavelli (1469–1527) of Florence.

Millenarianists Radical thinkers who believed in social reform whereby a kingdom's wealth would be distributed equally.

Nepotism The promotion or employment of family members and friends to important Church offices.

Non-residence Where priests did not live in their parish.

Orthodox Accepting doctrine without question, in this case of the Church.

Papal legate Personal representative of the Pope with the authority to act with full papal powers on ecclesiastical matters.

***Paraphrases* of the Gospels** Rewritings of the Gospels with commentaries by Erasmus.

Pastoral duties The duty of care exercised by a priest to his parishioners, such as baptism, marriage and burial.

Pluralist A clergyman serving more than one parish or holding more than one office.

Praemunire A legal provision, arising from three fourteenth-century laws, which forbade clerics to take any action that cut across the powers of the Crown – especially recognising any external authority without the monarch's explicit permission.

Predestination Belief that a person's life has been mapped out by God before birth and cannot be changed.

Propaganda Method by which ideas are spread to support a particular point of view.

Prorogue Temporary suspension of Parliament.

Purgatory A place where the souls of the dead are sent in order to undergo purification so as to achieve the holiness necessary to enter heaven.

Puritan Choir Coined by historian Sir John Neale to describe what he perceived to be an organised Puritan political group in the House of Commons.

Puritans Protestants who wished to reform the Anglican Church by eradicating all trace of Catholicism and Catholic practices.

Recusants Catholics who refused to conform to the State religion and refused to attend church services.

Regency Council Name given to the Privy Council during the minority of Edward VI.

Regular Church That part of the Church which consisted of monks, nuns and friars who lived and worked in monastic communities, usually in remote rural locations.

Renaissance An intellectual and cultural movement dedicated to the rediscovery and promotion of art, architecture and letters. It promoted education and critical thinking and ranged across subjects such as politics, government, religion and classical literature. Its spread was encouraged by humanist scholars such as Erasmus.

Sack of Rome Attack on and looting of Rome by Habsburg troops under Charles V. The attack was a result of the war between Francis and Charles for the control of Italy.

Sanctuaries Areas of land, ranging in size from the county of Durham to the environs of particular churches or monasteries, which were outside the jurisdiction of the law of the land.

Schism Literally meaning 'break', but used by historians to describe England's break with the Pope in Rome.

Schmalkaldic League A defensive alliance of Lutheran princes in Germany intended to defend their political and religious interests.

Secular Church That part of the Church which consisted of parish priests who lived and worked in the communities they served.

Sedition Speaking or acting against the government by inciting protest or rebellion.

Simony The selling of Church offices and holy relics.

Transubstantiation The belief that the bread and wine given at communion become the body and blood of Jesus Christ when they are blessed.

Treason Betrayal of one's king and one's country.

Unitary nation-state A country in which Church and State are united under a single authority or jurisdiction.

Urban radicals Educated artisans, tradesmen and merchants who had embraced the teachings and ideas of Protestantism.

Vicegerent The king's deputy in Church affairs.

White Horse Tavern A meeting place in Cambridge for English Protestant reformers who discussed Lutheran ideas.

Yeoman Class of richer peasants, just below the gentry, who either owned or rented their land.

Zwinglian Huldrych Zwingli was a protestant reformer as influential as Martin Luther and John Calvin. He was the leader of the reformation in Switzerland.

Further reading

General textbooks

A.G. Dickens, *The English Reformation* (Batsford, 1989)
A ground-breaking work on the causes and course of the Reformation

S. Ellsmore, D. Rogerson and D. Hudson, *The Early Tudors: England 1484–1558* (John Murray, 2001)
Accessible text designed for sixth formers covering the key issues with clarity

G.R. Elton, *England Under the Tudors* (Methuen, 1955)
An important work that became a reference point for all later studies of the period

N. Fellows, *Disorder and Rebellion in Tudor England* (Hodder & Stoughton, 2001)
A brief but very informative and up-to-date analysis

J. Guy, *Tudor England* (Oxford University Press, 1988)
Accessible and useful general analysis of the history of Tudor England

P. Gwyn, *The King's Cardinal: The Rise and Fall of Thomas Wolsey* (Pimlico, 1992)
Large and comprehensive biography of Wolsey with some useful comments on politics and religion

C. Haig, *English Reformation: Religion, Politics and Society Under the Tudors* (Oxford University Press, 1993)
An in-depth analysis of the nature, scale and impact of the Reformation

E.W. Ives, *The Life and Death of Anne Boleyn* (Blackwell, 1986)
This definitive biography of Anne Boleyn establishes her as a figure of considerable importance and influence at the court of Henry VIII

J. Loach, *Parliament Under the Tudors* (Oxford University Press, 1991)
Excellent study of the role and development of Parliament in Tudor government

D.M. Loades, *The Mid-Tudor Crisis, 1545–65* (Macmillan, 1992)
A focused account of the so-called 'mid-Tudor crisis'

J. Lotherington, *The Tudor Years* (Hodder & Stoughton, 1994)
A set of informed essays dealing with politics, government and religion in each reign **D. MacCulloch, editor, *The Reign of Henry VIII: Politics, Policy and Piety* (Macmillan, 1995)**
A set of informed essays dealing with politics, government and religion in the reign of Henry VIII

R. Rosemary O'Day, *The Debate on the English Reformation* (Routledge, 1986)
Excellent debate on key aspects of the Reformation

W.J. Sheils, *The English Reformation 1530–1570* (Longman, 1989)
Excellent synopsis with documents of the cause, course and impact of the Reformation

D. Starkey, *The Reign of Henry VIII: Personalities & Politics* (Vintage, 2002)
Thorough survey of the key characters, together with their role and influence in government, religion and the court

J. Youings, *The Dissolution of the Monasteries* (Allen & Unwin, 1971)
An absorbing look at the major social and religious upheaval caused by the dissolution of the monasteries

Chapter 1

E. Duffy, *The Stripping of the Altars* (Oxford University Press, 1992)
This profoundly influential book re-examines events leading up to the Reformation in England and illuminates our understanding of the period

E. Duffy, *The Voices of Morebath: Reformation and Rebellion in an English Village* (Yale University Press, 2003)
This study takes us inside the mind and heart of Morebath, a remote and tiny sheep-farming Devon village

R.N. Swanson, *Catholic England: Faith, Religion and Observance Before the Reformation* (Manchester University Press, 2013)
This book seeks to explore the nature of religious belief and practice in pre-Reformation England, using original source material to make the debates accessible

Chapter 2

D. MacCulloch, editor, *The Reign of Henry VIII: Politics, Policy and Party* (Macmillan, 1995)
A set of informed essays dealing with politics and government in Henry VIII's reign

R. Rex, *Henry VIII and the English Reformation* (Palgrave Macmillan, 2006)
An analytical account which sets out the reason for and nature of Henry VIII's short-lived Reformation

J.J. Scarisbrick, *The Reformation and the English People* (Blackwell, 1984)
Analysis of the reaction to and impact on the people of England of religious change

J.J. Scarisbrick, *Henry VIII* (Methuen, 1997)
Full coverage of Henry's life and career together with an analysis of the king's impact on religion and politics

Chapter 3

G.R. Elton, *The Tudor Revolution in Government* (Methuen, 1953)
A thought-provoking and controversial work on the nature and scale of the changes in Tudor government

G.R. Elton, *Thomas Cromwell* (Headstart History, 1990)
Short but incisive discussion of Cromwell bringing all of Elton's research up to date

R. Rosemary O'Day, *The Debate on the English Reformation* (Methuen, 1986)
Excellent debate on key aspects of the reformation

J. Youings, *The Dissolution of the Monasteries* (Allen & Unwin, 1971)
Solid revision of the causes, course and impact of the dissolution

Chapter 4

C. Davies, *A Religion of the Word: The Defence of the Reformation in the Reign of Edward VI* (Manchester University Press, 2002)
Focused account of the religious changes in Edward's reign

J. Loach, *Edward VI* (Yale University Press, 2002)
Biography of Edward VI, which reveals for the first time his significant personal impact on the history of his country

D. Loades, *John Dudley, Duke of Northumberland 1504–1553* (Clarendon Press, 1996)
In-depth analysis of Northumberland's role and impact as governor of England under Edward VI

D. MacCulloch, *Thomas Cranmer* (Yale University Press, 1996)
Large-scale biography of a man credited with establishing the Protestant faith

D. MacCulloch, *Tudor Church Militant: Edward VI and the Protestant Reformation* (Allen Lane, 2000)
Authoritative study of the Protestant revolution under Edward VI

Chapter 5

E. Duffy and D.M. Loades, editors, *The Church of Mary Tudor* (Ashgate, 2006)
A set of informed essays dealing with religious change but with useful references to wider issues in politics and government in Mary's reign

T.S. Freeman and Susan Doran, editors, *Mary Tudor: Old and New Perspectives* (Palgrave Macmillan, 2011)
A set of informed revisionist essays with useful references to issues in politics, religion and government in Mary's reign

D.M. Loades, *The Reign of Mary Tudor: Politics, Government and Religion in England 1553–58* (Routledge, 1991)
By far the best overall history of the reign to date

R. Tittler, *Mary I* (Longman, 2013)
Short but very useful biography of Mary with valuable selection of source material

Chapter 6

P. Collinson, *Elizabethans* (Continuum, 2003)
Examines the religious beliefs of Elizabethan England, as well as redrawing the main features of the political and religious structure of the reign

C. Cross, *The Elizabethan Religious Settlement* (Headstart History, 1992)
An excellent concise study of the settlement

C. Haigh, *Elizabeth I* (Routledge, 2001)
Excellent survey of the main features of Elizabeth's reign

P. Williams, *The Later Tudors: England, 1547–1603* (Oxford University Press, 1998)
An authoritative and comprehensive study of England between the accession of Edward VI and the death of Elizabeth

Index

Acknowledgements: Ashgate Publishing, *William Cecil and Episcopacy, 1559–1577* by Brett Usher, 2003. Blandford Press, *The Dissolution of the Monasteries* by G.W.O. Woodward, 1966. Cambridge University Press, *Reformation and Resistance in Tudor Lancashire* by Christopher Haigh, 2008. Collins, *The English Reformation* by A.G. Dickens, 1964. Headstart History Publishing, *The Elizabethan Religious Settlement* by Claire Cross, 1992; *The Reformation in Wales* by Glanmor Williams, 1991. Hodder, *Henry VIII and the Reformation in England* by Keith Randell, 1993. Jonathan Cape, *Elizabeth I and Her Parliaments 1559–1581* by J.E. Neale, 1953. Macmillan, *Sixteenth-century England 1450–1600* by Denys Cook, 1988; *The English Church in the Reigns of Elizabeth I and James I, 1558–1625* by W.H. Frere, 1904. Nelson, *The Tudor Century* by Ian Dawson, 1993. Palgrave, *The Later Reformation in England, 1547–1603* by Diarmaid MacCulloch, 1990. Royal Historical Society, *Faith by Statute, Parliament and the Settlement of Religion, 1559* by N.L. Jones, 1982. Yale University Press, *The Stripping of the Altars* by Eamon Duffy, 1992.